THE EUROPEAN UNION IN THE 21ST CENTURY

The European Union in the 21st Century

Perspectives from the Lisbon Treaty

Edited by
Stefano Micossi and Gian Luigi Tosato

Introduction by
Sabino Cassese

Centre for European Policy Studies
Brussels

The Centre for European Policy Studies (CEPS) is an independent policy research institute based in Brussels. Its mission is to produce sound analytical research leading to constructive solutions to the challenges facing Europe today. CEPS Paperbacks present analysis and views by leading experts on important questions in the arena of European public policy, written in a style aimed at an informed but generalist readership.

The views expressed in this report are those of the authors writing in a personal capacity and do not necessarily reflect those of CEPS or any other institution with which they are associated.

Cover: Claude Monet, Impression, soleil levant, 1872
Musée Marmottan, Paris

ISBN 978-92-9079-929-0

Centre for European Policy Studies
Place du Congrès 1, B-1000 Brussels
Tel: 32 (0) 2 229.39.11 Fax: 32 (0) 2 219.41.51
e-mail: info@ceps.eu
internet: http://www.ceps.eu

CONTENTS

PREFACE

Eventually, after fifteen years of agonizing negotiations among the member states and at times dogged resistance by segments of European society, the European Union has reached a form of constitutional settlement with the Treaty of Lisbon.

The new Treaty brings important changes to the European construction, including a significant expansion of common policies decided by the Community method, a stable President for the European Council, a strengthened framework for external policies, more transparent and effective decision-making and strict safeguards of subsidiarity.

Even in the wake of the new Treaty, however, the Union remains an entity in flux, in search of its destiny. Further institutional progress is by no means excluded, but it will have to be achieved explicitly rather than brought about by stealth. The presence among the member states and in the European Parliament of political forces staunchly opposed to further deepening of the Union makes the prospect of increased use of enhanced cooperation more likely.

Ultimately, the fate of the Union depends on its ability to respond to the needs of its member states and its citizens in providing external and internal security and economic prosperity in a global context of mounting economic and political instability, where the centre of gravity of world governance and strategic decisions is likely to continue to shift away from Europe and towards the Pacific and emerging economies.

Against this background, the essays in this volume analyse changing equilibria in common policies, institutional settings and legitimisation mechanisms of the European Union, which are being brought about by the new Treaty, and sketch out possible scenarios for the 21st century. The essays are organised in three sections devoted in turn to economics and consensus, international projection of the Union and the new institutional framework.

The contributors to this collection are all members of EuropEos, a multi-disciplinary group of jurists, economists, political scientists and journalists who first came together in 2002 to contribute to the deliberations of the European Convention and have developed into a permanent forum for the discussion of European institutional issues.

The views expressed in the essays in this volume are not always concordant, but they stem from a common commitment to the European construction. The title of the introductory essay, *Im zweifel für Europa*, is there for a reason.

Stefano Micossi and Gian Luigi Tosato

1. INTRODUCTION: IM ZWEIFEL FÜR EUROPA

SABINO CASSESE

1. The European Union: Reasons for success

The European Union represents the most successful establishment of a supranational system of government since the large empires of the past (the Holy Roman Empire or the Spanish, Ottoman, Habsburg and British Empires).

But none of these multinational structures developed in such a short space of time as the European Union, which in half a century has gone from being an association of 6 to 27 country states, from an economic union to a political union. And none of the structures that came before - unlike the European Union - was the product of a voluntary and equal association of nations, as opposed to a structure that coalesced around a dominant nation.

The Union has a third original feature as well. It unites states, but not on the basis of their traditional functions - defence, public order, justice, relations with foreign countries, budget - but on the basis of an element that is potentially external to the state, namely the market. That said, the European Union ends up exercising influence over traditional state functions as well: thus, it may not dispose of large sums of money (in terms of budget, it is dwarf-like), but it sets standards regarding states' spending power; it may not be responsible for public order, but it grants freedom of movement to European citizens; it may have little influence in defence matters, but it has guaranteed peace in Europe.

A fourth original feature of European construction is its support of nation states that internal centrifugal forces (separatism, regionalism) might otherwise fragment. National unity becomes necessary because of the need for dialogue, the need to speak with one voice with other nations. From this standpoint the traditional vision of a Union perpetually in conflict with its member states is turned around, and another emerges, that of a Union helping to strengthen national interests.

Fifthly, after barely half a century, the Union has become one of the pillars of a multipolar world. Most of the 350 cases submitted to the World Trade Organisation's Dispute Settlement Body involve disputes between the European Union and the United States. Conversely, in global fora, worldwide agreements are often based on an understanding between the United States and the European Union. The presence of the Union therefore helps preserve global plurality.

Sixthly, despite its rapid pace, the Union's development has been very much in accordance with the *19th century 'revolution in government'* mode, i.e. gradual: when a problem emerges, a solution is sought that is then shown to be flawed and incomplete, requiring correction, etc. Or solutions devised for one sector are transposed to another where they generate effects that are in part unintended and require adjustment. All this occurs in a self-feeding process, provoking angry tirades on the part of those who see in it nothing but the progress of bureaucratisation. The incorporation of successive compromises has built into Europe's legal system a rationale for slowness, but it has also encouraged a rationale for the 'essentiality'.

Finally the European Union crosses state barriers on a daily basis, in its quest to induce domestic reform. Domestic reform stems from a common European denominator (communications liberalisation, for instance), wherein it finds inspiration, but it ends up producing different outcomes, at a different pace. Hence the unstable balance between uniformity and differentiation, European solutions and domestic outcomes, the latter bearing the mark of local culture, style and institutions.

"Im Zweifel für Europa" (When in doubt, favour Europe) read the headline of a German paper a few years back, summing up the strength that has presided over Europe's development and led to its becoming the main point of reference for politics in Europe today.

2. The crisis and its paradoxes

Despite the Union's growing status as a world power and its increasing activity (evidenced by the reams of regulations produced daily by its numerous bodies), the standstill dealt by the Constitutional referenda held in France and the Netherlands and in Ireland over the Treaty of Lisbon induced a phase of apathy where the prevalent concerns focused on fragmentation and the prospect of a 27-gear Europe (and thus, a loss of collective momentum).

Yet even this critical phase is on various accounts paradoxical. There are those who deplore the Union's ineffectiveness not because it does too much, but mainly because it does too little. It is argued that it should intervene more pointedly in immigration, world trade, international terrorism, the environment, energy. At stake are functions that states cannot perform alone. Therefore, more Europe - as they say - is needed.

There are those who deplore the ineffectiveness of the Union's decision-making processes, ascribed to the facts that so many decisions require unanimity, the Council President's term is too short and Europe has difficulty in speaking with one voice vis-à-vis the rest of the world. European construction appears to be this machine ruled more by procedures than by products. But the complexity of the decision-making processes stems from the unavoidable compromises - as noted earlier - that are needed to run the machine and are what makes it stand apart. A driving force, not just a brake.

There are those who deplore the elitist character of the European construction: it brings together politicians, bureaucrats, business leaders. But in recent years citizens have been called to select who will represent them in the European Parliament and the referenda have at the very least involved many citizens in a European decision. So the Union is not an overblown superstructure set up by the ruling classes. The people too have a voice, and a direct one at that. And if the people feel fear and try to slow the process down rather than speed it up, one should try and understand why, rather than lament the collapse of the whole edifice. And in the meantime, steps should be taken to broaden and strengthen the 'elites' on which construction has long relied, trying out at the supranational level all the induction and socialisation tools that have helped establish national elites over the last two centuries.

There are those who deplore the re-emergence within the European Union of national interests, forgetting that its whole construction is based on reciprocal concessions, which have produced multiple benefits that no one can deny today. If a state decides to evade European constraints on a point that might damage its position, it must also be prepared to lose advantages specially tailored to its needs. This interplay of reciprocal favours is strengthened by the various ways in which costs and benefits are assessed by each individual nation and within each nation as well (favours and the benefits bestowed are not uniform), not to mention the fact that all supranational legal systems fragment national interests (one need but consider the conflicting interests of the retail and the textile industry in the face of expanding world trade).

Finally, there are those who deplore the fact that the Union has two governments and that the Commission is not fully answerable to Parliament. But this disregards the fact that in so doing, one is applying to a new construct rules devised for the old (state legal and political) systems, without first having investigated whether the new construct is not actually generating new ways of making the executive accountable. In other words, the dissatisfaction stems to a large extent from a defect in viewers' vision.

All these ambiguities and paradoxes give rise to a tormenting doubt – that the slogan *Im Zweifel für Europa* may no longer be appropriate.

3. A realistic agenda

The ambiguity with which the failings of European construction (which are in fact in part achievements, in part failings) are presented must not induce inertia.

One may have to renounce the idea of a European Constitutional Charter, but on the other hand there already is a European constitution. In any event this does not mean that a number of improvements are not required: in particular with respect to closer links between the Parliament and the Commission, a stronger connection between the Commission and the Council, a longer mandate for the Council President and a greater use of majority (and qualified majority) voting.

If on the one hand the Union is called upon to take on new functions and, on the other, it is still burdened with many other older ones, this does not mean that it shouldn't unburden itself through devolution to states, and mainly to sub-national authorities, while retaining powers of control.

If the composite power and joint committee system strengthens the Union but slows down its procedures, the decision-making process should be redesigned not to make it less collegial, but to make it speedier.

If elites and the general public enter into conflict, this conflict has to be changed into productive competition, into a balanced system of checks and balances. That may produce, in other words, more guarantees, not more conflicts.

And finally if national interests do fragment, steps should be taken to encourage their multinational re-aggregation, which is good for Europe (provided that it is not understood as a monolith, but as a network).

In other words, optimism should not lead to inertia. The strength of European construction also lies in the fact that it has never stopped during its first half century.

PART I

ECONOMICS AND CONSENSUS

2. PARTISAN PROTECTIONISM: POLITICAL CONSENSUS, THE EURO AND EUROPE'S RESPONSE TO THE GLOBAL CRISIS

CARLO BASTASIN

Far from providing an opportunity for better coordination, the global financial crisis has accentuated national differences among the member states of the EU. Although in line with the principles enunciated in the European Economic Recovery Plan, EU member states' responses to the crisis have shown a low degree of coordination. The impact of fiscal stimuli has not been coordinated even in the component of the fiscal packages (one-quarter of the total, according to the European Commission) carrying direct spill-over effects. In some cases, the amount of stimulus has been kept at a low level in order to 'free-ride' other countries' packages. Public money has been spent with an eye to support mainly local domestic activities, even at the cost of lower fiscal multipliers. Non-export industries, especially infrastructure, even though less affected by the crisis, have been supported by governments, thereby increasing demand for non-elastic production that could more easily adjust through higher prices than higher quantities, and actually resulting in a negative welfare effect.

Requests for banking transparency – and supervision – have caused uneasiness among national regulators and policy-makers. Banking opaqueness has been protected by national governments. There has not been an agreement on stress-testing, recapitalisation or restructuring of the financial system. The threat is still lingering that countries with problematic banking systems, little room for fiscal manoeuvre and low growth (Belgium, Ireland, Austria, Greece and the United Kingdom) will face increasing difficulty to manage their financial weakness and become destabilising for the whole EU. First-best solutions – fiscal cooperation or common financing instruments (Eurobonds) – remain unheeded as they typically require strong political commitment. This is inducing defensive attitudes by the banks themselves, resulting in less credit to the economy and less growth.

Exiting the crisis might prove a bigger challenge for the EU than the crisis itself. The area is divided between fast countries and slow countries. There is a risk that the growth divergence will reinforce these trends. Countries that grow faster can reduce public debt more easily, benefiting from less crowding-out and lower risk premia. Their banking systems can finance innovation instead of simply struggling to reduce losses.

If the implementation of short-term policies is disappointing, the long-term consequences of a lack of coordination are outright worrying. Countries without fiscal room of manoeuvre and with critical banking situations will need to be supported by countries with larger room of fiscal manoeuvre. Countries risking public-debt failure will also need support. Without macroeconomic coordination, current account imbalances, in an environment of low growth, will jeopardise public debt sustainability. All of this might trigger a chain effect from the weakest to the strongest links of the European Union.

Why is Europe drifting towards self-defeating non-cooperation?

The answer lies in the objectives of national governments. The system of national partisan politics in Europe defines itself in terms of its protective or, alternatively, protectionist stance with respect to globalisation. National consensus builds both on closure and openness. More precisely, it works on the basis of a principle one might call 'partisan protectionism': the protection of the constituency - labour for the left wing and capital for the right wing, identified with partisan ideologies of the past two centuries - while vigorously exposing the other constituency to the full duress and dynamics of global competition.

This duplicity - far from weakening it - is strengthening the grip of national ideologies on the imagination of the citizens of each European country. Traditional - national - politics become a structural hurdle with respect to coordination. The euro, for its many merits, has been the catalyst of the contradiction between an open economy and closed politics. Now, lacking an open European politics, the siren song of national protectionism, carrying us away from European cooperation, sounds irresistible.

1. A crisis in consensus

During the early decades, the European integration process elicited broad consensus as reflected in public opinion of the various member states.

Historical, political and cultural reasons had fed into a generally positive attitude towards the early integration initiatives and their rhetoric. Somewhat simplistically, this has been referred to as a 'permissive consensus', i.e. a consensus not preconditioned by the concrete political goals set forth in the European project, but rather by benign and not necessarily informed support for the long-term ideals evoked.

Prior to 1973, no statistical data were available on public opinion attitudes - a gap since filled by the Eurobarometer surveys, which have made it possible to demonstrate statistically that a significant change in public attitudes vis-à-vis the European Union has indeed occurred. The 1990s are the traumatic epicentre of this change. More specifically, up until 1991, explicit consensus among European citizens continued to rise, with the Single Market project marking the highest point in terms of positive answers to two standard questions: *Are you for or against the efforts currently being made to unify Europe?* and *Do you feel that in general terms your country's membership in the European Union is a good or a bad thing?* In 1991, 82% of all Europeans replied in the positive to the first question, and 72% to the second as well. A few years later, around 1997, positive answers to both these questions had dropped by 15 to 17 percentage points.

Public opposition to the European project emerged for the first time in a number of different countries during the critical years between 1991 and 1997: the Maastricht referendum failed in Denmark and Ireland and quite surprisingly, only passed with the slimmest of margins in France. Opposition to monetary union mounted in Germany, eroding the customary pro-integration majority (so much so that until 1998, two-thirds of all German respondents stated that they opposed the euro) with the support of the Karlsruhe Constitutional Court, and anti-Europe parliamentary votes in the UK garnered much attention and broad public opinion support, expressed via idiosyncratic anti-European media coverage. New localist political groupings in Italy, Austria, the Netherlands and Scandinavia began to gain ground through anti-European and at times outright xenophobic programmes, with some obtaining government positions by the year 2000. As of the 1990s, dwindling support for Europe had become an unavoidable issue.

But what exactly do we mean by 'consensus'? Strictly speaking, consensus is a positive *response* to a question, a second-tier request following that which led to the emergence of whatever is the object of the consensus. This is why British observers in particular have so often stressed the European Union's ability to *deliver* rather than to *deliberate*. There are many cases where joint achievements elicit consensus only after they have materialised: there are thus far fewer Germans opposed to the euro today than in 1998, as in this case European policy implementation has elicited consensus through its output. And the scope of this extra-democratic process subsequently extended even further, leading observers to speak of output-based 'legitimisation'.

But for various reasons, the process does not always work. In a number of cases, the ability of the European Union to deliver has not been appreciated by its citizens. Costs have remained more visible than benefits, and an inter-temporal balance between costs and benefits has not slotted into the rhetoric of politics. More specifically, according to some observers, the shift from negative to positive integration (ranging from the removal of obstacles to integration, a symbolic high point of which was the establishment of the Single Market, to projects establishing as *European* prerogatives that had hitherto been domestic, through institution-building and handouts of sovereignty) has made 'preventive consensus' harder to obtain. Telling Europeans "just wait and see, you'll love the outcome" is simply not enough when the process implies highly complex cost and benefit offsets within countries, among countries and, indeed, over time. This is particularly true when the stakes involve decision-making processes, the outer limits of which cannot be foreseen – no more than their end-points and thereby the full extent of their consequences: such decision-making processes, insofar as they are not devised for a single and specific project, tend to involve delegations of political sovereignty that are both broad and vague.

And thus the issue of consensus has become overlaid with that of Europe's democratic deficit, i.e. the lack of popular involvement and control that is notoriously the mark of decision-making processes within European institutions. Public opinion *detachment* has been linked to the issue of *remove* between citizens and European decisions. According to this interpretation, a dwindling consensus on things European corresponds to a demand for more democracy on the part of public opinion – handling this demand properly, through the appropriate institutions, would be the only way to grant legitimacy to European decisions.

Sounds convincing. But it isn't. Had this really been the case, had the low level of citizen support stemmed from citizens' frustration with their modest involvement in democratic decision-making processes, with the limited openings granted them to exercise control and demand accountability, why did the ratification process of the Constitutional Treaty fail when submitted to a popular vote in both France and the Netherlands and that of the Treaty of Lisbon more recently in Ireland? Both documents provided for more democratic decision-making, and one would have expected that European citizens would have been very approving of a fairly ambitious attempt at containing Europe's democratic deficit.

In other words, either the constitutional draft was actually not ambitious enough, or clearly the overlay of consensus and democratic deficit-based explanations doesn't do the trick. As shown - in the negative - by the drop in voter turnout in elections to the European Parliament, for an institutional and political organisation to elicit broader popular consensus, institutional forms or structures are just not enough. Channels through which consensus can mature - typically within a domestic context - must find an effective way of entering into dialogue with channels used for European deliberations. And for this to happen domestic policies must absolutely be consistent with European policies. Therefore the channels linking domestic public opinion to government-level policy decisions and European policy need to be watched closely, and no sweeping conclusions drawn.

A number of generic explanations have been put forth that aim to describe the consensus hiatus, which appeared between 1991 and 1997. A non-comprehensive list would include, indicatively, the following standard motivations: the relinquishing of too much sovereignty, Brussels' low legitimacy, less advantageous trade-offs between political autonomy, social identity and economic benefits, the rise of localist movements in the face of globalisation and the crisis experienced by ideological families in the wake of the collapse of communism. All of these are plausible explanations. But taken separately, or in the absence of a broader model that would lend them consistency, they do not shed much light on the dilemma. In practically all cases, they even appear to contradict one another: the relinquishing of sovereignty was perhaps somewhat excessive, and yet surveys show that citizens would be willing to accept even more in specific fields such as foreign or security policy; Brussels does not appear to have much legitimacy, but the citizens of some countries refuse to accept deeper or more democratic political institutions; localist movements are now waning in most countries; the ideological crisis has not benefited the European Commission, a model non-partisan institution. All these explanations of the 1992-97 crisis, therefore, appear to be impressionistic in nature, and therefore are unsuitable for further analysis.

The point I wish to make here is that the crisis in consensus primarily concerns domestic politics. And that in particular it has to do with the quality of public discourse, which to this day is still dominated by 20th century ideological categories in its upholding of the left/right divide as a leading, polarising criterion. Crossing this left/right opposition with another highly significant polarisation – that between closure to the outside world and openness – allows for descriptions of national politics in a context that highlights the global opening of European economies.

To the opening of societies and economies, domestic politics both left and right have responded according to a criterion that I call 'partisan protectionism', which in other words protects nothing but their basic constituencies in accordance with the ideological habits of the 20th century (with the right wing endorsing capital, and the left, labour) and opens up (i.e. exposes to global competition or to European integration) the rest of society, i.e. the political opposition's constituency. Against this backdrop – and it is no accident that the crisis in consensus should have occurred precisely between 1991 and 1998 – the euro proved to be *the* factor that revealed the inconsistencies of politics inspired by partisan protectionism. Because the euro did render inconsistent domestic policies anchored in the ideological rhetoric of the 20th century and, absent a response, a political vision consistent with openness, it eroded citizens' general trust in politics.

Partisan protectionism, in its defensive side, has been evident even in the public responses to the crisis. French right-wing government has supported businesses twice as much as jobs. British left-wing government has supported households three times more than firms. Germany's Grand Coalition has distributed public monies almost evenly between households (55%) and firms (45%). Once taken account of fiscal effects, the Italian right-wing government has supported firms more than jobs, and the Spanish left-wing government has protected jobs more than firms (excluding the hard-hit real estate and banking sectors).[1]

As long as partisan constituency protectionism continues to inspire national policies in their day-to-day grammar, European principles of openness and shared government will not find favour at the domestic level.

---

[1] See European Commission (2009).

On the contrary, their hostility to citizens' interests will be underscored. Demands for constituency-based political innovation will rise, in particular with the challenge of aging and managing healthcare systems, and this will call into question the universal rights that are at the very root of European feelings of equality and social identity that generated forms of 'social patriotism' in Europe after the war, when any other national feelings seemed unacceptable. In the absence of a political vision that can tackle not so much the opposition between state and market, but rather their cooperation, there will be no developing of either 'open' policies (unlinked to national borders) or efficient public responses. To sum up: protectionist and populist behaviour on the part of national political establishments – driven by the cultural legacies that have precluded coming to terms with the openness of global society – has eroded the pro-European consensus and may jeopardise the ultimate survival of the very project.

2. A crisis in politics

Even when European public opinion was at its most detached vis-à-vis the European Union and its plans for the future, Eurobarometer surveys continued to indicate that the crisis in consensus concerned domestic politics and institutions just as much as it did their European equivalents. The surveys showed that European citizens ascribed to their national governments and parliaments both more reliability, in terms of defending their interests (protection function) and more unreliability with discrimination being a risk: quite what one would expect when constituency protectionism prevails, as it posits that national governments do represent protection, but only for part of the country's voters.

Regarding national institutions, governments and parliaments, citizens expressing distrust have always outnumbered those expressing trust, whereas the opposite prevails when the same questions are asked with respect to the European Commission and Parliament. The greater degree of distrust shown for national institutions as compared to their European equivalents is self-evident and well known among various observers of all things European. Vivien Schmidt (2006) thus observes: "The institutional reforms envisioned in the Treaty could indeed have gone some way toward reducing the perceived problems of EU democracy. But they would not in any case have solved the real problem of democracy in the EU: the democratic deficit at national level." She considers that 'Europeanisation' has taken meaning away from domestic politics and further points out, incisively, that a "policy without politics" system has emerged at the European level while a "politics without policies" system prevails nationally. This, she feels, has led to disaffected voters and political extremism in member states. As the Constitutional Treaty aimed precisely to reconnect at least in part politics and policies, the ratification process failure may show that resistance to the idea of reconciling public opinion with European politics lies precisely at the political level and therefore at the level at which, domestically, public opinion is formed.

It is very often posited that in societies as complex as ours, citizens' political choices no longer correspond to simple left-right divides. In actual fact, ever since the 1950s, these categories have been viewed as decreasingly relevant. Nevertheless these two flexible and dialectic poles continue to inform the traditional choices that determine incentives and punishment for national governments. Citizens quite deliberately use constituency politics categories when bestowing or removing their consent where it matters most, i.e. in domestic political competitions.

And in actual fact, focusing on leading European Union democracies in the 1990s and the early years of the current decade, the *passé* concepts of right and left do provide us with a powerful key to understand constituency-protectionist politics and its consequences. In France, Germany, Italy and other countries as well, economic policies have highlighted the differences in stances taken by right- and left-wing governments. To simplify matters to a fault, the former have privileged labour market liberalisation while protecting the ownership of capital, and the latter have privileged financial market liberalisation while protecting labour markets. In simple terms, this is *partisan protectionism*.

In the years just after the fall of the Berlin Wall, the right- and left-wing continued to identify with capital and labour, i.e. the conventional socio-economic categories of ideological face-off politics. French privatisations were thus launched by Balladur's conservative government, which upheld golden share control by entrepreneurs with the right personal and political connections, while Jospin's socialist government went on to privatise capital through a stock exchange reform that impacted corporate governance and stressed the need for transparency in asset ownership. Similarly, in Germany, Helmut Kohl's conservative government launched a financial market reform, but protective networks, the real hallmark of German relational capitalism, were dismantled by Gerhard Schroeder's socialist government. The same occurred in Italy, with a left-wing government privatising and overhauling the tenets of corporate governance while the right-wing government that took over from it put an end to privatisations and market liberalisation, increasing the protective opaqueness of proprietary asset markets by passing legislation that favoured false accounting. The converse occurred regarding labour market reform: left-wing governments strengthened, in relative terms, labour protection and trade unions' protective role while right-wing governments, on the whole, attempted labour market liberalisation. In France, for instance, the 35-hour work week legislation adopted by left-wing governments has been eroded by right-wing governments introducing flexibility in starter job contracts and more recently still, in tax regimes applicable to overtime, not to mention limitations on trade union rights to strike in public services (also known as the 'service minimum'); in Italy, following the Treu reforms adopted by a left-wing government, the so-called 'Biagi legislation' proved to be a battle-horse for the centre-right government and its amendment or repeal is the focus of conflict, within the left-wing, between reformists and radicals. In Germany, labour market reform was initially planned, albeit somewhat reluctantly, by the Kohl government, but it had to wait six years and a 60% increase in the unemployment rate to actually wend its way onto the political agenda of the centre-left. Currently France's President Nicolas Sarkozy implemented explicitly right-wing protectionist policies: liberalising labour markets while protecting capital and national champions, and going so far as to de-penalise corporate crime. Consistently, Sarkozy is opposed to granting European antitrust policies constitutional status, wishes to limit ECB autonomy and temper common trade policy. Looking into individual economic policy measures clearly yields a more subtle picture, but partisan protectionism remains fairly prevalent in the rhetoric of both right- and left-wing European politics: the left tends to protect labour and open up corporate equity and capital markets, while the right tends to do the opposite.

With the opening of national borders to the global economy, national governments soon realised that opting for isolation vis-à-vis the rest of the world, and closing up borders, was impossible or in any event, counterproductive. The sophisticated response has been to protect on a priority basis only those segments of the economy in which vested constituency-based interests lie, while opening up the rest of the economy to the pressures of globalisation and making *them* bear the brunt of the adjustment. In so doing, both the right and the left have ended up referring back to traditional 20th century categories: capital for the right, labour for the left.

Partisan protectionism is at the root of a whole set of political paradoxes that have generated distrust of politics. By engaging in constituency protectionism, left-wing politics thus obtains right-wing results (insofar as exposing capital to competition increases its relative productivity as compared to that of labour) and vice versa; strengthens ideological confrontation (to the extent that only one voting constituency is made to bear the brunt of adjustment, political confrontation is exacerbated); challenges the credibility of politics (with one production factor flexible and the other rigid, the economy is bound to operate sub-optimally); strengthens the rhetoric of isolation (as adjustment to the outer world is entirely made to weigh on one part of society); favours non-political solutions (with the politically disfavoured production factor going for either the 'black' economy or tax evasion) or solutions that are not constituency-based (centrist or broad coalition governments that aim for protection rather than for openness); all of which encourages the rhetoric of isolation or of 'domestic' (in actual fact, constituency-based) interest protection, whereas policies could be embraced that aim to open up the economy.

Clearly, constituency-based protectionism stands opposed to the policies of openness that mark European integration and can therefore only make further inroads as support for Europe flags.

3. The euro as trigger – two examples: Germany and Italy

It is no accident that constituency protectionism emerged in the 1990s and more specifically between 1991 and 1998, as ideological confrontation rhetoric and trust in politics were then made inconsistent by the advent of the euro.

Prior to the liberalisation of capital flows, political comparisons in terms of income distribution were not really telling. Up until the early 1980s, small to medium economies with their own currencies, operating under limited capital flow regimes ('closed economies' for the sake of keeping things simple) could singly determine economic policies favouring either capital (in line with preferences voiced by right-wing voters) or labour (in the case of left-wing governments), knowing that the benefits directly deriving from such political decisions would be redistributed within national borders. Under a very simplistic closed economy model, right-wing policies would probably primarily benefit capitalists' profits, inter alia through lower capital taxation. But favouring return on investment also implies increasing the *supply* of investment, which in a closed economy in turn generates an increase in labour demand and, assuming production factor immobility, a subsequent increase in wage levels and increased income including for those who are not capitalists. Left-wing governments would probably adopt a different tack, supporting employment or wage levels, stimulating demand for consumer goods through increased household incentives, thereby laying the ground for increased yields on corporate productive investment. Setting aside for the moment business cycle issues, and thus remaining in a static medium-term world - a radical assumption that is nevertheless realistic in politicians' timelines - as well as the vigorous rhetoric of ideological confrontation, in terms of both income redistribution effects and the boost to growth, left- or right-wing policies would thus most likely be quite similar (ruling out radically anti-capitalist or anti-democratic policies). And should we assume - more realistically - a dynamic equilibrium in a quasi-closed economy, i.e. the typical position of European countries in the 1970s, conclusions would hardly differ. Poor resource allocation among domestic production factors would lead to balance of payments imbalances, which could in turn be remedied through monetary or exchange rate policies.

The economy's quasi-indifference to constituency-based policies has been acknowledged by analysts focusing on country performance as viewed via 'domestic models' centred on labour market institutions, rather than via policies specifically determined by the requirements of given political constituencies. This quasi-indifference assumption is a radical critique of conventional political analysis, which considers the rhetoric of right- and left-wing dialectics as an a priori significant interpretative key, because of values-related differences. In the real world, however, a quasi-indifference context presents parties with prime 'moral hazard' conditions, through which they can exercise radical dialectics as well as indulge in ideological proselytism, without in the end having to fear the consequences of their own economic policies, the potential inefficiencies of which can, if necessary, be offset through exchange rate-mediated balance of payments adjustments.

In this framework, monetary policy instruments clearly play a central role. Nearly all payments imbalances generated by poor, politically-biased, capital-to-labour resource allocation can be offset through exchange rate changes. And in some countries, exchange rate policies did indeed become the cornerstones of public policy.

Two countries – Italy and Germany – are emblematic of this centrality of exchange rate policies in the 1970s and 1980s, despite radical differences in their respective monetary philosophies.

Italy's recurrent devaluations helped the country rebuild a competitive edge eroded by constituency-based agreements – whether capital subsidisation or labour protection – entered into by governments and social partners primarily to defuse domestic social conflict and manufacture artificial political consent.

Germany, conversely, acknowledged that its central bank – the Bundesbank – was a fully independent monetary authority. While formally keeping a distance from the political fray, the Bundesbank in actual fact did interfere directly in capital-labour relationships. The German central bank was indeed ready to pre-empt all trade union wage hike claims that might have proved excessive in the light of its very restrictive inflation targeting through interest rate increases feeding into exchange rate appreciation, money supply decline and thereby a drop – in relative terms – in the demand for labour. The central bank played a crucial political role – rightly so from the point of view of *Ordnungspolitik*, to use the Freiburg definition – each and every time the balance of income distribution between wages and profits tended to generate inflation, or a balance of payments deficit. The very attractiveness of the D-mark as an investment currency helped keep investment flows within Germany's borders (in a *financially* effective form of 'competitive revaluation', as opposed to *trade*-effective 'competitive devaluations').

Both Italy and Germany's institutional set-ups, with central banks operating under different mandates, provided political groupings with the opportunity to engage in hard-edged rhetorical confrontation, without ever really going for conflict: whenever conflicts between capital and labour would generate inefficient economic policy 'fits', and therefore current account imbalances, the exchange rate would appreciate or depreciate, resetting the system to the same initial conditions for political confrontation on income distribution. The vibrant rhetoric of political and social conflict was therefore to a large extent all talk. In the years that preceded capital flow liberalisation, ideological confrontation may have appeared to raise life and death issues – in practice it was largely neutralised by foreign exchange policy.

With the adoption of the euro, exchange rate policies ceased to be an option. Biased decisions in terms of income allocation to capital or labour, generating payments imbalances, are no longer inevitably offset through currency management in the framework of a closed economy. On the contrary, in open economies with no control over exchange rates, worse case scenarios - where a given government adopts the wrong economic policies - lead to forms of factor mobility that penalise the least mobile factor, generally labour; best case scenarios - where political decisions are cogent with the development of an open economy - lead to situations where the relative advantage enjoyed by one production factor does not necessarily generate medium-term adjustment in favour also of the other. In an open economy, political decisions that favour one factor have more durable and imbalanced an impact than would be the case in a closed economy.

We tend to assume that we live in a post-ideological world, and that we are therefore sheltered from political conflict, whereas the conflicts implicit in right and left-wing policy decisions (both on the supply and the demand side) are far more loaded in terms of sustained consequences on equity today than was the case in the age of ideological confrontation. Protecting the interests of voter constituencies has taken on a much more concrete meaning, and has become more effective from the point of view of both distribution and advocacy for constituency-based policies. In other words, the adoption of the euro did mark the blossoming of partisan protectionism into an attractive electoral strategy for national politics, while it proved negative in terms of consent and support for Europe, insofar as it opposed the protective effectiveness of domestic policies to the claims to openness voiced by Europe.

4. Protection versus protectionism

We have just described the process by which the link between the euro and national political strategies gave rise both to constituency protectionism and a drop in support for the European Union (obviously, not only did those countries that joined the eurozone renounce autonomous monetary policy, but all of them did). Synchronicity with the crisis in support revealed by surveys is self-evident.

But can't constituency-based policies ever have protective features? This is a legitimate question that nevertheless requires moving away from the 'closed society' paradigm. In an open world where economic structures are highly dynamic and changing, upholding the interests of a given constituency does not necessarily correspond to specific allocative or distributive policies regarding production factors. Political splits are more often reflected in differing formulas and weights regarding equal opportunities, workers' participation in management, human capital investment, etc., or whether state or markets should be favoured in order to achieve goals of equity.

During the initial phases of globalisation, major episodes of domestic economy overhaul tended to coincide with forms of economic structural modernisation that concerned both capital and labour markets. Margaret Thatcher has gone down in history for having done away with the control previously exercised by trade unions over British industry, but an equally important achievement was the renewed dynamism in capital markets, which opened up corporate ownership and shareholding. More recently the overhaul of the German economy has gone through two phases: first the reform of capitalism, which occurred partly spontaneously, partly through corporate governance reforms, and secondly, with the Agenda 2010 reforms, which removed a number of rigidities in labour market regulation as well. Some economists have claimed that in order to be effective, product market liberalisation requires labour market liberalisation. Although the rule is not very well defined, non-constituency-based economic reform (at least in the 20th century acceptance of these terms) does appear to be effective.

As societies evolve towards knowledge economies, with service sector development and increasing dismantlement of borders in terms both of corporate ownership and production processes - with recent business theories talking of globally distributed tasks with no regard for the local production processes that used to ground specificity, as well as regional and community politics - we increasingly need a societal description that will not fragment around age-old splits between labour and capital: a society we could deem, for simplicity's sake, an open society. In open societies within a globalised economy, constituency protectionism has even less of a functional rationale than it did before.

Overcoming the reservations of the electoral interests/protection structures connection therefore requires one to spell out the true benefits to be derived from an open economy. If the European Union manages to convince voters in its member states of the political advantages and economic benefits to be derived from an open society, it will also manage in the process to repair the damage that has proved so detrimental to its future - but this will however not happen without the input of national policies. Domestic constituency-based political strategies need to focus on investing in human capital - according to different modalities, with different roles bestowed on public and private sectors depending on individual ideological preferences - and on making the most of global opportunities to date unconfined by domestic borders, so as to trigger a race towards controlled openness. Economic benefits, openness, joint government could thus become the terms of a new virtuous circle.

The whole issue of protecting citizens against economic and social risk cannot be swept under the carpet simply by passing negative judgment on protectionism, which uses it to manipulate matters politically. We would rather view support for the European Union as the outcome of a linear process: as economies become ever more open, innovation and productivity increase, and in turn generate jobs and prosperity which in turn elicit support in citizens both for national governments and for European institutions. This approach is reflected in the very history of European integration and the specific technical and economic 'vehicles' that have guaranteed its progress. In recent years, however, it has become ever clearer that the logical sequencing mentioned above - openness, reform, economic success, political support - does not correspond to the way most Europeans think. To quote Liddle & Lerais (2007), "the citizens of our countries think that globalisation, market liberalisation and the constant quest for competitive advantages are at least as much a threat as a cure". Citizens want some sort of risk insurance and failing this, the demand for protectionism will continue to rise. Globalisation is the reference framework within which the new finalities of the European Union must be defined. In the face of emerging new economic powers, of open borders, of major global phenomena - from climate change to terrorism - the European Union is positing itself as an institutional framework where demands for openness must adequately be met, alongside demands for security. Should this not happen, constituency protectionism shall prevail domestically, and support for the EU will decline. We may pretend that the need for security isn't there, but whenever European voters have their say we shall see that this 'perverted', obsessive search for protection does indeed exist.

Guaranteeing openness, while providing some form of security, assumes the ability to govern: the ability responsibly to reach decisions on the implicit choices underpinning trade-offs between growth and security or, for those who doubt that there are such trade-offs, between short-term insecurity and long-term growth. This inter-temporal bridging function also assumes the ability to govern, be it only because there is no systematic synchronicity between power and responsibility. It is no wonder that a significant number of European citizens feel that in the face of economic globalisation, their request for security has remained unanswered by the European Union. The Union, insofar as it has only integrated markets, is in fact perceived on a par with globalisation: that is, first and foremost, as an unaccountable player in the openness policy. Leaving aside a number of dubious initiatives such as the European Globalisation Adjustment Fund (EGF), to date its political response to the request for security has been to state that the issue was not its concern, and that all it could do was wait for the restructuring of European economies to yield economic dividends to the public at large.

Feelings of insecurity have further grown as other significant events have highlighted that the European Union is very often at loggerheads with member states when it comes to economic coordination. The need to engage in the structural reform of domestic economic systems has in fact coincided with fiscal consolidation in almost all member states, giving rise to financial re-balancing processes that have often proved painful and with no end in sight, and that have thus increased citizens' feelings of utter isolation in the face of the costs of globalisation. Rationales for fiscal consolidation include aspects of relevance to citizen support: the need for long-term sustainability as populations age (which is tantamount to securing welfare systems); a clearly defined efficiency requirement applied to the use of public monies; and a preference for lower tax burdens in view of the increased heterogeneity of our societies. But insofar as this process has coincided with the single (global) market's initial economic pressures, it has amplified contradictions between resource redistribution required locally for fiscal consolidation, and resource redistribution required by the opening up of our economies - which is now eliciting much (politically expressed) vexation.

Faced with the social costs of economic change and financial consolidation, individual member states and the European Union have often adopted opposing attitudes vis-à-vis citizens. Domestically, citizens have two basic references - their welfare systems and their protection (or closed economy) requirements, which they put to political parties as markets open up, and liberalisation proceeds apace. At the European level, fiscal consolidation and market openness requirements - in other words requirements that are the very opposite of citizens' protection requirements - are written into the very history of the Union. The EU has accrued long experience in coming to terms with issues of openness and challenges posed by structural reform. From the common to the single market, and then on to monetary union and the Lisbon agenda, the European Union has strengthened the dynamic vectors of border dismantlement and economic restructuring. And the same has obtained for fiscal consolidation: stability and fiscal discipline, convergence criteria, the Growth and Stability Pact all go to show European citizens that the political language of globalisation resides in Brussels, and not in their own national capitals and that moreover, this language is far removed from their possible control. However legitimate may be the criticism levelled against some national governments who indulge in 'Europe-bashing', one must acknowledge that a number of structural reasons do explain the fact that in the absence of a genuine ability to govern on the part of Brussels and therefore of an ability to promote both openness and security - citizens' dissatisfaction vis-à-vis uncontrollable social phenomena will quite naturally target the European Union.

It is therefore clear that in order not to fuel demand for protectionism, attention must be paid to this demand for protection: and thus forms of risk insurance must be provided that cover, first of all, the future of the welfare state. Because in the end, uncertainties in this respect may well explain the failure of so many polls on European issues.

5. Welfare

Thinking about the future of the welfare state in Europe requires a dynamic approach. It so happens that the factor that defines the priority ranking of the European social state is dynamic, including its productive structure, savings parameters and aggregate demand features. Clearly my reference here is to population aging, with its weighty consequences in terms of pensions and healthcare spending. According to UN data, people aged 65 and over will account for more than a quarter of the total population in 2030, as against 8% in 1950 and 14% in 2000. Population aging has a dramatic impact on financing schemes based on workers' contributions. In some European countries, such as Italy and Spain, the dependency rate of retirees vis-à-vis workers is going to double in less than 50 years, growing in Italy from 27.9% in 2000 (26% in Spain) to 64.5% in 2050 (63.5% in Spain). In most countries welfare reforms undertaken in the 1990s focused on the issue of pension scheme funding. Starting off with incremental corrections that slightly altered or somewhat tightened pension scheme parameters, reforms then focused on structural features including entitlements, indexation rules and retirement age. Currently, official EU forecasts for some countries point to dramatic growth in the impact of pension-related payments on public spending. In Spain, estimates point to a quasi-doubling, from 9.4% of GDP to 17.7%. Budgets will also have to contend with other increases in spending stemming from aging-related social programmes. According to estimates, the comprehensive increase is likely to total 3% to 10% of GDP, depending on welfare provisions and demographics. These fiscal consequences clearly show that unless measures are taken in time, the situation may well become politically untenable. As we know, within aging societies, voters' interests tend to increase the political cost of reform. Under the circumstances the issue of political compatibility between European economic, monetary and fiscal integration on the one hand, and the political and social sensitivities expressed at the domestic level on the other, must thus once again be addressed. One can easily envision domestic political costs being shifted to Europe. A risk that may however conceal an opportunity: couldn't European integration help member states safeguard welfare state *equilibria*, while strengthening citizens' trust in Europe?

Regarding the future of welfare systems there are at least three different possible outcomes, depending on the scope and quality of political initiative assigned to supranational bodies. The first is a European welfare system, modelled on national systems, administered by a continent-wide bureaucracy. The second is a system where national welfare schemes are not connected to European institutions, as these are not deemed to have any right to interfere in the social risk insurance models chosen by individual member states. The third is a regulated market for welfare schemes, where individual countries guarantee the universal coverage of their citizens at levels determined through regulation and redistribution, but where service provision by entities of all countries, both public and private, is allowed.

The first of these possible outcomes is not popular and governments advocating such a way forward would be headed towards political suicide. Delegating part of the responsibility for pension scheme management to a supranational institution such as the European Commission might help individual states reduce the political cost of reform, but would increase public distrust of Brussels and in the end might even risk weakening support for further European-level reform. The second outcome corresponds to the 'separate track' approach adopted so far. When the integration project was first launched in the 1950s, federalist discourse highlighting an 'ever closer to citizens' stance and various functional spill-overs was underpinned by the idea that the European Community should focus on opening markets in economic terms, while individual states retained control over welfare and social solidarity schemes. Starting in the 1980s this division of labour became somewhat unrealistic and with monetary union it has become downright counterproductive. To echo Ferrera (2006), insulating national welfare schemes from the dynamics of economic integration and supranational interference has long since ceased to be possible. This means that one should look into the third possible outcome, the only one that is both "realistic and European" (a point comprehensively addressed by Gareth Davies (2006): a European-wide regulated market for welfare services that would recognisably propose the European Union's social model, leaving the first pillar - which remains symbolically so important to national identity - under national jurisdiction, albeit within a European coordination and control framework, while developing a second pillar through a truly integrated market for voluntary pension schemes and supplemental health care coverage, eliciting public and private supply of increasingly efficient services, disconnected from territorial origin.

There are many forces driving market-based harmonisation of European welfare systems and in particular focusing on provision of services by both public and private players. The first has to do with the quest for more efficiency in public spending and is linked to citizens' tax preferences as well as to the need for effective public support at a time when private sectors are undergoing intense restructuring. Further impetus stems from economic coordination at the European level with a view to achieving greater convergence in public spending at least in terms of public policy stability and, to a lesser extent, quality. Another force has to do with 'negative' integration (i.e. the elimination of national protection) spurred by European jurisdictions wherever public services, because of their economic nature, come under European freedom of movement legislation, despite the well-known distinctions set forth in the Bolkestein Directive regarding welfare service liberalisation, in particular with respect to healthcare, but also more broadly to services targeting social objectives or presenting general economic interest.

The trend towards privatisation of a significant part of national welfare schemes can contribute to the harmonisation of European social assistance services insofar as private providers of welfare services, such as a German hospital, a British university or a Dutch pension fund, can provide similar services in a variety of different countries. These trends further reflect a number of other developments linked to the dismantlement of state economic monopolies, which has led both to an increase in the numbers of providers of public services and to a diversification in terms of quality. Thus, while continuing to uphold the right of all citizens to welfare coverage, an increasing number of countries handle health insurance and pension schemes through private providers; the privatisation process stems from the need for more rigor, and therefore more cost control in public spending. With public and private providers working in parallel, the former are encouraged to be more efficient, which corresponds to a general request on the part of public opinion. Finally, private providers, which are often able to break down the actual cost of services, allow for greater user choice.

The European Court of Justice has considered healthcare systems to be an 'economic activity', while it has refused similarly to define higher education as such. But if welfare services are considered to be an economic activity, one can hardly shield them from the freedom of circulation of services rule that in practice voids the nationality requirement for both providers and users of such services. The real obstacle to European action favouring welfare system integration lies therefore not in the European Union's history nor in its current legislation, but in an absolute lack of political will.

In discussions on the Bolkestein Directive, which liberalises markets for services, the idea of including healthcare services met with quite considerable resistance, despite the fact that the Court had deemed them to be an economic activity. There appears to be considerable resolve on the part of both governments and citizens to retain control over individual welfare systems, regardless of the clear efficiency gains that might derive from a broader market, more specialised providers and quality controls that would prove efficient even vis-à-vis state monopolies.

That said, welfare systems are one of the few fields addressed by politics in which each and every citizen has a concrete, direct and personal interest. It is quite understandable that citizens should wish to retain control over such interests, especially vis-à-vis European institutions the nature, efficiency and accountability of which they only dimly see. Resistance on the part of national political establishments, fearful of losing the power and influence they currently wield, is even stronger. This means that politically, no proposal to engage in positive welfare system harmonisation is likely to come forward, which paradoxically has the effect that markets will be left free to circumvent the regulatory obstacles defined by individual member states. Lack of governance or direction thus often leads to situations where citizens increasingly distrust politics and globalisation. Unregulated welfare service provision does not however guarantee that the solidarity dimension of current systems will be carried over, regardless of the significance of this dimension within citizens' more general request for security. The provision of private services of differing qualities actually tends to drive a wedge into the quality of social services on offer, but because of correlations between homogeneity and public solidarity, increased heterogeneity may transform the reasons for which citizens typically support European forms of solidarity. For changes to welfare systems - required to make them sustainable, efficient and 'open' - to be politically neutral, these changes must be governed and steered, and part of the political responsibility for this - even if only regulating private, non-national welfare service providers - shall inevitably behove European institutions.

In order to be credible in taking this responsibility over from individual member states, European institutions cannot avoid engaging in some serious thinking on how they themselves view individuals and societies. This is a difficult and demanding task, and it is no accident that to date it has failed to achieve one of its primary goals: laying constitutional ground for the whole structure. Positing a European welfare model based on regulated market services, rather than proposing a simple state model with monopoly over user choice, implies that European institutions have to become providers not only of rules and controls, but also of safeguards regarding citizens' freedom to choose.

According to Ferrera (2006), realistic approaches to the reconciliation of economic reform and social stability require political innovation to be even more structured at the common level, and demand that domestic welfare systems be slotted into a framework that currently lacks a multi-level European area of citizenship, on the basis of a joint catalogue of basic civil, political and social rights, including a European safeguard in terms of minimum (or sufficient) resources that could possibly be financed directly out of the European budget. This more ambitious qualification of the social dimension of European citizenship could open avenues to pilot initiatives aiming to address specific societal problems in Europe: combating youth poverty, setting up loan systems for higher education funding, supporting single mothers, easing cross-border mobility.

6. Beyond partisan protectionism

The framework described above assumes the ability to develop a new political vision that can focus on long-term goals, renounce 20th century social categories and encourage the opening up of a European welfare services market through state and market cooperation. This political initiative is consistent at the European level, but less so nationally. In order to respond to requests for innovation and political initiative, both relevant and accountable, a European space has to be opened up to political parties, so that they may reformulate their programmes at the European level in a consistent manner, and ultimately internalise goals of openness and inter-temporal consistency in their domestic programmes as well.

The fact that the European Union is still basically inter-governmental fuels interest in heterogeneity and keeps European parties from having a clear agenda. National parties that have regrouped at the European level all know that their preferences - and those of their voters - are essentially upheld by their co-nationals, regardless of party affiliation, more so than by their own political allies in other countries.

The functional and segmented nature of jurisdiction within the European Union is one of the factors currently hindering the development of European parties. Such parties, insofar as they are general players, put forth broad visions of society that connect a variety of different interests and different areas of activity, and that therefore do not lend themselves readily to the functional nature of European initiatives. That said, when addressing the issue of European welfare systems, broader social visions are difficult to avoid. Empirical surveys have furthermore shown that citizen and party positions on Europe are not only determined by national origin, but that a form of ideological polarisation is on the rise around left- and right-wing lines that is not being expressed directly through conventional opposition between capital and labour, but upstream from that, as openness versus protection. Analysing voting patterns in the European Parliament shows that it is the opposition between 'regulators' and 'open market supporters' that has determined the outcome of many a debate.

Integrated welfare systems require that a proper state-market mix be defined. This mix must be non-ideological, despite the fact that state and market have for decades now been the focus of ideological confrontation. Building a welfare service market with publicly set goals and regulations therefore needs to involve all major parties represented in the European Parliament.

This process must start at the national political level. Earlier in this chapter, I posited the view that national politics, which currently play a determining role in the generation of citizen support for the European Union, are conditioned by a specific operating principle that I have called 'partisan protectionism'. Within this principle, the right and left can be distinguished from one another by the fact that they protect capital and labour respectively - and therefore resist openness - while exposing the other production factor to external competition. Careful reading of the positions put forth by national governments in discussions on Europe, and more importantly still, of the policy stances they uphold on their own ground, that of national parliamentary debate, illustrates the explanatory powers of this partisan protectionism concept, which is in fact the coming together of the two forms of political polarisation we observe today: the coming together of demands for closure as opposed to openness, and demands for left-right polarisation. The political maturity required to overcome constituency protectionism has to do with how both right and left define their positions. More specifically, it has to do with the fact that the left needs to define itself as the political power upholding an open welfare service provision and labour market operation model - rather than express protective functions solely in terms of closed economies and markets, while the right needs quite as provocatively to open up capital markets to competition. It is only through an opening up of welfare provision to private market players that the left will prove able to save the social state. Just as exposing corporations to competition is the only way the right can guarantee that nationality doesn't become an obstacle. And it is only through the joint contribution of both left and right thus defined that an effective and non-national welfare provision system may emerge.

I am basically convinced that it behoves left- and right-wing politicians with a vision to formulate social programmes that provide for welfare system reform and the comprehensive opening of capital markets so that state and market can work together, each serving the other, and then resume confrontation, without antiquated diversions, as to what European citizens want in terms of equity or individual freedoms.

References

Davies, G. (2006), *The Process and Side-Effects of Harmonisation of European Welfare States*, Jean Monnet Working Paper No. 2/06, Jean Monnet Center for International and Regional Law and Justice, NYU School of Law, New York.

European Commission (2009), *The Economic Crisis: Its impact on Member States and how they are responding to it*, Occasional Paper No. 6-2009, Brussels.

Ferrera, M. (2006), speech at colloquium on The Social Dimension of the European Union: What are the Prospects?, Centre d'Analyse Stratégique, Bureau du Premier Ministre, Paris, 23 October.

Liddle, R. and F. Lerais (2007), *Europe's Social Reality*, A consultation paper from the Bureau of European Policy Advisers (BEPA), European Commission, Brussels.

Schmidt, V. (2006), *Democracy in Europe. The EU and National Polities*, Oxford: Oxford University Press.

3. A MORE SOCIAL EU: ISSUES OF WHERE AND HOW

MAURIZIO FERRERA & STEFANO SACCHI[*]

Introduction

Over the last few years, the two enlargements and the three referenda on new treaty texts have prompted a far-reaching debate on social Europe. To a large extent this debate has focused on the problems and prospects of national welfare regimes: their persistent difficulties, their comparative performance and their reform trajectories. But discussion has also focused, at least in part, on the social dimension of the EU proper: on what might be called the 'social EU'.

This chapter explores this second topic, the social dimension of the European Union as a political entity in its own right. In the process, we shall try to answer two sensitive questions:

Do we need a more social EU, that is, to engage in more supranational activism in the social sphere?

And if so, why and how?

1. The need for a more social European Union

Our answer to that first question is straightforward: yes, we do need a more social EU. We believe this to be the case for three broad reasons: the first has to do with social justice, the second with economic efficiency and the last with the legitimacy of the EU polity and its ability to command widespread positive support among European citizens.

---

* We gratefully acknowledge research assistance by Krzysztof Nowaczek and warmly thank Fabrizia Peirce for her valuable help in producing the final version of this chapter.

First, we need a more social EU in order to secure a fairer, more equitable distribution of life chances for EU citizens, both within and between member states. This is the 'social cohesion', or 'social justice' rationale. According to the treaties, the EU has a broad mission, that of promoting economic and social progress (Article 2, Treaty on European Union). Unless one believes in a naïve version of the trickle-down effect of growth, the pursuit of economic prosperity through efficient and open markets should thus be accompanied by an agenda for social progress, resting on key values (such as fairness, justice or social security) that are widely shared and deeply rooted in Europe's political cultures.[1] While there can be no doubt that this agenda includes areas and policies that legally come under national jurisdiction, it should be equally clear that the EU has a role to play, both directly (by exercising its legal powers to sustain and complement national social justice agendas) and indirectly (by mainstreaming, as it were, social cohesion/justice considerations within its own growth and jobs agenda, more so than it seems to have done so far under the new Lisbon strategy).

Second, we need a more social EU in order to improve the functioning of the internal market, and thus generate more growth and jobs (this is the 'economic efficiency' rationale). A wealth of political economy research has shown that social policies can play an important role not only as redistributive instruments and vehicles for social and political consensus, but also as 'productive factors'. This was one of the original assumptions of the Lisbon strategy and the 'modernisation' agenda set forth by the European Commission in the 1990s. At the theoretical level the positive (i.e. efficiency-enhancing) effects of social policy can be sketched out relatively easily: social insurance allows for riskier educational and occupational choices that increase the expected lifetime income of individuals, regardless of the risk-taking outcome: "Under the protection of

---

[1] However crude the indicator, it is telling that 17% of all European respondents listed the gap between the rich and the poor as one of their three main current concerns when offered a choice of 17 items, including pensions, terrorism, health, immigration, crime, the environment, globalisation and economic growth (see Eurobarometer, 2007b). In a more recent survey a vast majority of Europeans (87%) agreed on the following statement: "There should be policies ensuring that the gap between the rich and the poor is reduced significantly in our country" (Eurobarometer, 2008a).

the welfare state, more can be dared", to quote Hans Werner Sinn (1995, p. 507). At the practical level, however, identifying which policies can enhance productivity and competitiveness (and how exactly they do so) is a difficult task, as is quantifying the 'costs of no/non-social policy', or having one that is too limited, as illustrated by the ongoing debate on the actual effectiveness of active labour market policies. But the tasks are not per se impossible, and certainly such a *pars construens* is required (at the EU level) to offset the *pars destruens* of highlighting the negative effects that may stem from a status quo of social protection schemes in member states.

Thirdly, and possibly most importantly, we need a more social EU in order to secure continuing support for the integration process on the part of an increasingly worried public (and this is the 'social and political legitimacy' rationale). Recent opinion polls have provided growing evidence that the EU is perceived as a potentially dangerous entity by a majority of its citizens, as a threat to national labour markets and social protection systems, as a 'Trojan horse' serving the malevolent interests of globalisation.[2] Some initiatives on the part of the European Commission, such as the initial drafting of the Services Directive and some rulings by the European Court of Justice, as in the Viking, Laval and Rüffert cases, were received with great anxiety by large segments of the EU citizenry, particularly those more exposed to the consequences of economic opening. Mass perceptions can be factually wrong, but they do play a crucial role in politics. We know that post-war social protection systems and the welfare state have created extraordinary bonds between European citizens and their national institutions, bringing about a form of close allegiance, based on the institutionalised exchange of material benefits for electoral support. The EU, conversely, has been rather weak in terms of identity and allegiance-building. What neo-functionalist thinkers and statesmen had hoped for, and sometimes even forecast, never actually happened: European citizens have not systematically shifted their loyalties from domestic to supranational institutions. What binds European citizens (i.e. citizens of EU member states) to the EU is in fact a different kind of loyalty: a derived, secondary allegiance, which persists only as long the EU is

---

[2] As early as 2006, over 70% of all European citizens feared that 'the building of Europe' might entail the transfer of jobs to other member countries with lower production costs, while 50% feared that it might entail the loss of social benefits (see Eurobarometer, 2007a).

capable of providing resources to its member states, thereby reinforcing the direct, primary allegiance that links members of national political communities to their domestic institutions. The initial division of labour envisaged by the founding fathers of the European Economic Community (EEC) in 1957 had precisely this focus: the Community was to promote economic prosperity by opening markets and generating economies of scale, thus providing member states with resources they could use to power their own social protection systems, to engage in (welfare) state-building – or state-rescuing, in the wake of the Second World War, to echo Alan Milward (1992). As we shall see, in recent decades this division of labour has collapsed, and the European (economic) integration process has tended to encroach upon domestic social solidarity institutions, without rebuilding at the EU level what was being constrained domestically. Hence the widespread concerns that revolve around European construction.

In short: if voters' anxieties are not alleviated, if they are not convinced that 'the EU cares' (through direct and indirect action, or non-action), the integration process may be seriously de-legitimised and jeopardised by xenophobic sentiments and neo-protectionist demands voiced by those social groups that are most directly affected by economic opening. The economic crisis has undoubtedly intensified this challenge.

2. How to build a more social EU

The three rationales we have identified to show that we require a more social EU are analytically distinct, but they are of course interrelated and mutually re-enforcing. Judging by documents and official statements (such as the Presidency Conclusions of the 2007 Spring Council, the Berlin Declaration, signed on the 50th anniversary of the Treaty of Rome or the new Article 2 of the Treaty on European Union – Article 3 of the consolidated version – which states that the Union is based on "a highly competitive social market economy", promoting social justice and protection), they now seem to elicit a relatively broad consensus among both national and Community policy-makers. By the same token, opinion polls show that European citizens are quite unhappy with the EU's performance in the social field, and combating poverty and unemployment are consistently ranked as the top two actions that the EU should engage in as a matter of priority.[3] Recent surveys make it very clear that EU citizens want the EU to deliver more and better in the social field: in late 2008 employment and social affairs was the policy area with the greatest discrepancy between the perceived and desired resources spent from the EU budget (Eurobarometer, 2008b); in the summer of 2009, 34% of respondents asked for greater financial commitment from the European Social Fund (Eurobarometer, 2009). Moreover, a European welfare system, whatever that may mean, is seen as the best strategy to strengthen European citizenship (better than, among other things, adopting a European constitution).[4]

The problem is, where do we go from here? Answering our second question – provided that we need a more social EU, what purpose should it serve and what form should it take? – is indeed more complex. In which areas, exactly, should the social dimension of the EU be strengthened? What are the social challenges that require a response *at the EU level* rather than at national levels? In our quest for an answer, it may prove useful to recall a distinction often used in past debates on 'Social Europe', which remains heuristically valid: the distinction between *common* and *similar* social challenges.

Common challenges originate from a single exogenous factor or set of factors (e.g. cross-border liberalisations). These challenges affect all member states at the same time and require some type of joint response (national solutions are sub-optimal). It is on this front that a stronger social EU is needed urgently.

---

[3] "The protection of social rights" and "the fight against unemployment" are the two items ranked the lowest in a poll where respondents were asked to assess EU performance in a set of 15 policy areas including, inter alia, the protection of human rights, the fight against terrorism, equal treatment of men and women, and the promotion of democracy and peace in the world. ("Ensuring economic growth" also ranked poorly.) See Eurobarometer (2006). As for the steps the EU should take as a matter of priority, see for instance Eurobarometer (2007c) and Eurobarometer (2008a). Still, what the EU currently does in the area of employment and social affairs is positively evaluated by a majority of respondents in Eurobarometer (2009).

[4] See QA20, Eurobarometer (2006).

Similar challenges, on the other hand, originate from largely endogenous dynamics (e.g. demographic ageing or changing family and gender relations) and can be met through different, path-dependent national responses. On this front, a stronger social EU is less urgent, but can still play a crucial role, with some qualifications.

3. Supplementing the internal market with social rights

What is the most pressing *common* challenge currently confronting national welfare states? Undoubtedly, it is the internal market. In recent decades, and in the past ten years in particular, the internal market (and more specifically the free movement of labour and services) has come to strain the social policy and employment regimes of member states. Recent enlargements have significantly accelerated this process. As we have seen, the original treaties envisaged a division of labour between supranational and national levels: the Community was to be instrumental in opening up markets and helping achieve otherwise unattainable economies of scale, so as to generate resources that member states could use in the institutionalised exchange of social benefits - flowing from their national welfare institutions - for regime support on the part of their domestic political communities. "Keynes at home, Smith abroad", as Robert Gilpin (1987, p. 355) aptly dubbed this kind of embedded liberalism arrangement. This justified the weakness of the social provisions in the Rome Treaty: from equality of treatment for men and women (which incidentally was not meant to bestow rights directly upon citizens, but rather to ground supranational action and guarantee a level playing field for European companies) to the coordination of social security regimes. All the social provisions and articles contained therein were instrumental in the dismantling of non-tariff barriers to trade and the creation of a higher economic order featuring unconstrained economic trade flows. However, this supranational liberal order rested upon, or rather was embedded in national welfare states that were to be equally unconstrained in terms of social regulation capabilities, and in particular would not be constrained by the supranational authorities. This was the rationale behind the paucity of social provisions in the Rome Treaty, and for the economic instrumentality of those few included in it: social policy was the business of national institutions only. Put differently, this division of labour implied separating the jurisdiction between the supranational and national levels, thus establishing 'mutual non-interference' between market-making and market-correcting functions. European competition law and the four freedoms were not supposed to impinge upon member states' sovereignty in the social sphere (Giubboni, 2003).

This did not last. Firstly, international political economy conditions have changed since the 1970s, and the embedded liberalism compromise has floundered. Moreover, and more importantly still as regards European integration, the Community legal order has been constitutionalised - to quote Joseph Weiler (1999). More specifically, the supremacy of Community law over domestic legislation has, along with direct effect, torn the initial division of labour to pieces: if Community law trumps national law, then provisions geared to fostering unconstrained competition (i.e. the Treaty provisions) trump social regulation, as enshrined in national constitutions and laws, and ECJ judges, contrary to national constitutional judges, will be constrained in balancing economic and social interests whenever these clash (Scharpf, 2009). This state of affairs has of course become more apparent as the economic integration process has deepened: from the White Paper on the internal market through to the Single European Act and the Maastricht Treaty, and then to EMU, the integration of European economies has progressed at a spectacular pace, without being matched by anything similar in the social realm. What we have tried to argue so far is that reasserting the original competence allocation - market-making with the EU, social policy with the member states - simply will not do the trick, since social policy at the national level is no longer safe from 'intrusion' (or 'infiltration', as Gérard Lyon-Caen puts it (1992)) by the European economic constitution, as many ECJ rulings have by now made quite clear (Ferrera, 2005).

When it comes to social protection systems, it is the free movement of labour and services that poses the greatest challenge to the viability of domestic social solidarity arrangements as we know them, even though it is noteworthy that the ECJ has not always operated as a 'market police force', and has on several occasions granted some degree of 'immunity' against European market law to national welfare institutions and practices. However, in the absence of a Treaty 'hook', it has done so on the grounds of legal arguments that may well be overridden in the future. In addition member states are investing a lot of energy in cushioning their social protection systems against challenges stemming from European law, whether by not complying with rulings, agreeing among themselves to change European law or even failing to introduce new social programmes that could subsequently become the object of European court action. This may well be one of the reasons why such issues have not yet come to the fore of public debate in Europe and remain confined to insider circles: their potentially disruptive outcomes have so far been buffered by member states' reactions. But how long can this last? Member states may be compared to those cyclists who track stand - expending a lot of energy in order to maintain their position.

Let there be no mistake: freedom of movement for persons and services has opened up opportunities and brought about tremendous benefits for individual citizens, despite the challenges to national welfare systems. If unregulated, however, this enhanced freedom for individuals may come at the cost of severe systemic disruptions, or even failure - which may in turn result in diminished welfare provision for all. It is certainly a good thing that Mrs Watts and many in her situation all over Europe can now get prompt treatment abroad paid for by their own domestic healthcare schemes; however, when this comes at the risk of disrupting a basic organisational tool of contemporary health systems, i.e. waiting lists, clearly some direction is called for.[5]

To some extent, the European Union is experiencing a 'social question' (as well as a 'governance issue') that is not too dissimilar from that experienced by European nations in the second half of the 19th century, when the 'freedom to work' became a universal civil right and local labour markets merged to give rise to single 'domestic' labour markets, which were then subjected to common standards (labour laws, unemployment and more generally social insurance, national labour exchanges, etc.).

In his groundbreaking historical analysis of modern citizenship, T.H. Marshall (1950) suggested that the evolution of this institution involved a two-fold process of fusion, and of separation. The fusion was geographical and entailed the dismantling of local privileges and immunities, the

---

[5] We refer here to the ECJ ruling in the Watts case (C-372/04, decided on 16 May 2006). The Court ruled that a refusal to grant prior authorisation for treatment abroad paid for by domestic authorities could not be based solely on the existence of waiting lists intended to allow for the planning and management of hospital care supply on the basis of predetermined general clinical priorities, without there having been an objective medical assessment of the patient's condition. Where delays arising from such waiting lists appeared unacceptable, in the light of the patient's assessed condition, the competent institution could not refuse authorisation for treatment abroad.

harmonisation of rights and obligations throughout the national territory concerned and the establishment of a level playing field (the equal status of citizens) within state borders. The separation was functional and entailed the creation of new sources of nationwide authority and jurisdiction, as well as new specialised institutions for the implementation of that authority and that jurisdiction at a decentralised level.

The present historical phase is reproducing this double challenge of fusion and separation under new guises. As was the case domestically 150 years ago, freedom of movement can now be a tremendous trigger for growth and job creation in the EU's internal market, and can therefore enhance welfare for European citizens. But without adequate supranational norms and governance (a stronger 'social' EU), this new market will not work effectively and in fact runs the risk of reducing individual welfare. Again, fusion requires institutional innovation in order to fully bear fruit (under the economic rationale), and to safeguard the equitable distribution of such outcomes (under the social justice rationale) in a context of social peace and political stability (under the legitimacy rationale).

Managing the social implications of freedom of movement (or, to put it another way, securing the social complements of the internal market) ought to be the primary goal of a stronger 'social' EU, which would seek to eschew the risk of biting the hand that feeds it by not jeopardising the bond between citizens and their welfare states, and being made to bear the blame for whatever storm member states would then have to face. On the basis of what we have discussed so far, it is clear that only the EU can perform this task. But how should it go?

There already is, of course, an *acquis* of hard norms that have been introduced over time precisely (or primarily) with a view to paralleling market 'fusion' with a modicum of social harmonisation. Some of these norms (such as the Directives on non-standard employment, or on gender discrimination) also address new social risks in a post-industrial society. But what are the new and further steps that should be taken in this direction in the current post-industrial (and post-enlargement) context - also considering the deep impact of the crisis? We believe that the following would be the most natural candidates for the task at hand:

- Establishing (or strengthening) a common floor of labour law guarantees, especially for non-standard, irregular workers;
- Agreeing on common definitions and criteria regarding those areas (such as social security, services of general interest, etc.) that are

particularly sensitive to greater freedom of movement, thus finding a proper balance between the goals of 'dismantling local immunities and privileges' and that of preserving legitimate national diversities;

- Establishing common rules on a minimum wage on the one hand, and launching a Community initiative on a generalised minimum income guarantee on the other, in order to protect the most vulnerable;
- Updating and fine-tuning social security regimes for migrant workers;
- Establishing something along the lines of a 'European Audit Board' for the oversight of contractual practices, in order to avoid social dumping.

Progress on these fronts was advocated by a declaration on "Enhancing Social Europe" signed by the Labour ministers of eight member states (Belgium, Bulgaria, Greece, Spain, France, Italy, Cyprus and Hungary) in February 2007 – to little avail, in the end. Still, on each of these fronts a number of relatively detailed proposals has begun to circulate. To name but a few, the issue of a common floor of labour law guarantees, dealing with the working conditions of all workers, regardless of their work contract (and therefore also applying to irregular workers) was put forward in the 2006 Green Paper on labour law. The Lisbon Treaty, meanwhile, includes a Protocol on services of general interest and retains the so-called horizontal social clause written into the Constitutional Treaty Article 9 of the Treaty on the Functioning of the European Union, which introduced a form of 'social mainstreaming' by stating that, in implementing its policies, the Union should take into account social requirements (Ferrera, 2009).

The issue of a minimum income guarantee is also important, and deserves more attention insofar as it may well be a very promising way of securing the social complements of the internal market, according to our definition of the approach required. This might take the form of Community-wide legal provisions regulating minimum income schemes at the national level (a Community Directive on this topic was originally put forward by the Commission in 1992, but was downgraded to mere communication status following member states' opposition). This would regulate, and possibly improve, benefit provision in countries where such schemes exist, and spur into action those (such as Greece, Italy and Hungary – ironically, three of the signatories to the plea to "Enhance Social Europe") that do not have a generalised means-tested scheme. This might also take the form of a pan-European welfare scheme, locally administered but stemming directly from the EU. Certain concrete proposals along these lines have been circulating for some time in academic circles.[6] It is not our intention to assess the pros and cons of this thought-provoking idea here, knowing that in any event it would need to be carefully crafted lest it generate opportunistic behaviour on the part of citizens and national governments alike. It could however be instrumental in building some form of direct allegiance between European citizens and the EU, thus replicating at the supranational level, in a sense, the formidable bonding tool constituted of social protection schemes at the national level.

Another measure that addresses common challenges (albeit those posed by globalisation and now the economic crisis, rather than the internal market) and that – if well crafted and publicised – could help forge bonds between the EU and its citizens, thus providing legitimacy to the former, is the European Globalisation Adjustment Fund launched at the beginning of 2007. This aims at providing European workers made redundant because of globalisation (under trade-induced mass layoffs) with time-limited direct support in finding new jobs. The idea here is that funding is provided by the Community budget (more specifically, the scheme is co-funded by the EU and member states) only to active labour market policies. So far, the Fund seems to have been rather effective for those workers who have had access to the measures financed by it (some 70% of the 10,000 workers involved in 2008 have been re-employed), but it has on the whole delivered very little: out of €500 million available every year, only less than €50 million were distributed in 2008, owing to the lack of requests and the slowness of the procedures. In June 2009, the Fund Regulation was changed in order to make it a tool to counteract the economic crisis, thereby lowering the threshold of layoffs necessary to qualify (from 1,000 to 500), raising the share of co-funding on the part of the EU (from 50% to 65%), extending the period for which the funding is granted (from 12 to 24 months) and broadening the range of its applicability to crisis-related mass layoffs.

---

[6] See for instance, discussions published in various issues of the *Journal of European Social Policy* in 2001, with Philippe Schmitter & Michael Bauer's (2001a) proposed 'Euro-stipendium', the ensuing criticism by Philippe Van Parijs & Yannick Vanderborght (2001), as well as by Manos Matsaganis (2001), with a rejoinder by Schmitter & Bauer (2001b).

It is to be hoped that these changes will be accompanied by a quantum leap in the communication strategy of the European Globalisation Adjustment Fund, as until now this strategy has been virtually non-existent. The result is that over 70% of Europeans, when interviewed, declare they have never heard or read anything about it (Eurobarometer, 2009). This is in stark contrast to the strategy of massively publicising the European Social Fund, which is administered through national and regional authorities, while the European Globalisation Adjustment Fund, being directly administered by the EU, could be an important source of legitimacy for the Union as a political entity in its own right. Still, if the European Globalisation Adjustment Fund is simply there to co-finance existing national measures for which full credit is claimed by member states, the legitimacy return for the EU runs the risk of being negligible, if not outright negative (as would be the case if an application by a member state were to be rejected by the Community).

Be that as it may, in addition to important - in substantive and symbolic terms - but rather small-scale initiatives, what really matters at this stage is the forging of a consensus around a general concept: that of putting in place a basket of basic common social standards applicable to the entire EU space, as well as setting up the regulatory and governance prerequisites for the mutual recognition of social policy and employment regimes across member states. Without shared requirements and reciprocal trust, mutual recognition is impossible, and this is all the more important now, since the economic crisis has sparked a return to domestic, nation-specific interventions in the social field.

Drawing, once again, inspiration from the history of modern citizenship, a new regulatory and governance regime for the EU's freedom of movement legislation should be interwoven with a more basic institutional fabric: Fundamental Rights, as set out in the Nice Charter. In a way, the fact that the Charter is deemed to have the same legal value as the treaties can be seen as another form of 'mutual recognition' on a symbolic level. While member states reaffirm - in the Treaty of Lisbon - their acceptance of the EU's freedom of movement and competition regime, the Charter is the tool through which the EU acknowledges the supremacy of rights and their centrality in the EU's construct and mission, while accepting that member states may have their own legal proclivities concerning social citizenship, which are part of the basic EU constitutional order.

That the Charter has been given full legal status is an immensely valuable fact, since it will allow the ECJ to take fundamental social rights into account in its rulings, and thereby enable it to play its role in terms of constitutional balancing. One may regret the fact that this is merely recalled in the Treaty of Lisbon, however understandable it may be in light of British and Polish opposition. Symbols can go a long way in politics. A charter of rights that is swept under the carpet does not exactly fit the bill.

4. Less rhetoric, more forward-looking initiatives

Let us now briefly turn from common to similar challenges. Here, as mentioned above, there is less need and scope for direct and 'hard' supranational activism, but the EU can still play a significant role in encouraging and facilitating the modernisation of national social models, primarily in the context of existing demographic challenges. To a large extent, this is already happening through a set of instruments, most notably the Open Method of Coordination (OMC) and its various social processes. One of the latest institutional innovations on this front has been the adoption, by the European Council, of a number of solemn 'pacts', in which member states have committed to achieving shared goals and strengthening cooperation in the field of youth policies and youth mainstreaming (2005), equal opportunities and work-life balance (2006), and family policy (2007).

Even though there has been some disappointment regarding the effectiveness of these 'soft' instruments for the joint management of challenges of this ilk, they do provide valuable institutional capital on which to build, and their performance to date has been rather good, assuming one relinquishes the perfectionist, classic Community method angle.[7]

Without entering into the technical debate about how to fine-tune soft coordination from both a substantive and procedural viewpoint, some general suggestions come to mind for the purpose of stimulating debate and further thinking on this issue.

---

[7] The most thorough empirical assessment of social OMC processes so far is to be found in various chapters of Zeitlin & Pochet (2005) and Heidenreich & Zeitlin (2009), in particular in Jonathan Zeitlin's conclusions to both volumes.

The first two suggestions regard the OMC processes:

- Incorporating into the draft of the Integrated Guidelines for National Reform Programme, alongside macroeconomic, microeconomic and employment guidelines, a social chapter, so as to induce both Community and national policy-makers to take all angles into account;[8] and
- Introducing some 'OMC+', i.e. coordination processes supplemented with tangible and financial incentives. This is already at least partially happening with both the employment and the inclusion processes, but more could be done, especially as regards training and lifelong learning, child poverty and childcare in general.

A third suggestion regards the new 'pacting' approach that seems to be taking root alongside (or in anticipation of) more structured forms of open coordination. If properly designed, properly communicated and properly implemented, pacts and/or alliances centred around similar social challenges confronting all or most member states can indeed play a significant role and contribute to the strengthening of a social EU. Assessing the actual implementation of such initiatives is premature, as most were only launched in the past few years. But to date their design and the way in which they have been communicated to the public at large have been extremely poor. The initiative on the European Alliance for Families, a platform for exchanging information and experience on family-friendly policies received only a cursory description in the Presidency Conclusions of the 2007 Spring European Council Meeting and was not supported by any recognisable (let alone effective) communication campaign (but there is, however, a dedicated website).[9] This risks rapidly eroding the promising

---

[8] An attempt by some member states, the European Commission and the European Parliament to include some 'social' objective in the Lisbon Strategy for Growth and Jobs turned out to be unsuccessful, due to the opposition of many member states. The only change so far has been that the member states are expected to refer to the flexicurity principles elaborated by the Commission when drafting their National Reform Programmes 2008-10.

[9] In May 2009, an Employment Summit was held with the participation of national ministers, which confirmed the commitment to mobilise all EU funds and institutions to boost employment and social inclusion in the light of the financial crisis. Again, however, the Summit was not accompanied by any effective communication campaign.

potential of such instruments or, worse still, turning them into yet another signal of the EU's superficiality, opportunism and mere rhetoric in all matters that have to do with welfare and social policy. Why not take these instruments more seriously and re-configure them into a single "Pact for a New Social Europe", that could serve as a general symbolic and institutional framework for all OMCs? If this scenario does not prove feasible, then it might indeed be advisable to renounce all further proliferation of pacts and alliances, in order to avoid overload, confusion and the possible loss of legitimacy in this field (the EU's 'caring' dimension) – a field that should generate, rather than erode, EU legitimacy.

The fourth and final suggestion is that of considering the launch of a new policy initiative at the supranational level, with a strong 'signalling' potential on the three fronts mentioned at the beginning of this chapter: justice, legitimacy and efficiency. The most promising move in this direction would be one geared towards young Europeans. As we have seen, the EU already has a youth agenda, but it should consider taking specific action, and implement ground-breaking measures. Drawing on a paper prepared by the Bureau of European Policy Advisers to the President of the Commission on "Investing in Youth" (Barrington-Leach et al., 2007), a number of innovative measures with a high legitimising potential and the ability to reconcile social justice and economic efficiency could be considered for direct Community action. This might involve a 'European capital grant' to all children, that is a universal grant awarded to every baby at birth, which could be topped up (to a certain level) by parents and made available for use when the child reaches the age of 18; or a 'European Early Childcare Fund'; or a European student loan scheme, which could be made available through the European Investment Bank.

One rather alarming indication stemming from the latest Eurobarometer polls is that there is a widespread belief among all respondents that young people's life chances will be worse than those of their parents (Eurobarometer, 2007b). In the summer of 2009, almost half of respondents expressed strong concern about the prospect of their children losing their jobs in the wake of the recession (Eurobarometer, 2009). A stronger social EU should see to it that this does not happen: investing in youth should indeed become its flagship cause, its leading and most clearly recognisable priority.

References

Barrington-Leach, L., M. Canoy, A. Hubert and F. Lerais (2007), *Investing in youth: an empowerment strategy*, Bureau of Economic Policy Advisers, Brussels.

Eurobarometer (2006), *Special Eurobarometer 251, The future of Europe*, May.

Eurobarometer (2007a), *Standard Eurobarometer 65*, January.

Eurobarometer (2007b), *Special Eurobarometer 273, European social reality*, February.

Eurobarometer (2007c), *Standard Eurobarometer 66*, September.

Eurobarometer (2008a), *Flash Eurobarometer 227*, Expectations of European citizens regarding the social reality in 20 years' time.

Eurobarometer (2008b), *Standard Eurobarometer 70*, October.

Eurobarometer (2009), *Special Eurobarometr 316*, European Employment and Social Policy, July.

Ferrera, M. (2005), *The Boundaries of Welfare. European Integration and the New Spatial Politics of Social Solidarity*, Oxford: Oxford University Press.

Ferrera, M. (2009), "The JCMS Annual Lecture: National Welfare States and European Integration: in Search of a Virtuous Nesting", *Journal of Common Market Studies*, Vol. 47. No. 2, pp. 219-233.

Gilpin, R. (1987), *The political economy of international relations*, Princeton, NJ: Princeton University Press.

Giubboni, S. (2003), *Diritti sociali e mercato. La dimensione sociale dell'integrazione europea*, Bologna: Il Mulino.

Heidenreich, M. and J. Zeitlin (eds) (2009), *Changing European Employment and Welfare Regimes*, London: Routledge.

Lyon-Caen, G. (1992), "L'infiltration du Droit du travail par le Droit de la concurrence", in *Droit Ouvrier*, pp. 313-359.

Marshall, T.H. (1950), *Citizenship and social class and other essays*, Cambridge: Cambridge University Press.

Matsaganis, M. (2001), "The Trouble with the Euro-Stipendium", *Journal of European Social Policy*, Vol. 11, No. 4, pp. 346-348.

Milward, A. (1992), *The European Rescue of the Nation-State*, London: Routledge.

Scharpf, F. (2009), "Legitimacy in the Multi-level European Polity", *European Political Science Review*, Vol. 1, No. 2, pp. 173-204.

Schmitter, P. and M. Bauer (2001a), "A (Modest) Proposal for Expanding Social Citizenship in the European Union", *Journal of European Social Policy*, Vol. 11, No. 1, pp. 55-65.

Schmitter, P. and M. Bauer (2001b), "Dividend, Birth-Grant or Stipendium? - A Reply", *Journal of European Social Policy*, Vol. 11, No. 4, pp. 348-352.

Sinn, H.W. (1995), "A Theory of the Welfare State", *The Scandinavian Journal of Economics*, Vol. 97, No. 4, pp. 495-526.

Van Parijs, Ph. and Y. Vanderborght (2001), "From Euro-Stipendium to Euro-Dividend", *Journal of European Social Policy*, Vol. 11, No. 4, pp. 342-346.

Weiler, J.H.H. (1999), *The Constitution of Europe*, Cambridge: Cambridge University Press.

Zeitlin, J. and P. Pochet (eds) (2005), *The Open Method of Co-ordination in Action*, Brussels: Peter Lang.

4. Economic Policy Coordination and Failures in Europe to Counter Recession

Fiorella Kostoris[*]

I had too often observed the limits of coordination. It is a method which promotes discussion, but it does not lead to a decision. It does not allow us to transform the relations between human beings and between countries when union is necessary. It is the expression of the national power, as it is; it cannot change it, it will never create unity.

J. Monnet, *Mémoires*, Vol. I, 1976

Introduction

Economic policy coordination is not a clear-cut concept. This chapter first examines the different kinds of economic policies that are currently considered subject to coordination pursuant to Article 99 of the European Treaties and those which, according to the subsidiarity principle, should be common policies, being the exclusive competence of the Union, or should be coordinated between member states, being shared competences. Secondly, it shows under which conditions economic policy coordination is strong or weak, using the Stability and Growth Pact as a specific case study. It then analyses the implications of these general conclusions in order to show whether economic policy coordination in the EU is able to meet the challenges of the current recession. It concludes that European monetary policy - a common action in the single currency zone - is well-suited to

[*] Two previous versions of this paper were presented respectively in Berlin, at a seminar at the Freie Universität in May 2009, and in London, at a breakfast speech at the Business Club Italia in July 2009. The author is grateful to the participants of those meetings for their stimulating comments and questions.

addressing the systemic negative demand shock we see now. But European fiscal policy coordination is inadequate, because its basic instrument, the Stability and Growth Pact, is ill-conceived and needs urgent reform. The coordination of financial policies also needs to be much improved.

1. When is coordination appropriate?

Economic policy coordination within the European Union has increasingly come to be considered as useful, if not necessary, in debates among experts and in the public mind. Economic policy coordination has always been considered favourably in the European Treaties. Article 99 of the Treaties states that member states' policies are all "a matter of common concern" and are coordinated "within the Council". The same formula is repeated in the unapproved draft of the *Treaty Establishing a Constitution for Europe* and in the newly approved Lisbon Treaty. In particular, European federalists, who support the political union of the Community and think the best way to achieve it is by acting through Parliament from an institutional perspective, and through the single market/single currency from an economic viewpoint, complain that many Council decisions must be taken unanimously. Unanimity is of course difficult to reach so coordination is sometimes impossible.

But this fact need not affect the well-being of Europe. For instance, in setting tax rates, if unanimous coordination is reached, the outcome is worse than without it because, in the absence of unanimity, competition prevails. If it is not implemented in an incorrect and illegal way, competition is better than harmonisation, which would imply tax rates at an intermediate level between the minimum and the maximum in Europe, while the minimum rates, consistent with given public expenditure goals (themselves related to market failures), would be obtained by competition.

The latter does not meet with the favour of member states, as they prefer spending to please their electorate, whether they have to do it for rational economic reasons or not. Thus, it is no coincidence that, among the 12 points of the *Global Legal Standard* OECD (2009) paper approved at the 2009 G8 L'Aquila Summit, there is one inhibiting any 'race to the bottom' in labour markets or in social and environmental standards, while international agreements are longed for. In fact, this formula hides a sort of protectionism favouring residents versus immigrants, insiders versus outsiders, national rather than foreign investments. It limits incentives to attract both capital from abroad – as, for example in Ireland with detaxations - and workers from other European countries or from marginalised parts of the society - by adopting mutual recognition and country of origin principles, or by offering lower wages and potentially smaller welfare provisions, which might nonetheless be desirable as they are better than unemployment subsidies.

As a consequence, competition is often labelled as 'unfair' or 'wild' without explanation. It is so described in spite of the fact that the condition of voluntary exchange holds true, no law is evaded and no objective moral principle (as in the 10 commandments) is violated. True, the level playing field between different European member states or between different components of social systems is missing, but the essence of competition is precisely to use those differences to the advantage of the most efficient agents, inducing the others to find counterbalancing, compensating factors, able to reduce their weaknesses, while favouring the well-being of all.

Economic policy coordination, in the current European jargon, is an 'umbrella concept' being applied to a very wide range of interventions. It ranges from the exchange of information (sometimes partial, as has been the case up to now in banking supervision), to multilateral monitoring on the basis of commonly recognised best practices (as in the Lisbon Agenda). It may concern agreed principles of a philosophical nature (such as those on ethics and economics, as illustrated at the 2009 G8 Summit of L'Aquila by the *Global Legal Standard*, echoing Benedict XVI's Encyclical Letter *Caritas in veritate* on matters like CEOs' bonuses, which should be sustainable and consistent with an appropriate degree of risk aversion).

It further concerns more practical principles expounded in proposals regarding European institutions, for example those on Eurobonds supplied by the EIB, tending to finance the TransEuropean Networks managed by the EBRD. Conversely, economic policy coordination may become slightly more factual when it is the expression of agreed intentions regarding the management at member state level of some macro policy, such as the still-national stabilisation actions (for example, the Council Decision of 11-12 December 2008, in line with the Commission Communication of 26 November 2008, defines the European Recovery Plan with its major budgetary impetus worth 1.5% of GDP - about €200 billion - 1.2% of which is provided by member states; but those are mere intentions, because EU countries may avoid any intervention consistent with that Decision, as indeed happened according to the OECD and the IMF estimates).

Finally, economic policy coordination ranges from co-decided rules for fiscal deficits (as in the Stability and Growth Pact), or, more recently, for financial policies (as in the Euro Action Plan of 12 October 2008), to truly common actions (as is the case with monetary and competition policies).

The aim of this chapter is not to describe all these policies in detail, but rather to identify under what circumstances European coordination is strong and effective. Referring to the latter, the distinctions usually made are related to the degree of rigidity observed in the corresponding regulation, established by primary or secondary norms. For example, the Lisbon Agenda and the open coordination method of a qualitative nature are generally thought to be weak, while the Stability and Growth Pact and its numerical rules are supposed to be 'hard' forms of coordination. It might be said that they are both weak, perhaps not equally weak, as in this respect the fundamental difference in European policies is between those that are realised by the Council and those that are managed by the Commission or by some other European technical institution, like the European Central Bank or the European Court of Justice; this distinction being based on the subsidiarity principle.

When externalities beyond national borders are large and require a higher level of government capable of activating a policy, there is the necessity of a supranational intervention and the exclusive competence of the European Union leads to a truly common policy, which is not managed by the Council. When cross-border spillovers or redistributive purposes at the Community level are limited, the national public intervention is shared with the Union and policies are merely coordinated by the Council. Finally, in the absence of any significant cross-border externality, competences are exclusive to member states, remain local and presumably uncoordinated. The Council responds to national, not to European interests, as it is composed of national policy-makers subject to the tyranny of democracy: in a European perspective, coordinated policies are weak. Conversely, the Commission, the European Central Bank, or any other European institution managing a common policy, are technical authorities that do not have to be chosen equally by voters and are independent from the executive power. Their governing board being protected by the democratic deficit, common policies are much stronger as a result.

Two examples of this are worth examining: monetary and competition policies, which seem to be pretty effective, even under the present critical economic circumstances.

Monetary policy, since the birth of the euro in 1999, has been able to keep inflation under control, thus establishing the reputation of the ECB. During the whole recent financial crisis, expansionary monetary policy has performed brilliantly in the eurozone. It has alleviated both euro and non-euro countries' cyclical downturns, particularly in the second half of 2008 and in the current year. The ECB has been capable of reducing the recession effects and sustaining economic activity by massively increasing banks' liquidity in the eurozone, reducing discount rates, lengthening from 6 to 12 months the duration of banks' refinancing at fixed rates and for unlimited amounts and inventing new bank funding formulas, particularly through covered bonds (debt securities issued by them and backed by mortgages).

Competition policy, since the Rome Treaty, has been a fundamental pillar of the construction of Europe. By preventing abuses of dominant positions in the Single Market and state aid distortions, the Commission has been operating as an antitrust authority. Some of the Commission's recent actions monitoring competition have been much criticised but in fact have turned out to be flexible and rather intelligent. For example, in September-October 2008, Ireland appeared to violate the European rules on state aid by guaranteeing banks' debt issuance. The Commission did not intervene here and rightly so, since, immediately after Ireland, Greece passed the same policy and a few days later other member states also followed suit. This was certainly easy to forecast, as there is full competition in capital markets and banking, current accounts can quickly be transferred to other eurozone member states. Finally, on 12 October 2008, a European Summit decided to adopt the same policy of guaranteeing bank debt for the whole Union. In the end, therefore, the Commission was extremely effective in not sanctioning Ireland and Greece for distortionary state aid policies, knowing that competition would achieve the same outcome as its regulatory interventions.

2. Economic policy coordination under pressure

Exclusive EU competences are logically derived from the subsidiarity principle appearing in the Union primary norms, and are pragmatically defined by the European Treaties as well. There is some inconsistency between the principles and their practical application, but neither the former nor the latter can be easily redetermined and so for the time being have to be considered as a given.

As indicated above, other competences, listed equally in the treaties with some analytical inconsistency, are shared between the Union and member states and the corresponding policies have to be coordinated by the Council. The idea that this institution is always a source of weak coordination finds an exception when all member states have a common identical interest and decide to pursue their goals with a unanimous, co-decided intervention. In this case, *ex ante* coordination is not necessary, while *ex post* coordination is easy and sufficient, or, to put it another way, *ex ante* rules become self-enforcing.

A typical example of this condition is what happened over the weekend of 12 October 2008. The world's stock exchanges were fearing extreme volatility after September 15th when Lehman Brothers filed for bankruptcy, but in a matter of hours European countries managed to find a new governance formula to address their problems, namely an Ecofin Summit consisting not of finance ministers but heads of state and governments, for the occasion enlarged to include the British (eurosceptic) Prime Minister Gordon Brown. They agreed on three major solutions: state guarantees of bank debt issuance; banks' recapitalisation and governments' commitments to avoid their bankruptcy by buying, if necessary, all their assets; and transitory abandonment of the market-to-market formula, in order to strengthen the trust message of the first two initiatives, considering that this kind of transparent evaluation may lead to confusion between short-term liquidity and long-term solvency. The successful political outcome was certainly facilitated by the dramatic context of the European partners' meeting. As indicated by the Italian Minister of Finance, Giulio Tremonti (Sensini, 2009):

> At the IMF in Washington, on October 9, which was Friday, we understood that the London Stock Exchange could not open on the following Monday. During the night of May 9 Iceland declared bankruptcy. The turning point came on October 12 in Paris, when Governments and Politics took the right initiative.

But this rapid and efficient *ex post* coordination would have been impossible had each member state not had the same interest to back bank debts and boost market confidence in a unanimously coordinated way, all being well aware not only of the risk of contagion, but also of the threat represented by other European partners potentially able to provide even bigger bailouts to their banks.

3. A case study of the Stability and Growth Pace

In more 'normal' circumstances, Council coordination is generally mild, irrespective of what might be suggested by hard regulations. Moreover, it becomes even weaker the more ill-conceived is the governance of the institutions that have the duty to control the stakeholders' behaviour involved in coordination. The less effective are sanctions and incentives directed to those agents, the more mistaken are the intrinsic rules of the coordinated policy.

The Stability and Growth Pact can be taken as a case study to show the importance of these three elements. The rigidity of the Pact's rules are well-known, from the famous ceilings of 3% in the deficit-to-GDP ratio and 60% in the debt-to-GDP ratio (Article 104 of the Treaties), to the two 1977 Regulations shedding light on four further aspects (medium-term objectives, derogations to the excessive deficit procedures, mitigating factors to start the early warning procedure and sanctions), concluding with the 2005 Pact reform. Derogations, as reformulated in 2005 by two new Regulations, are particularly relevant in the current economic crisis: the excessive deficit procedure does not start if there are 'exceptional' economic conditions, such as when the annual GDP growth rate is negative or the output gap relative to the potential level is persistent, while the distance of the deficit-to-GDP ratio from the reference value is temporary and small.

To analyse the first of the three relevant aspects, it should be noted that the governance of the Pact is ill-conceived, mainly because the decision on whether a country is a fiscal delinquent is assigned to other, at least potentially, fiscal delinquents. Indeed, supervised finance ministers coincide with the supervisors and – in Juvenal's words – who shall guard the guards themselves? Such conflicts of interest seemed to arise in November 2003, when the Commission wanted to start an excessive deficit procedure against France and Germany, abundantly exceeding the 3% ceiling, while the Council decided not to intervene, probably influenced by the Ecofin President of that semester, Giulio Tremonti. Presumably a sort of implicit '*do ut des*' (reciprocity) was implemented, exchanging a current favour towards Paris and Berlin for a future favour towards Rome. In fact, Italy received an early warning on its excessive deficit only in July 2005, while in four out of the five years since 2001 its deficit had exceeded 3%.

As for the sanctions system, it proved even less effective after the European Court of Justice's Solomonic ruling of July 2004 on the above-mentioned 2003 controversy: on the one side, it agreed with the Council against the Commission but, on the other, it asked the Council to revise its Decision, considering it to be inconsistent with its previous ones. The reputation and credibility of the Pact have consequently been diminished because, admittedly, it appeared to be strictly applied to small countries and freely interpreted for large, powerful ones, thus lessening the moral weight of any sanction. Besides, the probability of sanctions decreases as the actual number of fiscal delinquents increases, as is happening at the moment. Finally, incentives to behave well from a deficit and debt viewpoint are correctly identified by the Maastricht Treaty in the convergence phase, as the member states' ability to satisfy convergence parameters is rewarded by entry into the Eurogroup, offering many gains in terms of nominal stability. On the contrary, once a country is in the club, the latter becomes non-inclusive in the sense that the treaties do not provide any rule to exclude a fiscal delinquent from the club, and the carrot of entering the euro area has already been eaten, while the stick of exclusion is substituted by unlikely and ineffective sanctions.

Third, the formula of the Pact is ill-conceived. To resume its basic rationale, described in the 1989 Delors Report, two underlying hypotheses can be recalled. First, member states' fiscal policies create small cross-border spillovers, not requiring common action but only some European coordination. While this assumption does not seem to be disproved by the empirical evidence, the second is factually more controversial. Accordingly, national fiscal policy spillovers are negative because, within a group of countries sharing the same currency, each member state hit by an asymmetric shock does not take into account the effects of its expansionary fiscal policy on the common reference interest rate. This creates a deficit spending bias, which is opposed by the European Central Bank. The latter ultimately succeeds in targeting European inflation, but this action raises interest rates and brings no advantage to anybody: it is therefore better to agree on an *ex ante* maximum deficit, avoiding free-riding problems.

A very simple mathematical model (presented in the Annex) conveys this message. It shows, however, not only the Delors Report rationale for the Stability and Growth Pact, but also its weaknesses. In particular, it clearly indicates that an optimal *ex ante* fiscal policy coordination in the Eurogroup cannot be set if three distinctions are missing: between demand and supply shocks and between weak and strong demand shocks; between asymmetric and systemic shocks.

Indeed, in the optimal solution, the 3% constraint appears to be too large when facing a negative supply shock - when essentially no deficit spending should be allowed. It may be correct, when facing a mild asymmetric negative demand shock, i.e. when automatic stabilisers are sufficient to restore output at the potential, but it is finally suboptimal when there is a strong and/or a systemic negative demand shock, hence a discretionary expansionary fiscal policy is called for, beyond automatic stabilisers. The coordination failure in fiscal policy is particularly absurd when there is a systemic demand shock, because each country is then positively, not negatively affected by the budgetary stimulus of other partners. A good proposal would therefore consist of a further reform under the Stability and Growth Pact, whereby the Commission and the Council should take into consideration whether a country faces a supply or a demand shock (strong or mild) and a common-systemic shock or an asymmetric one.

In order to make this proposal operational, one should avoid impossible changes to the Treaty. One should therefore amend the present formulation of the Pact either through a different informal interpretation of the 'exceptional' economic conditions inducing derogations to the excessive deficit procedures and/or through an innovative formal concept of 'exceptionality', defined by a new Council Regulation. Moreover, from a political viewpoint, a double question immediately arises. How hard is it for the European Commission and the Council to identify the nature of the country-specific (or of the systemic) shock? And is it possible to adopt a common methodology and harmonised European data to detect this in every member state?

Three data sets are currently available in the Union for the guardians of the Stability and Growth Pact, which have already been homogenised by the European Commission Services for all EU27 countries, and have existed for many years, though they have not been much exploited. They allow the quick supply (although still discretionary) of measures on qualitative and quantitative aspects of economic cycles. A negative demand shock can then be identified by the simultaneity of the increase in the unemployment rate, combined with the decrease in the inflation rate, while, on the contrary, a negative supply shock is characterised by rising inflation coupled with growing unemployment. In addition, a negative demand shock is identified as strong, if the inverse correlation between unemployment and inflation is accompanied by a percentage of firms declaring problems with insufficient demand rather than insufficient profitability above the normal trend. The strongly negative demand shock has to be considered systemic or common to all countries belonging to the same area, if each of them shows the same three features simultaneously. In Table 1 and Figure 1 below (with annual frequences except for the last quarters), a strong demand shock is detected when there is a contemporaneous upward movement in (u), a downward movement in (π) and (D-C)/Average (D-C 1997-2008) > 10 (it should be bigger than 1, but the variable is multiplied by 10, so as to make the graph more easily readable).

Looking at Table 1 and Figure 1, it is immediately apparent that we are living in the middle of a severe economic crisis. By mid-2009, firms were constrained in their demand 50% more than in the average trend of the previous 12 years, particularly in the eurozone. In the last 3-4 quarters and in the current year, unemployment is increasing and inflation is declining everywhere in the EU27. Starting with the second half of 2008, we observe not only that the cyclical downturn is larger than those emerging in other critical years of the period under consideration (1997-2009), but also that this strongly negative demand shock is, for the first time, common to all European countries. Germany, France and Italy are now all suffering from the same disease. This was not the case in 2002-03, when a country-specific shock hit some of the member states: the three combined quantitative indicators, used in Table 1, suggest that in those years Germany was the only big partner to bear a strongly negative demand shock, unlike Italy and France. In its most critical years, the latter was affected by a strongly negative supply shock. No doubt, if the Commission had adopted the distinction between demand and supply shocks, it would not have requested the early warning procedure against Germany, thereby separating the destinies of Paris and Berlin. Perhaps a joint viewpoint between the Commission and the Council could have been reached then, without damaging the reputation of the Stability and Growth Pact.

Table 1. Detrended demand-constrained (D) relative to capacity-constrained (C) business regime, unemployment and inflation rates in some European areas (1997-2009)

	Euro Area			**Germany**			**France**		
Years	(D-C)/ Average (D-C 1997-2008) (x 10)[1]	u (%): Unem-ployment rate[2]	π (%): Inflation rate[3]	(D-C)/ Average (D-C 1997-2008) (x 10)[1]	u (%): Unem-ployment rate[2]	π (%): Inflation rate[3]	(D-C)/ Average (D-C 1997-2008) (x 10)[1]	u (%): Unem-ployment rate[2]	π (%): Inflation rate[3]
1997	14.3	10.6	1.6	16.2	9.9	1.5	16.2	11.5	1.3
1998	11.7	10.0	1.1	11.5	9.3	0.6	11.5	11.1	0.7
1999	12.9	9.1	1.1	10.9	8.5	0.6	10.9	10.5	0.6
2000	7.6	8.5	2.1	4.2	7.5	1.4	4.2	9.0	1.8
2001	10.4	8.0	2.3	6.9	7.6	1.9	6.9	8.3	1.8
2002	13.6	8.4	2.2	12.1	8.4	1.4	12.1	8.6	1.9
2003	14.1	8.8	2.1	14.3	9.3	1.0	14.3	9.0	2.2
2004	9.7	9.0	2.1	9.9	9.8	1.8	9.9	9.2	2.3
2005	9.9	9.0	2.2	10.9	10.6	1.9	10.9	9.3	1.9
2006	6.2	8.3	2.2	8.7	9.8	1.8	8.7	9.2	1.9
2007	3.3	7.5	2.1	7.4	8.4	2.3	7.4	8.3	1.6
2007-Q1	3.0	7.7	1.9	10.0	8.7	1.9	6.7	8.7	1.3
2007-Q2	3.2	7.5	1.9	9.3	8.5	2.0	6.2	8.7	1.3
2007-Q3	3.1	7.4	1.9	5.7	8.3	2.0	3.8	8.2	1.4
2007-Q4	3.8	7.3	2.9	5.0	8.0	3.0	3.4	7.8	2.5
2008	6.2	7.5	3.3	7.0	7.3	2.8	7.0	7.8	3.2
2008-Q1	3.5	7.2	3.4	5.1	7.6	3.1	3.4	7.6	3.3
2008-Q2	4.8	7.4	3.6	4.1	7.4	3.0	2.7	7.7	3.7
2008-Q3	6.7	7.6	3.8	6.7	7.2	3.3	4.5	7.8	3.6
2008-Q4	9.4	8.0	2.3	11.3	7.1	1.6	7.6	8.2	2-0
2009	14.4	9.9	0.4	14.5	8.6	0.3	14.5	9.6	0.2
2009-Q1	13.5	8.7	1.0	13.6	7.4	0.8	9.1	8.6	1.5
2009-Q2	15.2	9.2	0.6	15.4			10.4		

	Italy			European Union		
Years	(D-C)/ Average (D-C 1997-2008) (x 10)[1]	u (%): Unemployment rate[2]	π (%): Inflation rate[3]	(D-C)/ Average (D-C 1997-2008) (x 10)[1]	u (%): Unemployment rate[2]	π (%): Inflation rate[3]
1997	11.3	11.3	1.9	12.9	9.8	1.7
1998	10.8	11.3	2.0	10.8	9.4	1.3
1999	11.8	11.0	1.7	12.7	9.1	1.2
2000	8.1	10.1	2.6	8.8	8.6	1.9
2001	9.7	9.1	2.3	10.6	8.4	2.2
2002	11.1	8.6	2.6	13.2	8.8	2.1
2003	12.7	8.4	2.8	13.6	9.0	2.0
2004	10.0	8.0	2.3	9.5	9,0	2.0
2005	10.0	7.7	2.2	9.4	8.9	2.2
2006	7.3	6.8	2.2	7.2	8.2	2.2
2007	7.2	6.2	2.0	4.5	7.1	2.4
2007-Q1	5.5	6.1	2.0	4.4	7.4	2.2
2007-Q2	5.8	6.1	1.9	4.3	7.2	2.2
2007-Q3	8.6	6.2	1.7	4.0	7.1	2.1
2007-Q4	8.8	6.3	2.6	5.1	6.9	3.0
2008	10.0	6.8	3.5	6.9	7.0	3.7
2008-Q1	8.9	6.6	3.3	4.7	6.8	3.5
2008-Q2	9.7	6.7	3.8	5.8	6.8	3.9
2008-Q3	10.1	6.9	4.0	7.3	7.0	4.3
2008-Q4	11.4	7.0	2.9	9.6	7.4	2.9
2009	13.9	8.8	0.8	13.6	9.4	0.9
2009-Q1	14.0			12.8	8.1	1.5
2009-Q2	13.8			14.4		

Note: Both numerator and denominator are given in detrended terms.

Sources: (1): Elaboration on Business Survey Data. Empirical evidence on 2009-Q2 is based on April data. (2): Eurostat data up to 2009. The 2009 annual data are provided by the European Commission in *European Economy, Economic Forecasts*, May 2009. The 2009-Q2 data, if data are available at least one month in the quarter, correspond to the latest observed. Eurostat data are integrated with information on the eurozone derived from *Banca d'Italia, Bollettino Economico*, n. 56, April 2009 and information on the EU27 coming from the Bureau of Labour Statistics, *Unemployment Rates in the European Union and Selected Member States 1995-2009*. (3): Eurostat data up to 2009. The 2009 annual data are provided by the European Commission in *European Economy, Economic Forecasts*, May 2009. The 2009-Q2 data are based on April data provided by the European Central Bank.

Figure 1. Indicators of demand shocks in the euro area, 1997-2009-Q2
(Quarterly data since 2007)

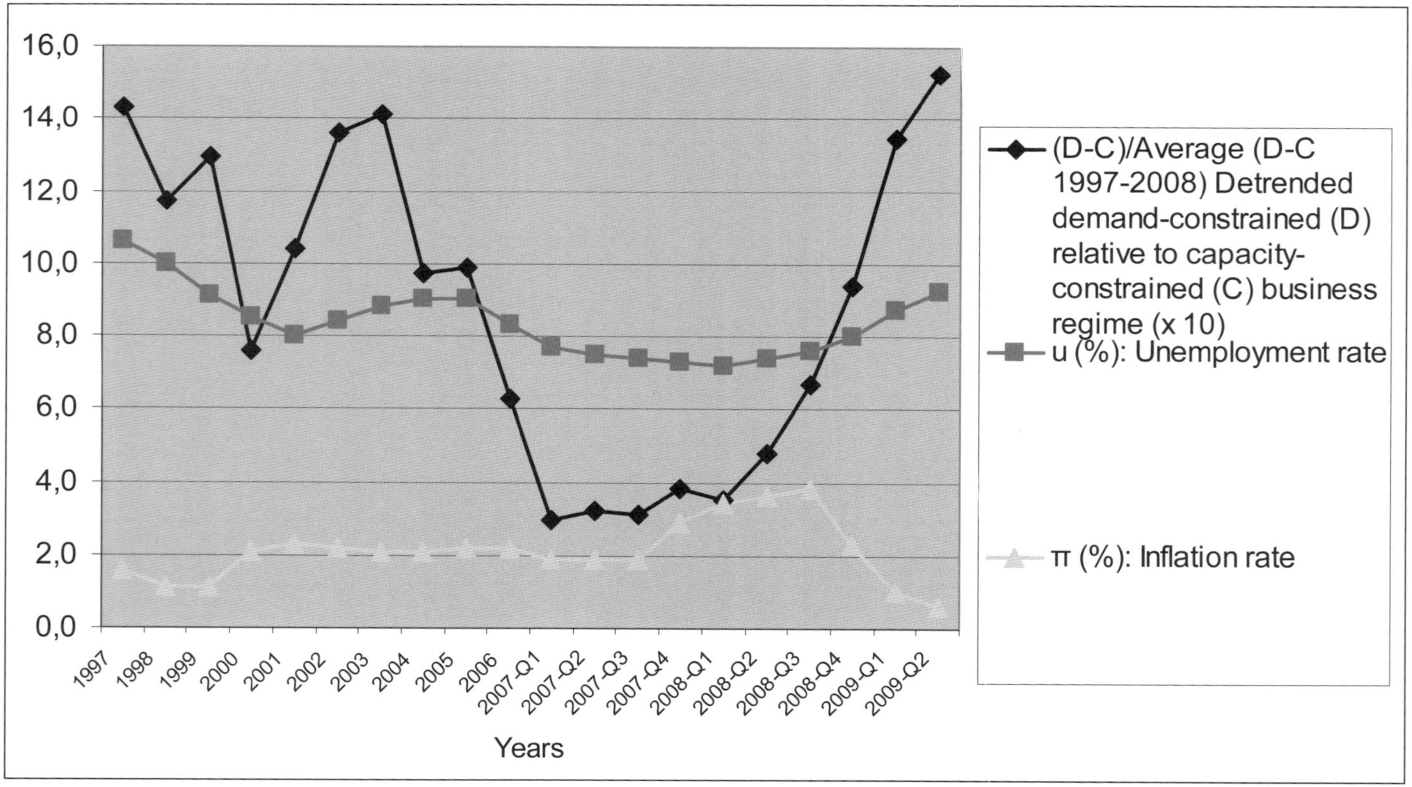

Sources: See Table 1.

4. Effects of the financial crisis

The origin of the present crisis in the real economy is elsewhere in the financial sector, when it started in summer 2007 with the bursting of the speculative bubble in the American housing market and the difficulties in debt repayment on subprime mortgages. The securitisation of these assets, made in complex and opaque ways, later induced a general diffusion of partly unobservable risks, with a consequent loss of confidence in the financial markets. Due to the globalisation of capital markets, the derived lack of liquidity and credit crunch reached all stock exchanges, from Wall Street to London, from Japan to Brazil. The existence of leads and lags explains why the real economy was hit approximately a year later. And it also explains why unemployment will keep rising even when GDP starts to recover, although it did not deteriorate immediately after the beginning of the cyclical downturn. Indeed this phenomenon is already being tested in some countries, like France and Germany, where the recession would seem to be at an end by the second quarter of 2009 and yet labour market performances are still worsening, even though they were improving up to the second semester of 2008 when a fall in output was starting to emerge.

In developed countries, the aggregate demand contraction observed since mid-2008 stems from a decrease in the incomes of firms and households, from a decline in confidence and from a credit crunch, with a consequent contraction in funding for the purchase of durables and non-durables and a delay in investment decisions. The fact that this happens at the same time in Europe and in the United States - which constitute major consumer markets for each other - means that foreign demand is also adversely affected. On the other hand, the fall in world trade leads to a cyclical worsening in BRIC and other developing countries, while OPEC is also suffering from the extreme volatility in oil prices. Everywhere, the recession in the real economy is caused by a systemic, strongly negative demand shock.

Focusing more on Europe, the recession began in the second quarter of 2008 in Germany and Italy, but later in other major countries like Spain, the United Kingdom and France. Indeed, on average, the euro and the EU economic systems started to observe a recession only in the third quarter of last year and the severity of the slowdown appeared particularly worrying after 15 September 2008. Not only was 2007 still a boom period for the whole Union, but even the GDP growth in 2008 remained positive in the vast majority of member states (the notable exceptions being Italy and Ireland), in spite of the fact that all European countries have experienced a recession since the second semester of last year. In some cases, the 2008 GDP dynamics seem remarkable (1.3% in Germany – slightly bigger than in the US, 0.7% in France, 0.8% and 0.9%, in the eurozone and in the EU). Forecasts for 2009, however, are worrying, despite clearly improving performances in large European countries since the second quarter of this year: estimates for 2009 growth are -3% in France, -4.4% in Italy, -5.4% in Germany, -4% both in the euro area and in the Union, also due to the very poor prospects of the Spanish and British economies. On the contrary, expectations for 2010 are generally positive. Looking ahead, it is to be hoped that the recession in the Union will only last 12-18 months, implying a much smaller cumulative GDP decrease than during the Great Depression, of a size similar to that measured during the first oil shock of 1973-74, the latter being, however, of a totally different nature (an asymmetric, strongly negative supply shock).

The 2008 average inflation rate was still growing (3.3% in the eurozone, 3.7% in the European Union). But the overall picture has deteriorated dramatically since the last quarter of 2008 and more so in 2009. The most recent data for the eurozone indicate a negative inflation rate in the three months since June 2009.

5. Conclusions

We should ask ourselves whether economic policy coordination in Europe is indeed apt to fight the recession that started in mid-2008. We know that, when faced with a strong and systemic negative demand shock, macro policies in the Union should be expansionary and decided upon and managed jointly in order to obtain the most effective results. While monetary policy is well-suited to these needs, fiscal policy in Europe is not, for reasons already outlined in the discussion about the Stability and Growth Pact, which is the only instrument available for budgetary coordination. Due to the Pact being ill-conceived, there is an explicit limitation on proper fiscal expansion: according to the Pact's rules, for example, but contrary to any economic rationale, on 18 February 2009, six EU countries (France, Spain, Greece, Ireland, as well as Malta and Latvia) were affected by an excessive deficit procedure due to their negative balance in 2008. The same procedure will presumably concern 13 out of 16 euro countries next year and it is difficult to understand how they will be able to avoid useless, indeed harmful sanctions foreseen by the Pact, unless the latter is quickly reformed - be it in a formal or informal way. Unfortunately, for the time being, this would seem to be difficult, as France and Germany do not agree on the direction to be taken: the former wants to spend more in order to oppose the current cyclical downturn, while the latter is sticking to the old rules, as it fears the inflation-boosting effects of deficits. Germany, moreover, is generally afraid of having to 'foot the bill', which is why Berlin is against many other innovative proposals, including the supply of Eurobonds.

A quick and successful exit from recession also requires some changes to financial markets: their performance is still less satisfactory than before the summer of 2007 and continues to suffer from excessive volatility. No doubt, public guarantees on bank debt and recapitalisation operations concerning financial and sometimes non-financial companies (as in the automobile sector) have played a positive role. Presumably the housing bubble is almost over and the subprime mortgage crisis is all but over, but the diffusion of toxic assets through risky securitisations is still considered as very dangerous; financial companies are supposedly not yet totally clean and full trust in transactions is still lacking. To restore 'initial conditions', two further public interventions would appear to be necessary:

- Bad assets should be completely eradicated from financial companies, particularly large multinationals. Up to now, governments have tried to set a conventional price for toxic assets that have no market. The problem is that if this price is too low, companies do not sell them, but if it is too high, tax-payers do not pay for them. Maybe it is necessary to use public money to buy the entire financial companies under critical conditions, whose market price is revealed on the stock exchange, and later separate the good from the bad, selling back the latter once finally cleaned up. It is not known, however, whether markets and agents would like these temporary forms of nationalisation, even though at least in the European Union they were explicitly agreed on 12 October 2008.
- The capital markets being globalised, the best corrective and preventive solutions to the problems of the financial sector should be decided at supranational level. European coordination would then be necessary, but probably not sufficient. The quality and extension of the supervision of financial markets should improve. Markets should become more transparent, all financial operators should be subject to

controls (beyond national borders if companies are multinationals), conflicts of interest should be eliminated, particularly in rating societies and the existing rules should be strictly implemented. Some steps forward are currently being taken both in the European Union and the United States in an uncorrelated, though possibly non-divergent way (Hamaui, 2009). Yet, fundamental changes on this side of the Atlantic appear to be difficult. This is because big European partners have always had different opinions on the optimal governance for microeconomic and macroeconomic prudential supervision: Paris feels that bank monitoring should be part of monetary policy (thus implicitly tending to assign such tasks to the ECB), while Berlin thinks it should be better managed by an institution having no control over monetary policy and reference rates. London considers that monitoring should be simultaneously extended to all financial intermediaries and insurance companies. As a consequence, the European Council Conclusions of June 2009, rather than imposing some Union coordination on financial supervision, only pay lip service to "the need to improve the regulation and supervision of financial institutions both in Europe and globally", *de facto* exclusively supporting the creation of a European Systemic Risk Board (previously envisaged by the Commission Communication of 27 May 2009). This new instrument should monitor any threat to financial stability caused by macro phenomena and risks of contagion, thereby providing a first partial answer to macro, but certainly not to micro, prudential supervision coordination problems.

References

European Commission (2008), "A European Economic Recovery Plan", Communication from the Commission to the European Council, 26 November, COM(2008) 800 final (http://ec.europa.eu/commission_barroso/president/pdf/Comm_20081126.pdf).

European Commission (2009), "European Financial Supervision", Communication from the Commission, COM(2009) 252 final , 27 May (http://ec.europa.eu/internal_market/insurance/docs/2009-markt-docs/communication-2009-252_en.pdf).

Council of the European Union (1997a), *Council Regulation (EC) No 1466/97 of 7 July 1997 on the strengthening of the surveillance of budgetary positions and the surveillance and coordination of economic policies* (http://eur-lex.europa.eu/smartapi/cgi/sga_doc?martapi!celexapi!prod!CELEXnumdoc&lg=EN&numdoc=31997R1466&model=guichett).

Council of the European Union (1997b), *Council Regulation (EC) No 1467/97 of 7 July 1997 on speeding up and clarifying the implementation of the excessive deficit procedure* (http://eur-lex.europa.eu/smartapi/cgi/sga_doc?smartapi!celexapi!prod!CELEXnumdoc&lg=EN&numdoc=31997R1467&model=guichett).

Council of the European Union (2008), *Brussels European Council of December 11 and 12, 2008, Presidency Conclusions,* 17271/1/08 REV 1 (http://register.consilium.europa.eu/pdf/en/08/st17/st17271-re01.en08.pdf).

Council of the European Union (2009), *Brussels European Council of June 18/19, 2009, Presidency Conclusions,* 11225/2/09 REV 2 (http://www.consilium.europa.eu/ueDocs/cms_Data/docs/pressdata/en/ec/108622.pdf).

Euro Area Countries (2008), *Declaration on A Concerted European Action Plan of the Euro Area Countries,* 12 October (http://ec.europa.eu/economy_finance/publications/publication13260_en.pdf).

European Commission (1989), *Report on Economic and Monetary Union in the European Community,* 12 April (http://www.ena.lu/mce.cfm).

European Court of Justice (2004), *Judgement of the Court of Justice in Case C-27/04,* Press Release No. 57/04.

European Union (1987), "Single European Act", July 1, *Official Journal of the European Union L 169,* 19 June 1986 (http://www.eurotreaties.com).

European Union (2004), "Treaty establishing a Constitution for Europe", *Official Journal of the European Union C 310*, Vol. 47, 16 December (http://www.eurotreaties.com).

European Union (2007), "Treaty of Lisbon amending the Treaty on European Union and the Treaty establishing the European Community", December 13, 2007, *Official Journal of the European Union C 306*, Vol. 50, 17 December (http://www.eurotreaties.com).

G8 Summit 2009 Declaration (2009), "Responsible Leadership for a Sustainable Future", From La Maddalena to L'Aquila, Declaration adopted at L'Aquila on 8-10 July (http://www.g8italia2009.it/static/G8_Allegato/G8_Declaration_08_07_09_final,0.pdf).

Hamaui, R. (2009), "America in vantaggio nella partita della vigilanza finanziaria", *laVoce.info*, 1 September (www.lavoce.info).

His Holiness Benedict XVI (2009), *Encyclical Letter Caritas in Veritate* (http://www.vatican.va/holy_father/benedict_xvi/encyclicals/documents/hf_ben-xvi_enc_20090629_ caritas-in-veritate_en.html).

Kostoris, F. (2006), *The 2005 Reform of the Stability and Growth Pact: Too Little, Too Late?*, Bruges BEER Working Paper, No. 6, College of Europe, November.

Kostoris, F. (2008), "Il coordinamento delle politiche economiche nell'Unione Europea", in S. Micossi and G. Tosato (a cura di), *L'Unione Europea nel XXI secolo. "Nel dubbio per l'Europa"*, Bologna: Il Mulino.

OECD (2009), *A Global Charter/Legal Standard. An Inventory of Possible Policy Instrument* (http://www.oecd.org/dataoecd/35/63/42393042.pdf).

Sensini, M. (2009), "Tremonti: autostrade, poste e Iva ci dicono che la caduta".

Uhlig, H. (2003), "One Money But Many Fiscal Policies in Europe: What are the consequences?", in M. Buti (ed.), *Monetary and Fiscal Policies in EMU*, Cambridge: Cambridge University Press.

Annex

Using an extremely simple model, itself an extension of a previous one (Kostoris, 2006), the rationale of the Stability and Growth Pact is shown, but also its main analytical weaknesses (which cumulate with those concerning its governance and its system of sanctions and incentives).

All variables are defined in terms of percentage deviations from their long-run values, except for the nominal interest rate, i, and are described by capital letters. All other small letters are parameters, assumed positive. The output differential of country a, Y_a, is assumed to depend only on the deficit gap of that country, Def_a, on the expected real interest rate, $(i - \Pi^e_a)$ with Π^e_a equalling the expected inflation rate in country a and on a demand shock, E_a. The inflation rate, Π_a, is an increasing function of the output differential and of a supply shock, U_a.

First consider in isolation the equilibrium of country a. Aggregate demand is

$$Y_a = c_a Def_a - v_a (i - \Pi^e_a) + E_a \,. \qquad (1)$$

The relation between the deficit and the structural deficit ($Defs_a$) depends on the economic cycle in two ways: the deficit increases when there exists an output gap in country a ($Y_a<0$) and, if negative shocks are common to other countries, when a similar shock arises elsewhere (the E shock concerning other countries has the same sign as E_a, unless there is an asymmetric shock, whereby $E_aE=0$). This is indicated by

$$Def_a = Defs_a - m_aY_a + d_a (E_aE) \,, \qquad (2)$$

where m_aY_a shows the automatic stabilisers and $d_a(E_aE)$ indicate the externalities created by a common (or systemic) demand shock. The latter element is usually ignored, as it is usually supposed that shock E_a is asymmetric.

Thus, the equilibrium output of country a is

$$Y_a = f_a Defs_a - k_a (i - \Pi^e_a) + h_aE_a + q_a (E_a E) \,, \qquad (3)$$

where

$f_a = c_a/(1 + c_a m_a)$; $k_a = v_a/(1 + c_a m_a)$; $h_a = 1/(1 + c_a m_a)$; $q_a = c_a d_a / (1+c_a m_a)= d_a f_a$; $(h_a + q_aE)>0$.

Aggregate supply of country a is

$$\Pi_a = n\, Y_a + U_a \quad . \qquad (4)$$

The nominal interest rate is supposed to be determined by the central bank so as to ensure expected price stability in the medium run, i.e. in the absence of shocks. Hence, $\Pi^e_a = 0$ and $i = f_a Defs_a/k_a$. This implies that in the medium run monetary policy is able to offset any effect of fiscal policy on output and prices via an appropriate level of the interest rate.

Let us assume that the government of country a fully internalises the reaction function of the central bank and the increase of i due to deficit spending. Let us also suppose that the government cares both about output stabilisation and about the fiscal rule, concerning $Defs_a$ (hence also Def_a), as it wants to minimise the following quadratic loss function L_a:

$$L_a = ½ [Defs^2_a + l_a Y^2_a] \quad , \tag{5}$$

where l_a captures the relative preference for output stabilisation relative to the fiscal rule.

Optimisation leads country a to the following decisions:

$$Defs_a = 0 \quad , \quad Def_a = - m_a h_a E_a + d_a h_a (E_a E), \tag{6}$$

with

$$Y_a = h_a E_a + q_a (E_a E); \quad \Pi_a = n [h_a E_a + q_a (E_a E)] + U_a \tag{7}$$

The optimum solution is a structural balanced budget, combined with a deficit spending in the short term, utilising automatic stabilisers to counterbalance any possible negative asymmetric demand shock ($E_a < 0$, $E_a E = 0$). Under these circumstances, the output gap becomes negative and inflation declines. The latter condition arises also with a positive supply shock ($U_a < 0$). Notice that, when the asymmetric demand shock E_a is negative, the deficit gap has to be positive and any numerical constraint on the deficit spending under the level $- m_a h_a E_a$ is not a first best: indeed, if there exists a strongly negative asymmetric demand shock, there may arise a logical inconsistency between $Defs_a = 0$ and $Def_a \leq 3\%$ of GDP. On the other hand, no logical inconsistency arises if the asymmetric negative demand shock is smaller, so that $-m_a h_a E_a \leq 3\%$ of GDP, or if there is a supply shock, given that in this event no deficit should be optimally chosen. Finally, if the negative demand shock hitting country a is common to other countries, a logical inconsistency may emerge with $Def_a \leq 3\%$ of GDP, even if the shock E_a by itself is not so strong: this is because the common shock determines a non-linear effect.

Let us now suppose that two countries, a and b, have a single currency and a common nominal and expected real interest rate ($i - \Pi^e$); while they take into account the feedback rule followed by the central bank in setting the nominal interest rate, they do not coordinate their fiscal policies, playing a Nash non-cooperative game.

Their aggregate demand and supply are functionally similar, but their parameters differ (i.e. $f_a \neq f_b$; $k_a \neq k_b$; $h_a \neq h_b$; $d_a \neq d_b$; however, n is common to both countries in order to simplify calculations). The monetary policy is now determined in a slightly more complicated way, so as to make the average expected inflation rate equal to zero, in the absence of shocks, i.e.

$$(\alpha Y^e_a + \beta Y^e_b) = 0 , \quad (8)$$

where the superscripts e indicate the expected values, α and β identify the weights of country a and b respectively, with $\alpha + \beta = 1$ and both positive. Hence the central bank sets

$$i = (\alpha f_a \, Defs_a + \beta f_b \, Defs_b) \, / \, (\alpha k_a + \beta k_b) \quad (9)$$

Countries a and b, taking into account the central bank reaction function (9), minimise their loss function L_a, as in (5), and similarly L_b, as follows:

$$Defs_a = Defs_b \, A - E_a \, (h_a + q_a \, E) \, C \quad , \quad (10)$$

$$Defs_b = Defs_a \, B - E_b \, (h_b + q_b \, E) \, D \quad (11)$$

where

$$A = \frac{\beta^2 f_a \, k_b f_b \, k_a \, l_a}{(\alpha k_a + \beta k_b)^2 + l_a (f_a \, \beta k_b)^2} \; ; \quad C = \frac{f_a \beta k_b \, (\alpha k_a + \beta k_b) \, l_a}{(\alpha k_a + \beta k_b)^2 + l_a (f_a \, \beta k_b)^2} \; ;$$

$$B = \frac{\alpha^2 f_a \, k_b f_b \, k_a \, l_b}{(\alpha k_a + \beta k_b)^2 + l_b (f_b \, \alpha k_a)^2} \; ; \quad D = \frac{f_b \, \alpha k_a \, (\alpha k_a + \beta k_b) \, l_b}{(\alpha k_a + \beta k_b)^2 + l_b (f_b \, \alpha k_a)^2}$$

$$\text{Hence } Defs_a = \frac{- E_b AD \, (h_b + q_b E) - E_a C \, (h_a + q_a E)}{1 - AB} \quad (12)$$

with $0<AB<1$

and similarly, $Defs_b$ is calculated. They both depend on demand shocks of countries a and b and on common shocks (if the latter arise).

Equations (10), (11) and (12) show why there are negative spillovers created by the existence of a single monetary policy, without any coordination between fiscal policies. Each country attaches only limited importance to the impact of its deficit on the interest rate, effectively free riding in its fiscal decisions. On the other hand, each country reacts to the deficit change of the other country, leading to an excessive structural deficit. This bias is, however, lower if there is a systemic shock, as this provides a positive externality. In fact, the structural deficit spending of other governments does not only induce negative spillovers, but possibly also positive ones.

Each country's structural deficit is not set to zero any longer and this is due to a coordination failure. To show why this is indeed the case, it is sufficient to see that, if the quadratic loss function (L) where calculated on the basis of a common target, consisting of minimising the joint preference for a fiscal rule and for output stabilisation, as in

$$L = \tfrac{1}{2} [(\alpha\ Defs_a + \beta\ Defs_b)^2 + l\ (\alpha\ Y_a + \beta\ Y_b)^2] \ , \qquad (13)$$

with l equal to the average of l_a and l_b, the optimal solution of (13), given (8), would be $Defs_a = 0 = Defs_b$.

Consequently, (6) and (7) would hold true for country a and similarly it could be calculated for country b. This consideration is supposed to provide the rationale for setting the limits on deficit spending in the eurozone through the Stability and Growth Pact. Indeed, according to Uhlig (2003):

> Ideally fiscal policy should respond to the country-specific 'fiscal demand shocks', leaving it to the European Central Bank to respond to the average of the country-specific cost-push shocks. However, each fiscal authority will be tempted to try to improve the situation for its own country by, for example, expanding government demand or government deficits precisely when the ECB needs to combat cost-push shocks via higher interest rates. With all countries doing so, the ECB ends up combating not only the cost-push shocks, but the additional fiscal demands as well. Institutions need to be found that will ensure that country-specific fiscal policies stick to the task at hand and avoid this free-riding issue. The Stability and Growth Pact can be seen as doing exactly that: by limiting country-specific deficits, the temptation in each country to seek an improvement in its situation at the expense of all other members of EMU will be limited.

However, further elements emerging in (10), (11) and (12), which are ignored in the Stability and Growth Pact, should be taken into consideration: a distinction in the binding constraints on the fiscal behaviour of member states belonging to the single currency should be made, depending on whether there exists a negative supply or a negative demand shock, whether it is strong or mild and asymmetric or systemic. First, in the optimal solution, the ceiling on deficit spending should be different in the case of a supply and of a demand shock. The 3% constraint may be too large, facing a negative supply shock, i.e. when essentially no deficit spending should be allowed, according to equation (6). It may be correct, when facing a mild asymmetric negative demand shock - when the automatic stabilisers restore output at the potential level within the limits of the 3%; it may finally be sub-optimal when there is a strong and/or a systemic negative demand shock (hence automatic stabilisers are not sufficient and a discretionary expansionary fiscal policy is called for). The coordination failure is particularly absurd when there is a systemic negative demand shock, because each country is positively affected by the budgetary stimulus of other countries.

5. MARKET INTEGRATION AND COMPETITION POLICY: THE CHALLENGES AHEAD

GINEVRA BRUZZONE & LUIGI PROSPERETTI

1. Introduction

While several objectives have been assigned to Community institutions since the very beginning and new targets and tasks have been added over time, the establishment of a single market in which competition is not distorted is still the core of the European project. It has been and remains an extraordinary experiment of integration that is respectful of national diversities.

There are good reasons to keep a central role for market integration in the EU of the 21st century. Indeed, the European project cannot dismiss its freedom-oriented compass without losing much of its identity. The incentives for European undertakings to increase efficiency in order to meet world competition would become muted and the prospects of economic growth would dim.

The accomplishment of the single market requires both negative and positive integration, i.e. the elimination of obstacles to the free movement of goods, services and factors of production and the adoption of common policies to ensure the proper operation of market forces.

The objective has not been fully attained yet. The ratio of intra-US states exports to GDP is around 70% higher than the ratio of intra-EU15 exports to GDP. For services, which account for some 70% of GDP and employment in advanced countries, markets are still organised along national lines and cross-border trade remains relatively underdeveloped.

Only 22% of public procurement in the EU is published for tender and therefore open to competition.[1] The establishment of a Community patent is still blocked by apparently insurmountable linguistic obstacles, although it is widely acknowledged that it would substantially reduce the costs for protection of intellectual property rights in Europe. The transposition of directives is slow and of low quality. The implementation of Community rules, contrary to what would be expected in a truly integrated area, leads in some cases to highly divergent results.

It may be argued that the attainment of a single market where competition is not distorted is a moving target, which will never be reached definitively. It is necessary not only to remove barriers that still hamper the fundamental freedoms, but also to ensure that new barriers are not created, that competition rules continue to be applied so as to avoid distortions resulting from the conduct of companies or from state measures. Common policies have to be adapted to changing market conditions and technologies. And yet there is room for improving the current situation with new distortions arising from national interventions to cushion the impact of the economic slump.

As to the political economy of regulation, it has long been recognised that removing barriers to open markets must confront a fundamental difficulty: the costs of greater market freedom inevitably fall on incumbents, who will therefore resist liberalisations, whereas those likely to benefit from them are usually less aware of the attendant advantages and therefore will not make their voice heard.[2]

Over time, there have been several waves of low popularity of economic integration in the EU internal market, owing either to legitimate concerns regarding the protection of social values and cohesion, or to the lack of visible benefits, or, naturally, to the impact of market opening on vested interests. When the economy is down, the problem worsens, as many recent examples confirm once again.

In autumn 2008, the outburst of the economic and financial crisis was followed by widespread calls for a suspension of the application of EU state aid policy so as to allow member states more room for manoeuvre in

---

[1] See Ilzkovitz et al. (2007).

[2] On these issues, see Amato & Laudati (2001).

managing the crisis. In the main the European Council managed to resist. However, the member states have taken quite a few measures designed to protect domestic industry and employment; in a number of cases they have notified the Commission aid measures which clearly discriminate in favour of national companies and therefore required adjustment before being considered compatible with the common market.

A paramount example was provided by the process which led, in 2006, to the adoption of the Directive on services in the internal market.[3] In the context of the enlargement of the European Union, the initial proposal by the European Commission, aimed at removing residual obstacles to the fundamental freedoms in the services sector, was perceived as threatening social dumping within Europe and therefore met strong opposition by trade unions in several member states. Prolonged negotiations led by the European Parliament eventually succeeded in reaching an acceptable compromise, but numerous amendments weakening the original text were required before the Directive could become politically acceptable.[4]

More generally, in recent years the demand for protectionism mounted in several member states.[5] In this perspective, it has been widely debated whether some of the changes introduced by the Lisbon Treaty imply a weakening of competition policies.

As is well known, following strong pressure by the French government, undistorted competition is no longer included among the objectives of the EU, although it has maintained its place among the instruments necessary to achieve integrated markets. Article 3 of the new Treaty on European Union states that the Union shall establish an internal market and shall work "for the sustainable development of Europe based on balanced economic growth and price stability, a highly competitive social market economy, aiming at full employment and social progress, and a high level of protection and improvement of the quality of the environment"; the promotion of scientific and technical progress is also mentioned, but the protection of competition is not. In order to find the statement whereby the internal market as set out in Article 3 of the EU

---

[3] Directive 2006/123/EC on services in the internal market.

[4] See Micossi (2006).

[5] See contribution by Bastasin, in this volume.

Treaty includes a system ensuring that competition is not distorted, one has now to turn to a recital of Protocol 27.[6]

One argument playing down the anti-competitive signal implicit in the removal of undistorted competition from the Treaty goals maintains that the protection of undistorted competition never was an end in itself (but is the promotion of technical progress an end in itself?). Furthermore, all the substantive rules on competition and the internal market contained in the EC Treaty have survived in the Treaty on the Functioning of the Union,[7] which in addition requires that the economic policy of the Union and the member states be based on the principle of an open market economy with free competition, and explicitly acknowledges that this principle favours an efficient allocation of resources.[8]

Importantly, Article 86 of the EC Treaty remained untouched: therefore, services of general economic interest remain subject to the rules on competition "in so far as the application of such rules does not obstruct the performance in law or in fact of the particular tasks assigned to them", although in its application the Courts will also have to take into account a new Protocol 26 on services of general interest, which emphasises the importance of services of general interest in the interpretation of the rules of the Treaty.[9]

---

[6] In Protocol 27 the High Contracting Parties specify that, to this end, the Union shall if necessary take action under the provisions of the Treaties, including Article 352 of the Treaty on the Functioning of the EU. Under that article, the Council, acting unanimously on a proposal from the Commission and after obtaining the consent of the European Parliament, shall adopt the appropriate measures.

[7] It remains to be seen whether, without an express mention of the target of undistorted competition in the EU Treaty, Community courts will still be willing to adopt an extensive interpretation of the illegality, under EU law, of restrictions of competition resulting from state measures. In the past, several important judgments in which the Court of Justice upheld the alleged illegality of anti-competitive measures adopted by member states referred to Articles 3.1.g and 10 of the EC Treaty as a legal basis. See, for instance, Court of Justice, judgment of 9 September 2003, case C-198/01, *Consorzio industrie Fiammiferi (CIF).*

[8] Articles 119 and 120 of the Treaty on the functioning of the EU (formerly Articles 4 and 98 of the EC Treaty).

[9] Interestingly, Article 16 of the EC Treaty, introduced by the Amsterdam/Nice Treaty, and now transposed in Article 14 of the Treaty on the Functioning of the

A pro-competitive single market agenda requires an active marketing effort vis-à-vis citizens and stakeholders so as to make the resulting benefits visible and understood by the public. There is also a need for effective measures supporting those who find it more difficult to cope with the consequences of integration. These measures will have to give particular attention to creating the conditions for enhanced flexibility of economic structures and factor markets, including appropriate support for human capital investment and employability.

In this paper we focus on four main challenges that must be met by European market integration policies in the coming decade: i) becoming closer to citizens; ii) keeping stable principles while avoiding unjustified rigidities that can feed opposition to pro-competitive policies, and improving the integration of structural policies in Europe; iii) reaching the right level of harmonisation of common rules; and iv) improving the institutional arrangements for their implementation.

2. Becoming closer to citizens

In principle, the protection of competition and the completion of the internal market are viewed favourably by European citizens. However, there are differences between member states. For instance, the responses provided by citizens of the larger countries to the assertion "Free competition is the best guarantee of economic prosperity" (Table 1) show heterogeneous social welfare functions, and these are quite stable, being only weakly affected by the financial crisis.

Moreover, in responses to the question "Which aspects should be emphasised by the European institutions in the coming years, to strengthen the European Union in the future?", the European internal market ranks tenth, after economic affairs, social and health issues, immigration, the fight against crime, environment, energy, solidarity with poorer regions, the fight against climate change and education (Figure 1).

EU, was weaker since, while requiring the Union and the member states to take care that services of general economic interest operate on the basis of principles and conditions that enable them to fulfil their missions, it expressly recalled the Treaty competition provisions.

Table 1. Responses to the (2009) Eurobarometer assertion "Free competition is the best guarantee of economic prosperity" (%)

	I agree	I do not agree	I do not know
EU-15	63	26	11
Germany	75	21	4
France	48	40	12
United Kingdom	63	22	15
Spain	57	27	16
Italy	69	23	8

Source: Eurobarometer, September 2009.

Figure 1. Responses to the question: "What aspects should be emphasised by the European institutions in the coming years, to strengthen the European Union in the future?" (%)

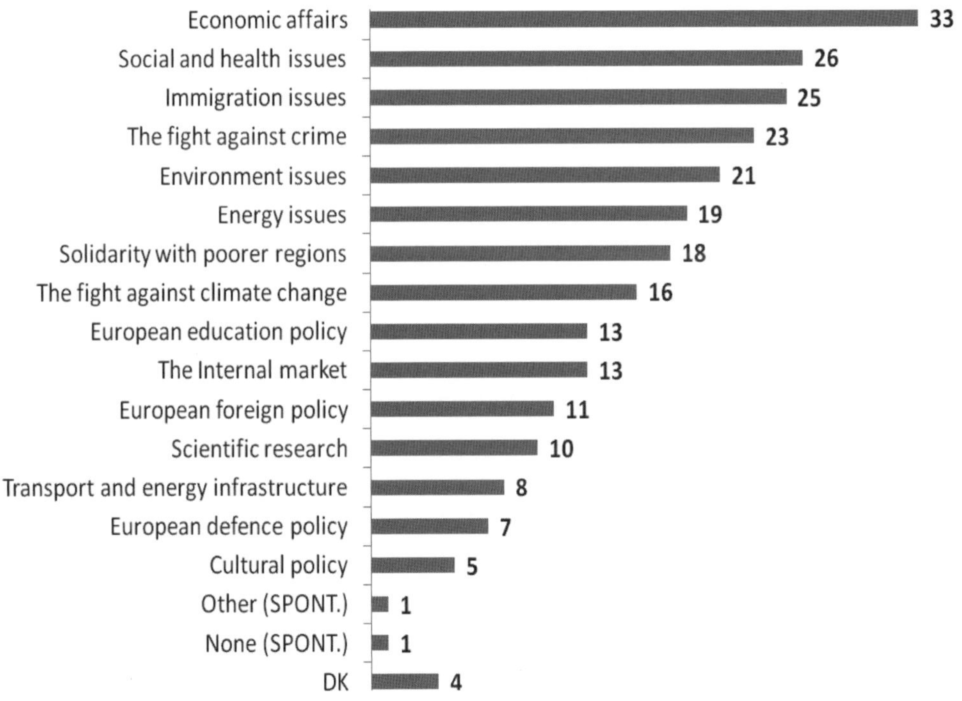

Source: Eurobarometer, September 2009.

Looking at the very different policy areas, this ranking is no surprise and clearly reflects the increasing demand for security by European citizens. However, it also shows that proactive measures are needed to create a sense of ownership by European citizens as far as the policies for the market are concerned.

There are several ways in which Community institutions can try to make such policies closer to stakeholders and, more generally, to citizens. They include, for instance, better regulation initiatives aimed at improving the quality of Community legislation, including extensive use of public consultation and *ex-ante* and *ex-post* impact assessment.

It is also useful to try to quantify the costs of non-integration and restrictions of competition so as to increase awareness of the potential benefits of pro-competitive policies. Since publication of the authoritative Cecchini report on the 'costs of non-Europe' in 1988, increasingly sophisticated empirical studies have been undertaken for this purpose by the Commission and private researchers. For instance, when the discussion on the services Directive was raging, economic analysis usefully pointed out that the productivity gap between the EU and the US is largely explained precisely by the obstacles to the establishment of a single market for services.[10] In preparation of the recent Single Market Review, it has been stressed that, as a result of the progress made over the period 1992-2006 in achieving an enlarged internal market of 25 member states (including liberalisation of network industries), "GDP and employment levels have increased significantly. The estimated gains from the internal market amount to 2.2% of EU value added and 1.4% of total employment (or 2.75 million jobs). Moreover, these gains could be doubled with the removal of most of the remaining internal market barriers."[11]

Other empirical studies have purported to assess the effects of competition policy in promoting productivity growth, again with evidence of positive effects.[12]

As to the enforcement of competition policies, in the last decade the Commission has strived to 'modernise' the system, with the ultimate aim of

---

[10] Micossi (2006); van Ark et al. (2008, p.38).

[11] See Ilzkovitz et al. (2007).

[12] See Buccirossi (2009).

increasing the awareness that enforcing competition rules is not a matter reserved to antitrust experts, but produces important economic benefits ultimately accruing to European consumers. Both in antitrust and the control of state aid, several notification requirements have been eliminated. In antitrust, the Commission placed an increasing emphasis on clear priority-setting by public enforcers, so as to focus on the infringements more likely to harm consumers, notably cartels.

Under the new approach, the Commission is also making intensive use of fact-finding sectoral investigations in sectors that are crucial to European consumers, such as retail banking, gas, electricity and the pharmaceutical industry. Recent conferences promoted by the Directorate General for Competition address issues that, only ten years ago, would have appeared odd, such as "How has competition policy benefited European consumers?" or "How can we deliver continuous improvement in consumer relations?"[13] Community institutions have also undertaken to make the control of state aid more intelligible to laymen. Procedures have been made more transparent and the Commission has started to explain its strategy concerning state aid in plain language, unprecedented in this area. Notably, it has tried to convey the message that EU member states should tend towards a system with "less and better targeted state aid" and that state aid measures can be justified only when they aim to remove clear market failures. It has also begun promoting private actions for damages arising from state aid.[14]

Although it remains unlikely that policy areas such as antitrust and the control of state aid will ever become truly popular among European citizens, the efforts to make pro-market policies perceived by citizens as less distant from their private interests are indispensable, in order to avoid that the single market and competition policies continue to be viewed as matters for Eurocrats.

---

[13] See the programme of the Conference on Competition and Consumers in the 21st Century, 21 October 2009, on DG Comp's website (http://ec.europa.eu/competition/consumers/events/2009/index.html).

[14] See the study conducted for the European Commission on these questions by Jestaedt et al. (2006).

3. Stable principles and integration of structural policies

As anticipated, with the outburst of the economic and financial crisis, European control of state aid risked being set apart, and this scenario would certainly have had permanent consequences. The challenge for the Commission was to keep the basic principles unchallenged, while showing sufficient flexibility to meet the demands for state aid that were justified by the need to address a crisis of unprecedented gravity. The Commission was sufficiently capable of meeting the challenge. It founded its criteria for the assessment of state aid during the crisis on a special legal basis, namely Article 87.3.b of the Treaty, which allows the Commission to consider compatible with the Common market state aid measures needed to "remedy a serious disturbance in the economy of a Member State". In so doing, it was able to rely on more flexible assessment, without prejudice to the normal criteria that will continue to be applied to state aid when the system will return to normality. The Commission, although proceeding amongst harsh criticisms and, somehow, also by trial and error due to the novelty and complexity of the economic environment,[15] succeeded in avoiding wrecking the system. Member states have always notified aid plans, the Commission has swiftly examined and generally approved them, in some cases requiring some changes and the removal of clearly protectionist measures. Not only has the system of state aid control held out, it has also helped governments to discriminate on the merits between requests of aid during the economic turmoil. Unexpectedly, although several problems remain unresolved, the European regime has come to be viewed as a best practice internationally.

A call for flexibility in the enforcement of pro-competitive policies also emerges from the requests for a better exploitation of the synergies between different European structural policy instruments.[16] It can be

---

[15] Some changes are evident, for instance, in the position taken in the December 2008 Communication on the recapitalisation of banks, compared with the October 2008 Communication on State aid in the banking sector.

[16] For instance, Ilkowitz et al. (2007) argue that "internal market policies contribute towards creating the appropriate framework conditions for European firms to be competitive at world level. Other policies, including in particular competition (state aids, merger control and antitrust) and innovation (R&D, education, ICT) policies, have similar objectives. Potential gains from integrating these different policy instruments within a systemic approach are substantial."

argued that the quest for integration of policies entails the risk that industrial policy objectives will systematically prevail over the objective of maintaining an open market economy based on undistorted competition. But it is not necessarily so: a more integrated approach to structural policies can also be undertaken without weakening the fundamental principles of each policy area.

For instance, the need to reconcile competition policy with the promotion of efficiency and competitiveness does not necessarily require external constraints, but only the application of proper competition principles. In modern competition policy, it is clear that the goal is not the maintenance of a fragmented market structure, but the protection of the competitive pressures that are essential to the operation of the market process. Efficiency is seen as a value, not a risk for competition. Competition rules are not, in themselves, an impediment to the growth of European companies, even through mergers and acquisitions. Acknowledgement that cooperation among competitors may, under certain conditions, produce positive results, for instance in standard-setting, is also fully compatible with a modern approach to the application of antitrust rules.

On the other hand, when requests of weak enforcement of market principles are justified on the basis of social concerns, giving up the objective of a single market with undistorted competition does not seem the right response, because of the negative impact it would have on growth prospects. A much better strategy is to support further progress in market integration, including the removal of still high barriers to the mobility of labour, with a renewed social agenda and better functioning welfare regimes.[17]

4. The proper degree of harmonisation

4.1 Supranational regulation

From the very beginning, the search for the proper degree of harmonisation in the definition of rules for the internal market has been a matter for discussion. In order to assess these issues, it may be useful first to address

---

[17] On these issues, see the two contributions elsewhere in this volume by C. Bastasin and M. Ferrera & S. Sacchi.

the more general question of regulatory models in a multinational context such as that of the European Union. Considering our goals here, we will refer to the very broad definition of regulation set forth by Stigler in 1981, whereby regulation is any "attempt on the part of government to use its authority to influence the economic behaviour of non-government agents".[18]

There are three main economic reasons for supranational regulation: i) the need to remove barriers among states that reduce trade flows and therefore welfare, ii) the presence of domestic market failure spillover effects towards other countries and iii) the greater effectiveness of supranational, as opposed to domestic, regulation stemming from regulatory economies of scale.

The first of these reasons underpins the whole Treaty. Article 5 perfectly captures the other two, in stating:

> in areas which do not fall within its executive competence, the Community shall take action, in accordance with the principle of subsidiarity, only if and in so far as the objectives of the proposed action cannot be sufficiently achieved by the member states and can therefore, by reason of the scale or effects of the proposed action, be better achieved by the Community.

As pointed out by Pelkmans (1998),[19] regulatory effects of scale and cross-country effects are therefore two necessary preconditions for Community regulation.

Where these conditions are met, supranational regulation can therefore be efficient, assuming one does not underestimate the extreme complexity of the general backdrop: market failure-derived problems can indeed take on varying degrees of severity depending on the country concerned, just as perceptions of said severity by different national communities may vary widely.

As for the instruments of supranational regulation, they can be analysed as coming under two main categories: *ex-ante regulation* and *ex-post regulation*. *Ex ante regulation* is generally based on Articles 94 and 95 (1) of the Treaty, traditionally used to remove obstacles to the exercise of

---

[18] Stigler (1981).

[19] Pelkmans (1998).

fundamental freedoms, as well as to eliminate significant competitive distortions. According to Barnard's taxonomy (2004),[20] this type of regulation can take on different forms:

- Full harmonisation uses regulation to set *mandatory standards*, the adoption of which prohibits member states from introducing different standards, including more stringent ones. Typically, these are 'slow' harmonisation measures, with member states attempting to negotiate instruments to defend their own firms, as the harmonising regulation may be good or bad for them.
- Minimal harmonisation sets *minimum standards* and leaves member states free to adopt more stringent ones.
- Optional harmonisation sets standards that producers in any given country *may* adopt for sales in their domestic markets, but which they *must* adopt for sales in other countries.

Article 94 empowers the Council to issue directives "for the approximation of regulations which directly affect the establishment or functioning of the internal market"; it requires unanimity and produces full harmonisation. It proved cumbersome and ineffectual, and was eventually superseded by the Single Act (in force since 1987) with Article 95, a far more flexible instrument.

Article 95 empowers the Council, acting by qualified majority voting, to adopt measures for the approximation of regulations of member states "which have as their object the establishment of the internal market". It was underpinned by the famous 1979 *Cassis de Dijon* decision by the Court of Justice,[21] which had strengthened the presumption in favour of freedom of circulation of goods, services, capital and people, under the principle of mutual recognition of national legislations and had subjected the introduction of restrictions to the strict tests of imperative need, adequacy and proportionality of the restrictive measures. From that moment onward, the Commission could concentrate its attention in harmonising legislation on the measures that were required to eliminate restrictions that could be justified under the *Cassis de Dijon* test.

---

[20] Barnard (2004).

[21] Case 120/78 *Rewe Zentrale v. Bundesmonopolverwaltung fur Branntwein* (1979).

Article 95 achieved a delicate balance between the requirements of freedom and the protection of legitimate national interests of protection of consumers, workers and the environment; it was revised by the Treaty of Amsterdam in order to strengthen these protections. Thus, the Commission, in its proposals to the Council concerning health, safety, environmental protection and consumer protection, must take as a base a high level of protection. After the adoption of a harmonisation measure, a member state can maintain national provisions for major reasons pertaining to public policy objectives recognised by Community law,[22] but has to notify the Commission and the other member states, setting in motion a review procedure that can approve or reject the measure. New measures can also be introduced by member states in harmonised areas, but only on the basis of new scientific evidence relating to the protection of the environment or the working environment. All Community measures are subject to safeguard clauses that make it possible to reassess their adequacy in the face of evidence of insufficient protection.

The Court of Justice made it clear that Article 95 can be used to eliminate likely obstacles to the exercise of the fundamental freedoms as well as appreciable distortions of competition in the internal market.[23]

Recourse to these instruments has evolved over time.

4.2 *Common rules for products*

Initially, full harmonisation measures under Article 94 were used extensively to standardise all products from a technical standpoint, and their application would be sought whenever a country barred the goods of another from access to its domestic market, with obvious costs in terms of competition and innovation.

As was mentioned, the Court of Justice's *Cassis de Dijon* ruling represented a turning point. It clearly stated that full harmonisation was normally unnecessary, and that different countries could legitimately opt for different forms of regulation, provided that regulatory restrictions complied with necessity and proportionality criteria for the pursuit of

---

[22] Article 95 refers to the objectives mentioned in Article 30 of the EC Treaty, as well as to the protection of the environment and of the working environment.

[23] Case C- 376/98, *Tobacco Advertising* (1998).

regulatory goals recognised by Community law.[24] The ruling thus sanctioned a principle of mutual recognition for regulatory regimes, subject however to green-lighting on the part of the country receiving goods regulated in their country of origin. The principle obviously allows for regulatory competition, insofar as national regulations that do not meet the criteria of necessity and proportionality are made to compete against those applied in other countries.[25]

As of the 1980s, the focus of full harmonisation measures was thus gradually restricted to product security purposes, and flexible harmonisation based on essential requirements of protection became the rule. This evolution was favoured by the so-called 'New Approach' to internal market legislation developed by the Commission after the entry into force of the Single Act. The New Approach was aimed at limiting the scope of harmonising directives to the task of defining the essential requirement of protection, while leaving the determination of technical details to voluntary standards, prepared under Community procedures by official standardisation bodies and published in the Official Journal, the adoption of which gives rise to a compliance presumption.

Therefore, as far as the features of products are concerned, there has been a clear trend away from full harmonisation in favour of increased flexibility.

---

[24] In the case in point, Germany was ruled against for having imposed, absent adequate justification, limitations to the sale of goods that had received all the required authorisations in their country of origin.

[25] This principle is however far from implying a home-country rule, insofar as the verification of the equivalence of the levels of protection is performed by the host country, and not by the country of origin. A country-of-origin rule would conversely assume that compliance checks have been performed once and for all by the product's country of origin. This distinction assumed great relevance in discussions on the Services Directive, as the Commission initally tried to push through a country-of-origin principle, while the solution ultimately adopted was that of mutual recognition under the control of the country receiving the service. There are currently no examples of country-of-origin rule application within the Community except for cases of full *ex ante* harmonisation of substantive rules.

4.3 *Commercial relations between business and consumers*

It would be misleading, however, to view the evolution of Community regulation as a one-way trend towards flexibility of regulatory choices at the national level. The most prominent counter-example is in the area of consumer protection and pertains to commercial practices aimed at reaching consumers in the different member states. In this area, the absence of common rules, including the minimum harmonisation approach followed by the 1984 Directive that set common rules on misleading advertising, led to significant divergences in member states which increased the cost to business of exercising internal market freedoms and made consumers uncertain of their rights. Therefore, Community institutions decided to shift to a maximum harmonisation approach: uniform rules establishing a high level of consumer protection are adopted at Community level and member states are prevented from adopting stricter rules. A maximum harmonisation approach has already been followed in the 2005 Directive setting common rules for unfair commercial practices in relations between business and consumers.[26] The same approach also inspires the recent proposal of a broad Directive on consumers rights, which will consolidate four different directives in the area of consumer protection.[27]

4.4 *Common rules for services*

Since the 1980s, the Court of Justice acknowledged that the mutual recognition principle can also be applied to services. However, it soon became clear that the barriers to the establishment of a single market for services cannot be removed solely on a case-by-case basis, by relying on the direct application of the rules of the Treaty on the freedom of establishment and the freedom to provide services. The removal of barriers required coordination of national regulatory models, i.e. common rules.

Most directives follow a sectoral approach. They cover, for instance, the regulated professions, insurance, banking and financial services, services relating to travel and tourism, television broadcasting, air and rail

---

[26] Directive 2005/29/CE.

[27] Sale of consumer goods and guarantees, 99/44/EC; unfair contract terms, 93/13/EC; distance selling, 97/7/EC; and doorstep selling, 85/577/EC.

transport, electronic communications, electricity and gas and postal services.

The sectoral approach, however, was not able to tackle the barriers to the freedom of establishment and the freedom to provide services existing for a myriad of ever-evolving services that would never be covered by ad hoc directives. Therefore, the 2006 Framework Directive on services was adopted with the aim of removing all remaining barriers to the internal market for services through horizontal framework rules.[28] The Directive requires member states to adopt measures of administrative simplification and to remove unjustified regulatory restrictions. For restrictions included on a black list, there is a irrefutable presumption of incompatibility with Community rules. For restrictions included on a grey list, the presumption is rebuttable. As for the provision of services, the Directive introduces a statutory requirement for member states to apply the mutual recognition principle and allows them to impose additional requirements only for a narrow set of public policy reasons. Moreover, it strengthens administrative cooperation mechanisms.

4.5 *...including network industries*

The experience of Community rules in network industries provides important hints on the preconditions that must be met for a successful setting of common rules.

Pro-competitive Community regulation of such industries has traditionally met strong opposition due to the influence of public ownership and the political weight of employee unions, and therefore common rules aimed at opening markets to competition, as a rule, have progressed slowly.

A relevant exception is provided by telecommunications, but it is easy to show how the success of European regulatory policies in this area should be attributed to rather unusual occurrences in the first half of the 1980s. In that period, at the international level, the fall in prices and the very high growth of the US telecommunications industry, unleashed by the structural separation of AT&T in 1982, were worrying developments to

---

[28] The scope of the Directive covers all services with the exclusion of some activities already covered by specific Community regulation and some specific services such as, for instance, gambling activities or services provided by notaries.

European policy-makers, who feared for Europe's competitiveness. The very same developments were worrying for European producers of telecommunications equipment, who feared falling irremediably behind their American competitors, who were enjoying such exceptional market growth. These parallel worries helped to foster a highly effective alliance between the Commission and hardware producers, which was successful in overcoming the strong resistance of telecommunications services incumbents. Such a success was greatly facilitated by the widespread perception that these operators were highly inefficient, as it became immediately obvious in the UK, when the privatisation of BT and the partial liberalisation of the market yielded immediate benefits in terms of price and quality. Nothing succeeds like success, and this convinced even the countries that were initially most reluctant towards liberalisation, such as France and Italy, to gradually accept these policies.

The policy mix put in place to liberalise the sector was an interplay between Council directives, based upon Articles 94 and 95, and Commission directives, based on Article 86, which were politically feasible because of the lack of significant opposition to the liberalisation measures. Regulatory policy in telecommunications was strongly supported by the antitrust provisions of the Treaty. In the early 1990s, the European Commission indeed clearly signalled that it intended to extensively use Article 82, together with Article 86 of the Treaty, in order to promote competition in network industries. In the *Sealink/Stena* case, in which it developed its 'essential facility' doctrine, it - unusually - decided to publish the full text of a decision, despite the fact that the companies concerned had in the meantime settled the controversy, and in so doing, it naturally set an effective precedent.

Experience in the telecoms sector continued to provide important hints in the following years. The new regulatory framework for electronic communications, enacted with five directives in 2002, endorses the principle whereby regulation should be used only where the application of competition rules is insufficient, includes rules for the access to the network and establishes common minimum rules concerning universal service and consumer protection. The package of proposals was very well prepared by the Commission, with a clear indication of the objectives and the proposed measures. It has been observed that "this greatly helped to put the debate on a concrete track for a constructive solution, which was acceptable to all major players. When it came to negotiations in the Council and in the

European Parliament, the basic structures for a solution had largely been accepted and the debate could be based on this common ground".[29]

The experience in the energy sector, whether gas or electricity, was completely different. For a very long time there was no convincing threat that procedures would be opened by the Commission against incumbent operators on the basis of Article 82 of the Treaty, with reference to the essential facility doctrine. A few attempts were made at national level, but these were rather rare, and often late: in the *E.ON Ruhrgas* case, the *Bundeskartellamt*'s objection was not endorsed by the German authorities, and elsewhere no significant case occurred prior to 2000. This time lag proved very costly in terms of regulatory policy, as it allowed incumbent operators in the energy sector to prepare for liberalisation (it should be remembered that drafting the various versions of the gas and electricity Directives took about a decade), by thoroughly saturating existing power and gas lines through the simple expedient of renegotiating take-or-pay supply contracts, while extending their duration and increasing their amounts.

Not having intervened during such a drawn-out 'bottleneck engineering' phase, the Commission was subsequently faced with considerable difficulties when new competitors repeatedly met the objection by incumbents that they couldn't access the grids because of near-total capacity saturation. Following an extensive sector inquiry, the Commission published a not particularly incisive Green Paper still identifying – nearly 15 years after the submission of the first draft Directive on the electricity market – harmonisation measures as the main way forward, and proposing a goal, that of "developing a European grid", to be furthered through the setting up of a European gas and electricity regulator.

Now, although the advisability of Community intervention in this field is hardly challenged in theory, since there are clear cross-country effects and equally clear economies of scale to be achieved in regulating these sectors, a number of obstacles exist. In a strategic situation where security of supply is all but certain, both for gas and electricity, different national communities will no doubt react quite differently to the risk of

[29] See Renda et al. (2009, p. 7).

supply disruption, and for that matter have different degrees of tolerance vis-à-vis competition-distorting measures in energy markets.

Moreover, it isn't immediately clear that (let's say) French consumers would be willing to ration their own electricity supply in order to provide power to (let's say) Italian consumers, should the latter be in need. In this framework, where the calls for market and policy harmonisation strategies are morally uplifting but devoid of any concrete impact, the Commission finally concluded to resort – on a much larger scale than it had done previously – to antitrust policy. After a detailed sector inquiry in electricity and gas,[30] the Commission has initiated foreclosure cases against E.ON, EDF, ENI, Electrabel, Distrigaz and other companies, thus supplementing possible local regulatory and antitrust slackness.[31]

5. Coordinated implementation

The application of the subsidiarity principle involves not only the level at which rules have to be established (Community versus national versus local), but also how centralised the application of Community rules should be.

In its recent recommendation on measures to improve the functioning of the single market, the Commission stresses that it is essential for a well functioning single market to have a proper system of transposition, application, enforcement and monitoring of the common rules and that further work is still necessary in this area.[32] Internal market scoreboards show that timeliness and quality in the transposition of single market directives are still scarce. Even when directives have formally been transposed, the frequency of infringement proceedings against member states is a signal of bad implementation. Supplementary provisions that are not necessary to transpose a directive are often added in the implementing legislation, well beyond cases of shared competence where this is justified by Community rules setting only minimum requirements.

---

[30] The final report is in SEC (2006) 1724, 10 January 2007.

[31] On the policy challenges in the energy sector, see the chapter by V. Termini in this volume.

[32] C(2009) 4728 final. See also the Commission Communication, "A single market for 21st century Europe" (Single Market Review), COM (2007) 724 of 20 November 2007.

The Commission therefore recommends that member states take a more pro-active role in managing the single market, ensuring that it functions well. In particular, it advocates a better coordination on single market issues within member states, as well as initiatives aimed to facilitate coordination and promote closer links between the administrations of different member states. It envisages exchanges of officials responsible for single market issues between national administrations and active cross-border cooperation on single market issues becoming part of the national administrative culture. These can be viewed as the embryonic stages of an integrated European public administration.

Further steps have already been taken in specific policy areas. An important reference is provided by the institutional architecture for the application of Community competition rules. For the control of state aid and for merger control, enforcement is fully centralised, i.e. the Commission has exclusive competence; for the application of Articles 81 and 82 of the Treaty, on anti-competitive agreements and abuse of dominance, however, the task of public enforcement is shared by the Commission and the competition authorities of member states. The Commission and national competition authorities operate as a network (European Competition Network), with its own rules for the allocation of cases. For instance, the Commission is considered well placed to deal with cases involving more than three member states and when a new competition issue arises, since only Commission decisions are subject to the scrutiny of the Court of Justice. The European Competition Network also works as a forum for 'soft harmonisation' in the use of instruments and procedures for the implementation of competition rules, i.e. in an area that has not been harmonised by Community law.

While European Community agencies have been established in several technical areas and for specific scientific or managerial tasks,[33] so far neither in network industries nor in financial sectors have proposals aimed at full centralisation of supervisory and regulatory tasks at the European level met a sufficient consensus. The idea to set up a European

---

[33] The tasks of European agencies include, for instance, fisheries control, aviation and maritime safety, disease prevention and control, the safety of chemical products, food safety and the implementation of Community rules on trademarks and designs.

regulatory authority for telecommunications meets the opposition of a number of leading countries (United Kingdom, France, Germany). For similar reasons, the proposal of a European regulator for gas or electricity is unlikely to succeed, at least in the near future. Also the need to strengthen prudential supervision in financial markets, strongly highlighted by the recent financial turmoil, led to new institutional arrangements but not to the establishment of fully centralised European authorities.

In most sectors, however, there is a clear trend towards closer forms of coordination for the implementation of Community rules. The arrangements emerging in the different areas are worth studying.

Groups or networks linking up the regulatory or supervisory authorities of member states have been established in areas as different as electricity and gas,[34] consumer protection,[35] public procurement[36] and the protection of personal data.[37] More ambitious institutional arrangements have been developed for electronic communications and financial services.

In electronic communications, the 2002 framework regulatory package established a dynamic relationship between the Commission and national regulatory authorities. It is not the Commission alone who decides what markets should be regulated. The Commission issues a list of candidate markets, which it periodically updates, but the decision concerning whether, and with what instruments, to regulate each of these markets in any country, is bestowed upon the national regulatory authority (NRA).

The NRA needs to assess each of the candidate markets in order to ascertain if they are sufficiently competitive. If they are not, it must impose obligations upon operators having a significant market power; the

---

[34] European Regulators Group for Electricity and Gas, with the task of advising and assisting the Commission in the preparation of draft implementing measures and to facilitate coordination of national regulatory authorities, contributing to a consistent application of Community rules (2003/796/EC).

[35] Enforcement network for consumer protection, established by regulation (EC) 2006/2004.

[36] Public procurement network.

[37] Data Protection Working Party, set up by Directive 95/46/EC with an advisory role on Community initiatives and with the task to promote a uniform application of the principles contained in the directives in all member states.

appropriateness of such obligations must be assessed in the light of the competition provisions of the Treaty, and of relevant jurisdictional precedents. The draft decisions of the national authorities must be notified to the Commission, which has one month to analyse them, and, if it feels it necessary, to send its comments to the national authority. If the Commission considers that the proposed measures create barriers to the internal market, or has doubts concerning their coherence with Community law, it can undertake an in-depth analysis for two more months, and it may eventually request that the proposed measure is cancelled. The Commission's view of this consultation mechanism is that it has ensured a consistent approach, in particular regarding market definition and SMP analysis across Europe, brought sound economic analysis to the market review process and resulted in increased transparency. Overall, this form of cooperation between the Commission and NRAs led to better regulation based on competition principles and contributed to the development of a common European regulatory culture.

The Commission's comments on the proposed remedies gave guidance towards a consistent regulatory approach across Europe, whilst taking into account specific national circumstances. The Commission focused on ensuring that remedies are appropriate, i.e. based on the nature of the problem identified, proportionate and justified in the light of the objectives laid down in the Framework Directive. Implementing a similar approach in the electricity and gas markets would probably be quite useful, especially if we consider the fact that national regulators in such sectors have to bear strong pressures from their national incumbents, which often limit their effectiveness. Moreover, it could help to reduce divergences in the way national regulators are proceeding on a number of relevant matters, such as network access and the rules to be applied to customers that become eligible.

For financial services, since 2000 a new decision-making structure has been established under the 'Lamfalussy approach' with the aim to improve regulation across the EU. Initially it concerned only the security sector, but afterwards was extended to banking, insurance and investment funds. Under the Lamfalussy approach, framework directives set out broad regulatory principles (level 1), while detailed secondary legislation is entrusted to sectoral committees made up of officials from national governments and chaired by the Commission (level 2).[38] Further sectoral committees composed of national supervisory authorities[39] play an advisory role on secondary legislation and monitor the implementation of common rules in the member states, with the task to ensure convergence but without binding powers (level 3).

Recently, the Commission has approved a new package of draft legislative proposals aimed at strengthening the European system of financial supervision following the financial crisis.[40] As far as the implementation of Community rules is concerned, three sectoral European Supervisory Authorities,[41] which will be composed of representatives of national supervisory authorities and of the European Systemic Risk Board, will take over all the functions of the previous level 3 committees with key additional powers, including the power to issue binding technical standards in specific prudential areas, as well as binding interpretations of EU rules and orders to comply in individual cases. They will also be able to settle disagreements between national supervisors and will play a coordination role in emergency situations.

Interestingly, even in the much less technical area of the Directive on services in the internal market, special institutional arrangements have been deemed necessary to ensure an effective and coordinated implementation of Community rules. In particular, each member state is required to present a report to the Commission on the authorisation regimes and the potentially restrictive regulatory provisions that it intends to maintain, demonstrating their compatibility with Community rules.

---

38 European Banking Committee, European Insurance and Operational Pensions Committee, European Securities Committee and Financial Conglomerates Committee.

39 Committee of European Banking Regulators, Committee of European Insurance and Occupational Pensions Supervisors, and Committee of European Securities Regulators.

40 The proposal provides for a two-tier system, with a totally new upper level focusing on systemic risk and macro-prudential supervision (European Systemic Risk Board - ESRB) and a lower level for micro-prudential supervision (European System of Financial Supervisors - ESFS).

41 European Banking Authority, European Insurance and Occupational Pensions Authority and European Securities and Markets Authority.

Each report will be forwarded to all member states and will be subject to mutual evaluation. Moreover, the introduction of new restrictions has to be notified to the Commission and reviewed under a Community procedure. The notification and mutual evaluation procedure is essential to bring out in the open and subject to review all measures potentially violating Community law. Notably, the provisions of the Directive do not entail any new legal principle since they basically incorporate general principles already established by the case law of the Court of Justice. However, by imposing transparent procedures and a systematic review of restrictions, which have to be notified to the Commission and member states and justified one by one, they strengthen the presumption in favour of free movement and open access.

6. Conclusions

Any supranational regulatory activity faces a highly complex scenario, where market failure problems may be rather different, and of different degrees of seriousness, from country to country. Furthermore, there are bound to be substantial differences across national communities concerning the perceptions of such seriousness. Citizens of different countries will also have different stances vis-à-vis regulation, because they will have different value systems, and different views concerning the correct degree of consumer protection.

Supranational regulatory intervention dictated by the overall aim of defending free trade among member states cannot ignore the fact that there are potentially relevant trade-offs between such aim and other relevant objectives of economic policy. It cannot ignore, either, the costs of regulation: if it's true, in general, that free trade fosters welfare, social welfare can be negatively affected also by regulatory intervention.

Trying to implement extensive harmonisation policies is bound to foster diffuse resistance to regulation. In some instances (e.g. popular English press), this can be explained with historical factors, such as the remaining fragments of imperial culture and the insularity of the policy debate in the United Kingdom. In others - such as for *services publics* in France - it can be explained by differing political-economic traditions.

But a quick search on the internet concerning European regulation quickly reveals hundreds of sites, blogs and discussion fora, airing violent opposition to one or more Community regulatory measures, and it seems doubtful that they can be liquidated by simply labelling them as the result of ignorance or manipulation.

Over-regulation at Community level is certainly not the answer to the current challenges. The strategy for internal market and competition policies in the 21st century requires a more sophisticated combination of measures: better regulation initiatives to make Community policies closer to citizens and their benefits more easily perceived; the safeguard of the fundamental market principles without undue rigidities; appropriate flanking measures to meet social concerns and a careful pursuit of the right degree of harmonisation in the different policy areas. Finally, it requires the search for more effective forms of interaction between EU and national public administrations, with a view to eliminate the current weaknesses in transposition and application which undermine the establishment of a true single market.

References

Amato, G. and L. Laudati (eds) (2001), *The Anticompetitive Impact of Regulation*, Cheltenham: Edward Elgar.

Barnard, C. (2004), *The substantive law of the EU*, Oxford: Oxford University Press.

Buccirossi, P. (2009), "Competition Policy and Productivity Growth: An Empirical Assessment", paper presented at the Lear Conference on What Makes Competition Policy Work?, Rome, July.

Ilzkovitz, F., A. Dierx, V. Kovacs and N. Sousa (2007), "Steps towards a deeper economic integration: The internal market in the 21st century – A contribution to the Single Market Review", *European Economy*, Economic Papers No. 271, January.

Jestaedt, T., J. Derenne and T. Ottervanger (2006), "Study on the Enforcement of State Aid Law at National Level", study produced by external consultants for DG Competition, European Commission (http://ec.europa.eu/comm/competition/state_aid/studies_reports/studies_reports.cfm).

Micossi, S. (2006), *Fixing the Services Directive*, CEPS Policy Brief No. 100, Centre for European Policy Studies, Brussels, 26 April.

Pelkmans, J. (1998), "A European Telecoms Regulator?", in P. Vass (ed.), *Network Industries in Europe*, Centre for Regulated Industries, London.

Renda, Andrea et al. (2009), *Policy-making in the EU: Achievements, Challenges and Proposals for Reform*, CEPS Paperback, Centre for European Policy Studies, Brussels.

Stigler, G.J. (1981), *A comment on Joskow and Noll*, in G. Fromm (ed.), *Studies in public regulation*, Cambridge, MA: MIT Press.

van Ark, B., M. O'Mahony and M.P. Timmer (2008), "The productivity gap between Europe and the United States: Trends and causes", *Journal of Economic Perspectives*, Winter.

6. ENERGY AND EUROPEAN INSTITUTIONS

VALERIA TERMINI

1. Background

As was the case at the end of the 1950s, Europe today faces an extraordinarily difficult situation in the energy sector. The Rome Treaties had then provided a solution and long-term prospects to the energy supply problems of the previous decade. The European Atomic Energy Community Treaty entered into force on 1 January 1958, with the aim to guarantee a shared approach to energy security. These institutions not only provided Europe's civilian nuclear energy industry with a common strategy: they also contributed to the launching of the European Economic Community.[1]

Today, for the European Union, the energy issue is even more complex. Externally, the issue involves negotiating with primary-source producing countries 'with a single voice' and facing competition from high-growth countries that are currently the largest energy consumers. Between now and 2030, over 87% of the incremental demand for energy will be accounted for by emerging economies, and just over half of the increase

[1] Together with the Treaty establishing the European Economic Community, the participants in the Rome Conference also signed, on 25 March 1957, a Treaty establishing the European Atomic Energy Community (Euratom) which entered into force on 1 January 1958. Subsequently, at the Rome Summit convened for the 10th anniversary of the EEC and the EAEC (or Euratom), held 9-30 May 1967, a decision was reached to unify the bodies of the three communities: ECSC, EEC and EAEC (initially separate, with the exception of the Assembly and the Court of Justice); on 1 July 1967, the Treaty merging the executive bodies entered into force.

will be represented by China and India (International Energy Agency, 2008). A further difficulty is that of negotiating with countries and regions whose use of energy sources is basically political, as is the case with Russia, Venezuela and Nigeria.

Measures must also be taken internally. The EU countries' industrial development strategies require innovation; the huge investments needed to develop alternative energy sources have to be planned and implemented; the transmission infrastructure has to be developed and cross-border connections strengthened so as to broaden the spectrum of potential primary source supply, inter alia in terms of countries, and interconnect domestic markets. Policies are also needed to contain energy demand growth (European Commission, 2007).[2]

The role and mandate of European institutions remain crucial in this respect. Experience has shown that long-term European energy policies readily revert to wishful thinking when European institutions are not given a clear mandate.

True, the Lisbon Treaty is innovative. It stresses the need for European solutions regarding energy and environment, especially considering the urgent need for global strategies. But if we focus on the ability to implement a common energy policy, we see that unfortunately the Treaty is only innovative in terms of recommendations to national governments. Also, this is not enough to overcome the major contradiction between domestic policies and the European energy strategy – a contradiction that continues to jeopardise the emergence of a European market. And that explains the limited effectiveness of policies and the consequences described below. Before analysing policies in substantive terms, section 2 will however attempt to recall the main institutional phases that have led Europe from Euratom to the Lisbon Treaty.

2. European Institutions: A necessary but insufficient precondition. From Euratom to the Lisbon Treaties

With the 1958 Treaty establishing the European Atomic Energy Community (EAEC), the six founding countries, including Italy in a significant momentum-giving role, aimed to share – in the new nuclear

---

[2] Under a business as usual assumption, European energy demand is scheduled to increase at an annual rate of 1.7%.

industry – the definition of joint safeguard and security criteria, and the implementation of an investment policy no single state had ever contemplated. Furthermore, the Treaty aimed to "ensure that all users in the Community receive a regular and equitable supply of ores and nuclear fuels", to quote the fourth mission listed under Title I of the Treaty, and defined measures to this end.[3] The achievement of this goal was to be guaranteed through the newly set up International Atomic Energy Agency (IAEA). The IAEA was granted a right of option on ores, source materials and special fissile materials produced in the territories of member states and an exclusive right to conclude contracts relating to the supply of ores, source materials and special fissile materials coming from inside the Community or from outside.

In the face of this institutional architecture, the European energy policy outlined in the Lisbon Treaty appears to be a more or less ordered set of wishes and invitations to show goodwill towards member states.

Institutions, however, are only a precondition, necessary but not sufficient, for the development of a common energy policy strategy. Even then, in the wake of the original treaty, a contradiction had quickly appeared between the domestic policies of a number of member states, such as France and Italy, and the European strategy for a common nuclear policy. Interestingly, this contradiction inevitably ended up weakening not only Europe's energy policies but also its very institutions.

In particular, the European medium- and long-term strategy soon entered into conflict with the foreign policy of President De Gaulle, who by 1958 had significantly dampened the French push for European political integration. He opposed in fact the United Kingdom's entry in 1963 and refused to bind France to the pact on civilian uses of atomic energy. It was also De Gaulle who opted for the *'force de frappe'*: a nuclear arsenal aimed at granting French foreign policy the power of nuclear deterrence. France thus embarked on its nuclear testing programme: starting with Gerboise Bleue, tested in the Algerian Sahara in 1960, through to the first H bomb in 1968, and the explosion in the Polynesian atoll of Mururoa in 1995.[4] Euratom's role was thus made weaker.

---

[3] Article 52 of the Treaty.

[4] This approach was reaffirmed in 2006, when President Jacques Chirac, addressing military staff stationed at a nuclear submarine base in Brittany, stated that France,

As we know, France's opposition was at the time compounded by Italy's difficulties. Italy was then at the vanguard of research and development work for the first facilities implementing the peaceful use of nuclear energy. Following projects launched in 1953 by the National Committee for Nuclear Research (Comitato nazionale per le ricerche nucleari - CNRN) with the United States and with World Bank funding, following the building of the first nuclear power plants in Garigliano, Latina and Trino Vercellese, in the early 1960s Italy was forced to scale down its role for domestic reasons[5] until the referendum eventually put a 'final' stop to Italy's nuclear policy. The dismantling in Italy of transatlantic nuclear research projects, together with France's attitude and De Gaulle's opposition, gradually led to a scaling down of Euratom. Having come into conflict with the domestic policy of two of the leading founding states, the Community's energy strategy shattered and since then has proved difficult to rebuild.

The oil crises of the 1970s, with the inflation, industrial restructuring and even lifestyle changes they brought in their wake, were contended with individually by the European countries. Given the lack of a common policy, industrialised countries found themselves singularly deprived of bargaining power when faced with the new primary energy producers' cartel, and were thus vulnerable to severe consequences for their economic growth. To this the Germans responded by adopting policies geared to major industrial restructuring and currency revaluation, while the Italians and the British conversely went for a set of competitive devaluations.

In other words, during the first energy crisis, Europe did not speak with one voice. Euratom's Agency was still there. But its history had already shown how difficult it is to set up institutions capable of giving Europe this one voice in terms of energy security, while avoiding conflict with member states' domestic strategies.

---

if threatened with a terrorist attack, could resort to nuclear retaliation. According to Chirac, "the vital interests to be protected would include both the security of strategic supplies, such as energy, and the defence of allied nations".

[5] See Rigano (2002) for a review of the changes in Italy's strategy, which led it from front-line involvement in early civilian nuclear projects to their scrapping in the mid-1960s.

The issue was to arise again, albeit with different connotations, after signing the Maastricht Treaty. Europe decided to go for deregulation of both electricity and gas markets in order to develop a European energy market, contain energy prices and improve member states' security of supply. But European institutions were given no mandate regarding energy; the project of bringing together domestic energy policies in order to liberalise electricity and gas markets was ultimately watered down, yielding a general stance, sanctioned by directives as of the mid-1990s, and the hope that the Competition Authority would contribute to the *ex novo* emergence of competitive markets, thereby making up for other institutional deficiencies.

At the institutional level, Directives on the liberalisation of domestic power and gas markets[6] focused on promoting national mechanisms to ease liberalisation in diluting the market power of dominant operators and introducing elements of competition. In particular, they called for the setting up of independent domestic sectoral supervisory authorities to support the liberalisation process; the creation of wholesale electricity exchanges to provide markets with transparent pricing and a platform accessible to new producers; and finally – underpinning the whole process – they required that natural monopoly activities (managing the electricity transmission grid and gas transport) be unbundled from the potentially competitive activities both upstream and downstream of the grid (energy production and sale). This entailed a fragmentation of activities pertaining to the production, transmission, distribution and retail sale of electricity and gas, which had traditionally been carried out in an integrated fashion by major public utilities with national monopoly powers in these sectors.

Europe's stance carried on in the decade following 1996, the year of the first Directive; new targets were added – liberalising consumption, promoting energy conservation, suggesting improvements in energy efficiency and compliance with new environmental criteria – but the European energy policy remained unchanged, anchored to the role of

---

[6] Directive 96/92/CE of the European Parliament and the Council of 19 December 1996 concerning common rules for the internal market in electricity, Italian Gazzetta ufficiale n. L 027 del 30/01/1997; Directive 98/30/CE of the European Parliament and the Council of 22 June 1998 concerning common rules for the internal market in natural gas, Italian GU L 204 del 21.7.1998.

existing European institutions and the setting up of national mechanisms to promote energy market liberalisation, against a backdrop of considerable diversification.[7]

A break in the institutional set-up only occurred in 2007: environmental issues were directly introduced in the stance, goals and mechanisms of European energy policy through the 'third energy package' and the signing of the Lisbon Treaty which modified segments of the Rome Treaties relating to energy and the environment.

With the Lisbon Treaty,[8] European institutions did not actually make any significant step forward to develop the instruments required for a common European energy strategy.

The Lisbon Treaty includes new articles concerning energy and climate change, in both the revision of the Treaty on European Union and in the Treaty on the Functioning of the European Union. The Euratom Treaty is added thereto, in a partly revised version that had not been added to the Constitution. Energy is introduced through the solidarity provisions, by which states agree to support one another in case of need.[9] The need to fight climate change through international action is also specified. Competition, however, is no longer included in the Union's fundamental goals, and is mentioned instead in an additional protocol. This latter provision meets a request put by France, which had asked for the elimination of references to a common market subject to free competition.[10]

---

[7] The institutional architecture gained an additional dimension with the establishment of the EU emissions trading scheme or ETS, which is part of the EU's commitment to comply with agreed targets under the Kyoto Protocol (see Directive 2003/87/CE of the European Parliament and the Council of 13 October 2003 establishing a scheme for greenhouse gas emission allowance trading within the Community).

[8] Signed by Heads of State and Government, 13 December 2007.

[9] See Article 122 of the Treaty on the Functioning of the European Union.

[10] Title XX has been replaced by a new title and by a new Article 176A on energy, which reads: "1. In the context of the establishment and functioning of the internal market and with regard for the need to preserve and improve the environment, Union policy on energy shall aim, in a spirit of solidarity between Member States, to: (a) ensure the functioning of the energy market; (b) ensure security of energy supply in the Union; (c) promote energy efficiency and energy saving and the

Despite these provisions, the authority and ability to act effectively in the field of both energy and the environment remain quite modest.[11] There is still no mandate and no authority conferred to Council regarding energy.

Furthermore, on the institutional structure, discussions still focus on the need to provide the European Union with a regulatory authority entrusted with supporting liberalisation in the energy sector. Some have claimed that the institutional vacuum could be filled by assigning a more extensive and incisive role to the antitrust authority, but this step would not help resolve a glaring contradiction between market liberalisation policies and energy security policies, to be analysed in greater detail in section 3 below. Realistically, in order to overcome this contradiction, what is needed is an explicit mandate regarding energy policy that would allow the European Union to negotiate supply contracts on behalf of all member states. Moving forward with liberalisation is indeed difficult without the support of a European sectoral authority or a board of national regulators with a European mandate and the right authority. What is at stake is both the institutional dimension defining the relationship between the Union and the member states in the field of energy, and the ability to stimulate and coordinate member states' industrial strategies regarding energy; but a significant factor is the spectrum of possible mechanisms.[12]

Integrating national markets into a European energy market does indeed require adaptation to common rules on the part of countries or

---

development of new and renewable forms of energy; and (d) promote the interconnection of energy networks."

[11] Article 4 of the Treaty thus reads: "The Union shall share competence with the Member States in energy, as in the following principal areas (…)e) environment, f) consumer protection, g) transport, h) trans-European networks."

[12] These range from the definition of concerted strategies in the guise of Council recommendations, directives or regulations, to the activation of the enhanced cooperation modes taken up and redefined in Title IV of the Lisbon Treaty on the Functioning of the European Union regarding energy and the environment (see contribution by Giacinto della Cananea elsewhere in this volume). Title IV takes over the heading of Title VII, "Provisions on Enhanced Cooperation" and Articles 27A to 27E, 40 to 40B and 43 to 45 are replaced by Article 20, which also replaces Articles 11 and 11A of the Treaty establishing the European Community. The same articles are also replaced by Articles 326 to 334 of the Treaty on the Functioning of the European Union.

governments starting off from starkly different positions. As regards primary source availability, for instance, some countries have access to considerable supply: either because they have nuclear power plants, as do France and Finland, or because they have oil, as does Norway and to a lesser extent the UK, or because they have coal, as does Poland, or yet again because they have opted for renewable sources of energy, as have Germany, Denmark and the Netherlands. But other countries, such as Italy or Spain, are conversely far more dependent on external supply. From another point of view, that of market openness, the reality shows large differences, which translate into highly asymmetric public policies and corporate strategies.

The issues raised in Ferdinando Salleo's contribution to this volume regarding European identity in connection with enlargement policies are quite relevant here as well. Is the Union in the process of building a model that will feature a variety of different levels and densities? Will Europe end up having a variable geometry, based on enhanced cooperation schemes? Or in an attempt to break the standstill on institutions and authority that is currently jeopardising the construction of a European energy market, will we witness in the field of energy and environment the same granting of opting-out rights that the UK and Ireland have insisted upon in justice and home affairs?

In all these issues, European policy has to deal with a genuine conflict between the definition of its own energy strategy and the national demands that undermine its effectiveness. Brussels has been calling for liberalisation and market openness as a first step in the construction of a common European energy market. But national states, which have to bear the burden of singly ensuring security of supply, cannot sign on to this in the required fashion. This induces divergence among domestic policies, as they are necessarily involved in more or less explicit support of their national champions. This leads to free-rider behaviour in negotiations with producers. Which in turn generates a vicious circle that weakens both the Union and all its member states in international negotiations – as we will see in the following section.

3. European strategy and domestic policies: Goals, conflicts and proposals

The starting point is that the European Union has never had a mandate to implement a common energy policy. It has therefore from the very onset been forced to adopt a gradual and indirect strategy, at times resorting to general policy statements, at others to the definition of shared rules.[13]

And precisely because both instruments and institutions were indirect and inappropriate, the path ended up being unnecessarily tortuous. As mentioned above, an initial approach was outlined by the 1996 and 1998 Directives on domestic market liberalisation, which aimed to reduce internal barriers within the Union's markets for electricity and gas in order to develop a European market. But the European Commissioner for energy did not have an explicit mandate to do anything more than indicate a general stance and address recommendations to member states.

Member state responses have proved quite asymmetrical. At one extreme, France, with its very strong state sector, was keen on defending its national champions, with their vertically integrated production structure. At the other extreme, the UK and to some extent Italy as well, from 1999 to 2007, subjected their electricity markets to significant change, involving unbundling, production break-up, market liberalisation and supervision by a sectoral authority.

On the other hand, in the absence of a European regulator empowered to impose unbundling rules, in order to dissociate upstream monopolies from downstream distribution and sales of gas and electricity, the only way forward was to suggest that governments and if applicable, industry-level authorities, consider separating grids from service provision: in terms of ownership, functions, corporate structure or simply from an accounting standpoint.[14]

In reality, at the beginning of the process, there was indeed a strong liberalisation push: electricity exchanges were set up by most member states, although unevenly and with quite varied fortunes. The UK's 'Pool' was thus highly liberalised, with initial guidelines in 1990 making it mandatory for all wholesale electricity contracts to be brought to the

---

[13] See Article 249 (former Article 189) of the EC Treaty.

[14] Of the two modalities set forth once again in the Commission's recent Recommendation (2007) – namely the corporate separation of companies owning the grid/network from those entrusted with operations, or the setting up of an Independent System Operator or ISO (under which the vertically integrated utility retains grid/network ownership and receives an administered return rate, but is not responsible for grid/network management or development).

exchange; ten years later, in 2001, it was closed down and replaced by a number of platforms for the bilateral exchange of energy contracts (Neta).[15] The Spanish Exchange has conversely retained largely administered pricing for wholesale transactions. And finally Italy complied completely and relatively quickly to all the European directives, but it then reverted to unified management and ownership of the national electricity grid with distinctly unsatisfactory governance.

The unfavourable international context at the beginning of the new millennium - such as the Enron failure in 2002 and the Californian electricity crisis of 2001, even if caused by bad management and/or control and regulatory mistakes - increased government reluctance to renounce tried and tested practices such as entrusting security of energy supply to major public monopolies. Support for the European single market development strategy, to be achieved through domestic market liberalisation, thus dwindled to a bare minimum. And gas market development experienced even more difficulties, inter alia because of Europe's notable dependence on Russian gas fields.

This push to liberalisation occurred at the end of the 1990s, at a time when fossil fuel prices appeared to be contained - notwithstanding the fact that 53.8% of Europe's consumption is met by fossil fuel imports (see European Environment Agency, 2008).[16]

The contradiction between liberalisation policies and energy security strategy has eventually blown up. It has blown up with the rise in oil prices; it has blown up with the Russian gas crisis, triggered by Putin both for reasons of domestic politics and to raise his bargaining power internationally. By this token, the Russia-Ukraine dispute regarding natural gas provision in January 2006, and the further dispute involving Russia and Belarus in January 2007 are just the tip of an iceberg that could in the end dramatically highlight Europe's vulnerability (Stern, 2006 and 2007).

---

[15] Neta was introduced in March 2001, and Betta (British Electricity Trading and Transmission Arrangements) on 1 April 2005.

[16] Europe's dependence on hydrocarbon imports is growing. Under a business-as-usual assumption, primary source imports are forecast to rise from 50% of current consumption to 65% in 2030; more specifically as regards gas, imports are scheduled to increase from 57% of total gas consumption today to 84% in 2030; for oil, the rise will be from 82% to 93%.

It was only then that the contradictory nature of asking member states to break up their major public utilities appeared for what it was worth. Or rather, the contradictory nature of asking them to do so prior to having set up the institutions, authorities and mandates needed to ensure the European Union's security of supply through unified negotiation. A process, the incompleteness of which became obvious with the gas crisis and even before that, with the fallout from the 9/11 attacks and the subsequent increase in oil prices, heralding ever more uncertain trends.

It has become terribly obvious that neither Brussels' incentives nor its recommendations ever yielded the desired outcomes. But hoping they would was unreasonable. And the outcome of a number of policies introduced by the European Commission shows that it wasn't only the instruments that proved inadequate, but the general strategy.[17] A few examples suffice to highlight the consequences of this contradiction between European strategy and domestic policies, as in the case of the plans for the Trans-European Networks (TEN-E) – those cross-border networks designed to facilitate the interconnection of domestic markets.[18] And the strategy aimed at improving gas supply by building liquid gas vaporisers highlights similar problems in the gas sector.

The TEN-E has a complex procedural architecture: it involves an incentive policy aimed at strengthening cross-border connections between electricity transmission grids on the European continent, so as to broaden the benchmark electricity market. Ten years after inception, it has yielded one-tenth of its expected outcome. And attempts at importing liquid gas via sea, supported by the widespread building of vaporisers, with a view to freeing gas-importing countries from their dependence vis-à-vis a small

---

[17] The reference framework is provided by amendments to Directives 54/03 and 55/03, amendments to the Electricity and Gas Regulations (1228/03 and 1775/05) and by the European Council decisions of March and December 2006. Currently, Directive 2005/89/CE requires that national regulatory authorities report annually to the Commission on security of supply in electricity; Directive 2004/67/CE introduces this same reporting requirement for gas supplies as well as for legal frameworks aimed at developing investment in infrastructure.

[18] Trans-European Networks (TEN-Energy) concern projects of common interest defined and regulated in 1996 with subsequent updates in 1997, 1999 through to 2003. See "Trans-European Energy Networks. Policy and Action", Lux. 1997 and http: //europa.eu.int/comm/ten/energy/legislation/index_en.html.

number of producers - in particular Russia - and transportation systems have yielded equally minimal results.

Setting utopia aside, it is clearly difficult to convince utilities to invest in cross-border transmission infrastructure with a view to broadening the domestic markets from which they currently derive significant oligopoly profits. The only way to do this would be to involve these very same utilities and national governments by having them espouse the medium-term advantages they stand to derive from a unified European energy market: in terms of security strategy, joint bargaining power, more competitively priced supply, increased growth opportunities, corporate synergies beneficial to innovation, research and transfer of cutting-edge technology. All in all, these are all long-term benefits that would accrue to Europe's industry, upon completion of the liberalisation process, including in terms of competitiveness.

However, the real difficulties concern Europe's energy security policy and the lack of a corresponding mandate. If responsibility for ensuring gas supply - an essential tenet of energy security - rests exclusively with national governments, which in recent economic history, since the end of World War II, have shifted this responsibility to domestic utilities (the former public monopoly incumbents), the utilities end up representing citizens in the negotiation of contracts with non-EU producer countries such as Russia, Nigeria, Algeria, Turkmenistan and Azerbaijan. And governments must then, together with their utilities, assume the full risks of political uses of primary sources and political instability in transit countries. Add to this the absence of supranational rules and guarantees regarding network/grid access. Even the Energy Charter, designed to guarantee state reciprocity and third-party access to networks/grids, is pending ratification by Russia. And Russia can thus decide to not tie itself down in its bilateral negotiations with European countries' utilities. So far these utilities' strategy has been to enter into bilateral contracts with the gas monopolies in the upstream segment of the production stream, especially in Russia. And this is a strategy shared, more or less openly, by their governments.

The political insecurity is now compounded by economic insecurity regarding supply availability. Faced with Putin's new programme to diversify exports by increasing Asia's share, one is beginning to wonder whether Russia will be able to deal with growing internal demand while continuing to export the amounts of gas required by Europe. One also wonders whether Putin's strategy, which involves nationalising and using energy as a priority foreign policy instrument, is compatible with the investment policy required to develop this sector. The low level of gas prices, strictly correlated to those of oil, in the 1990s has not encouraged any significant investment to improve the extraction efficiency and network infrastructure functionality. Similarly, even when prices were high, the additional profits accrued by the gas industry were used to offset low-income growth (Gaddy & Ickes, 2002).[19]

Faced with these difficulties, European governments and their utilities have attempted to negotiate an increase in supply contract duration. Putin has in fact granted European countries 10- to 15-year extensions, thereby ensuring in 2006 additional profits of about €39 billion.[20] However, as these contracts have a *take or pay* structure, they require rigid long-term buyer programming: the amounts acquired will in any event have to be paid for, regardless of whether they are actually taken.

For this reason too, the opening up of the gas market that can be activated through the building of vaporisers does represent, in the long run, an alternative programming model, that may introduce supply flexibility and competition, by diversifying both sources and suppliers. But in the short run, by introducing demand flexibility, it would go against national energy security policies, weakening the bargaining power of major utilities - having to pay in any case the predetermined offer - compared to a small number of producers, the leader of which is Gazprom.

In this context, the way in which vaporisers fit into a highly sophisticated process requires further thinking to devise a comprehensive strategy covering all the phases of player and country involvement in the gas industry. Initially devised to make gas supply more flexible, vaporisers have in fact yielded quite disappointing results in terms of unifying the European energy market through virtuous and incentive-driven processes, as has been the case with TEN-E. In this case as well, the problem was not

---

[19] The situation is similar with respect to oil, where Russia ranks second in terms of global output after Saudi Arabia, with a 2007 average output of about 9.5 million barrels a day.

[20] While it has maintained a policy of annual contracting with CIS states, at significantly lower price levels.

only inadequate funding. What really emerged was a radical conflict between Europe's medium- and long-term vision on the one hand, and the goals pursued by players assumed to orient their corporate strategies to the achievement of common objectives, on the other.

4. Europe's relationship with the rest of the world: Energy security and climate change

A third crisis dimension - that of environmental sustainability - has latched on to the above-mentioned difficulties, which may nevertheless open up new prospects. This is an issue where Europe has conquered a leadership role even though so far results have been more significant in political terms, with the driving role taken on by Europe in the Kyoto Protocal process, than in strictly environmental terms, i.e. that of containing emissions levels globally.[21]

It is therefore essential that we now reflect on the EU's interests, but without losing track of the role it may play in the emerging multipolar scenario and the promotion of multilateral negotiations.

At the international level, as well, the issue of which institutions to empower with responsibility for process support is crucial. Clearly there is a need to move beyond the 'divide and conquer' policies that often characterise US bilateral negotiations with primary source producers in Latin America and Asia, or its strategic and military approach to Middle Eastern producer countries.

It is equally essential to further the development of the world's poorest countries. It is a known fact that today 2.5 billion people produce energy by burning wood, plant waste and dung, in a very damaging use of biomass, while another billion is totally deprived of any access to energy.

---

[21] The United Nations Fourth Report on Climate Change, a reference for policies aimed at improving climate conditions, indicates that by mid-century global emissions of gas pollutants will need to be reduced by at least half as compared to 1990 levels in order to halt the increase in global warming. The contemplated 20% unilateral reduction in European emissions by 2020 corresponds to less than 4% of the reduction called for globally. According to computations, by 2020 CO_2 emissions will exceed the 1990 levels by over 60%, especially as a result of rising energy - and in particular fossil fuel - demand, with China, the United States and India coming in first, second and third (Skinner, 2006).

Not even towards Africa does the EU have a unitary strategy capable of standing up to China's new aggressive policy (consider for instance the close political connection to Angola, thanks to which China has acquired offshore exploration rights in exchange for loans; or to Nigeria, which has granted off-shore exploration rights to the Chinese state utility in exchange for roads and infrastructure).

Even the flexible mechanisms provided for in the Kyoto Agreements (Joint Implementation and Clean Development Mechanisms), which aim to promote investment in clean energy production and use through partnerships between businesses based in the industrialised countries that have ratified the Kyoto Protocol (and that are therefore listed in Annex I), and in developing countries (not in Annex I), would require dedicated structures and institutions, in addition to a far more active and coordinated European Strategy.

According to the World Energy Outlook 2008, investments totalling $22,000 billion, nearly $4,000 billion in China alone, will be required by 2030 (see IEA, 2008). Clearly, this raises the issue of where the money is to come from, considering that major uncertainties regarding both political context and primary source rules and prices are likely to distort very long-term decisions. International financial institutions will obviously have to be the first to provide answers.

In this field as well Europe tends to put forth the multilateral approach it embodies. This was clear in Bali where for the first time Finance Ministers had been invited to take part in negotiations aimed at defining financial rules and instruments for the post-Kyoto period. This was equally clear in the agreement signed last October in Lisbon by a subset of European countries that has given rise to the International Carbon Partnership (Icap). The idea underpinning the agreement is precisely that of setting up a joint fund on the basis of a broader emissions market than the one we currently have, so as to gain access to significant funding for both technology transfers and climate change mitigation and adaptation measures for the least developed countries. That said, it also reflects economic principles according to which the negative externalities of emissions generation must be priced and factored in so as to reduce industrial free-riding. The multilateral approach has been well received: significantly, the agreement was also signed by a number of US states (in particular New York, New Jersey and California) that have been exerting pressure on the US Administration to participate in the new multilateral agreements launched by Europe, and thereby correct its refusal to participate in the Kyoko Protocol.

By its very nature the energy/environment problem calls for concerted global solutions. This method, supporting multilateralism and the United Nations' role for the management and direction provided to global negotiations for the post-Kyoto period, has proved positive; it has inter alia allowed for the participation in the negotiations of industrialised countries that had not signed on to the Kyoto Agreements, such as the United States and Canada,[22] and the active involvement of China and India, countries that are contributing the most to emissions growth globally, as well as that of Indonesia, Malaysia and African and Latin American countries. It was the latter in actual fact that forced industrialised countries to give serious attention to the slotting into the negotiations of programmes, in particular financial, for adaptation and mitigation in the face of climate change, and support for the transfer of low-emissions technology and combating deforestation.

The European Union has therefore scored points in terms of methodological process and leadership, but it is proving to be much weaker in terms of content and policy efficiency. As a result it is unclear whether it will manage to preserve its 'multilateralist' leadership position vis-à-vis countries such as Japan and Canada, or vis-à-vis Asia.

The US administration for its part is currently involved in developing various alliances, based on a corporate approach, through bilateral agreements and pragmatic action, the development of public-private partnerships to support the feasibility of investment in new technology and the promotion of environmentally-compatible industrial development, directly activated by private sector businesses.

The issue of process governance is clearly highlighted by the comparison between the US bottom-up and Europe's top-down approach to the ongoing adjustment process. Will the post-Kyoto process elicit interest in the United States, the Asian countries and the poorest countries for a multilateral agreement approach, by way of a strategy shared with the United Nations (through the UNFCCC - United Nations Framework Convention on Climate Change) that aims to define a joint responsibility

---

[22] And Australia, which ratified the Kyoto Protocol at just about the time of the Bali meeting.

with differentiated obligations and burdens? If so, Europe will have contributed to significant change. The adjustment process can indeed not be separated from the role played by dedicated institutions, even internationally. But it is precisely internationally that Europe risks in the meantime losing credibility, for not having managed to restore order within its own borders and for not having figured out how to put an industrial development spin on environmental issues.

In other words, the European Union has to contend with two issues at one and the same time, while not remaining anchored to old paradigms. It must, first, put its own institutional house in order. That is, provide Council with powers and a mandate regarding energy; set up a European regulators coordination mechanism; and develop the control instruments required to make a single market possible. Secondly, it must define not only the role to be played by Europe in international negotiations but also the basic tenets of an industrial strategy involving businesses and investors in post-Kyoto developments. Time has really run out on unilateral, EU-wide commitments to reduce GHG emissions, and this last aspect warrants some further words of analysis.

Using its own unilateral commitment to promote the design of joint responsibility and differentiated burdens, Europe has shown its leadership capability in its very best light, with its wish to promote sustainable development in the poorest countries. This vision, underpinned by the need to promote integrated policies with respect to energy and the environment has filled the vacuum created by the US administration's lack of interest in pollution issues; it has helped overcome the divide and conquer policy in the US security of energy supply strategy, based on the one hand on the ramping up of military relationships in the Middle East, and on the other on bilateral negotiations, in Latin America and the Pacific, with primary-source producer countries.

It is important that this action continue, strengthening the role of international institutions, including financial ones, in order to launch both the technology transfer process and coordinated support for the development of the poorest countries. But once these political outcomes are achieved, Europe will still have to contend with the issue of policy efficacy. It is a known fact that the Kyoto Agreements' contribution on this is quasi-nil. As regards instruments and policies, Europe risks making a serious mistake if it does not broaden the spectrum of what it considers acceptable action along the lines of what the US administration, for example, has done to develop cooperation among businesses.

Technological innovation appears to be the keystone in terms of addressing and solving the problems of energy and environmental security now facing the industrialised economies. Businesses' contributions will prove essential. Market instruments such as emissions trading, especially if extended on a global scale, will no doubt prove important in the short and medium term to price carbon emissions and force businesses to internalise these negative externalities. But this approach has to be implemented in conjunction with strategies to promote and facilitate long-term investment, in order to activate the engine of industrial transformation and development. This will require huge funds and cooperation between enterprises, public and private sector and European and developing countries. And it involves much more than the cap-and-tax mechanisms devised by the Commission.

Environment, calling for focused technological development, is a growth opportunity that Europe cannot neglect. And this is a road that industrialised economies could in part travel together, cooperating in order to allow countries such as China and India to accomplish the technological shift demanded by the protection of our planet, and to help move the poorest countries out of poverty. But to date there have been but occasional signs of a shared awareness of these issues.

The crucial problem is that a rigorous and for the time being unilateral (in terms of content) European strategy, neglectful of its impact on corporate competitiveness, opens the door to industrial relocation solutions favouring countries that do not yet have binding environmental targets, such as China or India, and are far less efficient in complying with environmental criteria. Their industrial processes, for the same goods, generate more emissions than Europe's. Consequently, taking the global view that environmental issues necessarily require, this policy - very costly for a number of European industries - may well lead to no progress whatsoever in terms of goal attainment, and no containment of global emissions.

In other words, the energy/environment package just launched by the Commission, however careful in using objective and unchallengeable indicators such as per capita GDP in computing national commitments, seems to stem more from an administrative logic than from efforts aimed at activating the engines of technological innovation in energy and industrial renewal in Europe, by fostering partnerships for research, transfers of technology, and the testing of new industrial models likely to get a boost from environmental challenges.

Finally, in terms of policy efficiency, even if this costly and unilateral effort on the part of the European Union were to be on target in 2020, and assuming improbable zero growth for the rest of the world's emissions, its impact on global targets aimed at stabilising environmental pollution growth and global warming, as uniformly computed by international agencies and the United Nations' experts, would be under 4%.

5. Conclusions

The issue of European energy policy governance has become ever more central, as a result of the emergency affecting security of supply of primary energy sources and the environmental emergency of global warming deriving from excessive GHG emissions. Speaking with one voice, the European Union has managed to exercise leadership in sensitising the planet to the Kyoto Agreements and in suggesting a method and a vision based on multilateral agreements. But this has not been matched by corresponding effectiveness and results at the policy level. For these to materialise, the Union still requires institutions with powers regarding energy.

The Union will have to strengthen its institutions if it wishes to move beyond the contradictions that currently plague it and are in practice jeopardising the construction of a single market. As a first stage in a security of supply strategy, the Union has pushed market liberalisation and opening, so as to construct a European energy market. But this liberalisation and this opening up cannot elicit sufficient support from those states that have had to bear the full burden of ensuring security of energy supply for their citizens. This has led to diverging national policies, as governments became involved in supporting, more or less explicitly, their national champions. And this has also led to free-riding in negotiations with producers. In short, this is a vicious circle that is weakening the European Union's international bargaining power.

On the other hand, only the awareness that a single market will provide value added is likely to convince governments they should sign on wholeheartedly to a European plan to open energy markets, convinced that this single market will represent a positive externality for domestic markets in terms of increased security. But to reach this point, Europe needs institutions to support and coordinate domestic market liberalisation, to provide guarantees as to rules and stances to those utilities that will be called upon to face up to competition and invest in the market.

Recent years have shown quite clearly how disappointing it is to think that one can offset the institutional vacuum of a mandate-less Council and a European regulator that is simply not there, simply by extending inappropriately the missions and functions of the antitrust authority.

The second message is that the European Union, however significant the role it has played in promoting and supporting internationally a multilateral vision of energy policies and climate change, will not be able to continue playing this role, if it hasn't beforehand put its own house in order. Nor will member states be in a position singly and separately to face up to Asian competition, the growing demand of which is putting pressure on the very same primary sources they use. European institutions will therefore have to play an essential role over the next few years if they wish to avoid having piecemeal interests prevail in energy policy.

However, institutions are a necessary but not sufficient precondition for cooperation in the field of energy. The outcome so far shown by the European Commission's policies demonstrates that their focus remains far removed from one target: that of starting up the engine of industrial development, inter alia in the energy sector.

Technological innovation, and this is the third conclusion, appears to be the keystone to address the issues of energy and environmental security with which industrialised and developing countries alike now have to contend. Business contributions will prove essential. Such is the approach that underpins the bilateral negotiations between governments and businesses that are at the heart of US policy. But it is also a road that industrialised countries could travel under the aegis of a necessary form of multilateralism, cooperating to allow countries such as China and India to accomplish the technological shift required for the protection of our planet, and to help the poorest countries pull out of poverty.

This is also a growth opportunity for industrialised countries - and one that Europe can ill-afford to ignore.

References

European Commission (2007), *An Energy Policy for Europe*, Directorate-General for Energy and Transport, Brussels, January.

European Environment Agency (EEA) (2008), *Energy and Environment Report 2008*, European Environment Agency, Copenhagen, June (http://www.eea.europa.eu/publications/eea_report_2008_6).

Gaddy, C.G. and B.W. Ickes (2002), *Russia's Virtual Economy*, Brookings Institutions Press, Washington, D.C.

International Energy Agency (IEA) (2008), *World Energy Outlook 2008*, OECD/IEA, Paris (http://www.worldenergyoutlook.org/2008.asp).

Rigano, A.R. (2002), "La Banca d'Italia e il progetto ENSI: Fonti per la storia dello sviluppo energetico italiano degli anni cinquanta nelle carte dell'Archivio della Banca d'Italia", *Quaderni dell'Ufficio Ricerche Storiche*, No. 4, June.

Skinner, R. (2006), *Strategies for Greater Energy Security and Resource Security*, Oxford Institute for Energy Studies, Oxford, June.

Stern, J. (2006), *The Russian-Ukrainian gas crisis of January 2006*, Oil, Gas & Energy Law Intelligence (OGEL), Oxford Institute for Energy Studies, Oxford.

Stern, J. (2007), *Gas-OPEC: A distraction from important issues of Russian gas supply to Europe*, Oxford Institute for Energy Studies, Oxford, February.

Part II

The International Projection

7. EUROPE ON THE INTERNATIONAL SCENE: A UNION OF NECESSITY AFTER A UNION OF CHOICE?

CESARE MERLINI

European foreign policy will only come into being when capitals acknowledge that relinquishing jurisdiction to Brussels doesn't weaken them, but makes them stronger, because the policy shift increases the influence of all EU States worldwide. (…) The European option - "make law not war" - could however turn into a lie worthy of social romanticism, if Europe's security policy rules out a military component.

Ulrich Beck[1]

Thus far the role of the European Union (formerly, the Community) on the international scene has been largely passive, in the sense that it has been less the outcome of policies or political will than the consequence of its very existence. The EU has been a conspicuous and expanding reality, an area of prosperity and the sum of important or at least not irrelevant states. Moreover the Union has been an atypical player in the world system, because of the implicit, irreversible peace among its member states, and because of its unparalleled and unprecedented hybrid of federal and intergovernmental institutions - a model possibly to be copied in other contexts. The magnetic effect on neighbouring states has been remarkable and has led to the view that the EU has so far exerted its geopolitical influence mostly through enlargement, in particular with the latest accession of ten plus two countries.

---

[1] Ulrich Beck, *Das kosmopolitische Blick oder: Krieg ist Frieden*, Suhrkamp Vrelag, Frankfurt aM, 2004.

With respect to enlargement to include Eastern European countries formerly belonging to the Soviet empire or even the Soviet Union itself, it may be noted, by the way, that it has taken place while the West has seen its global presence and influence shrinking and/or declining. This applies particularly to the Asian continent, with the unsuccessful wars the US has fought in it, following the historical demise of the European empires. In other words a sort of counter-cyclical Western expansion has been achieved through the attractiveness of its institutions, above all the EU but also NATO, rather than through the action of its armies.

The perception of the EU as an international player by its shear existence, not only in economic terms (the euro, trade, competition law) but also, at least potentially, in political terms is also gaining ground abroad. Robert Kagan, for instance, an analyst not generally known for his softness vis-à-vis the Europeans, who he famously said are from Venus while the Americans are from Mars (Kagan, 2002), subsequently wrote that the European Union is a *"geopolitical miracle"* that *"in its own way, expresses a pan-European national ambition to play a significant role in the world, channelling German, French and British ambitions* (…)" Kagan (2007). Former Italian Foreign Minister D'Alema likes to recall a meeting he had, together with two other European leaders, with Chinese President Hu Jintao, who told them, "We are a great power that will be called upon (during the first half of the 21st century) to manage Chinese-American bipolarism" - at which point, realising he was addressing a group of Europeans, he added, "Obviously, Europe will also be there,... if it is united" (D'Alema, 2007a).

To stay with the United States, the expectation that an integrated Europe will take a more active role internationally is also remarkably high in the public opinion. In this respect, data recently published by *Transatlantic Trends* - an annual survey conducted by the German Marshall Fund of the United States to measure broad public opinion in the United States and 12 European countries - are worth noting: in 2009, 63% of Americans surveyed have a positive view of the EU and seven out of ten believe that its leadership in international affairs would be desirable. This is only marginally down from the 77% who, being asked the same question in 2007 had answered "yes", with 30% adding "very", while only 16% answered "no".[2] This apparent US "enthusiasm", particularly high among

---

[2] *Transatlantic Trends* (2009 and 2007), various tables.

registered Democrats, has remained fairly stable over the last seven years (and is consistently higher, by the way, than that shown by the British in similar surveys).

In contrast with this passive, but relevant role, is the EU's formal foreign policy, which has been conducted prevalently with a technocratic approach, drawing from mechanisms, almost as if the real world and its power plays did not exist. The results have not been entirely negligible, as demonstrated by the various small and medium-scale missions in the areas of security and defence, and by the activity of the High Representative, whether independently or jointly with the Ministers of member states, but they have been marginal.

The saying currently goes that there has been a re-nationalisation of various European policies over the last decade or two, including foreign policy. However it would be hard to say that national initiatives and strategies have achieved much more. Sarkozy's activism has had limited impact, except possibly for the second half of 2008, when France held the rotating EU Presidency (in application of the Kagan paradigm of the European 'multiplier' of national ambitions). The UK foreign policy seems not to be at one of its highest points. Italy's unsolicited mediations have not met with success. Neither have, so far at least, the efforts of such groups as the so-called EU-3 (the British, French and German foreign ministers with or without the EU High Representative) or 5+1 (the five permanent members of the UN Security Council plus Germany), both marking the dominant diplomatic aspiration of re-unified Germany, i.e. of being formally recognised again as a great power and consequently becoming a permanent member of the UNSC – a prospect that seems to have become more remote with the current US administration.

That said, the ambition for a shared, or at least coordinated, capability in the fields of foreign affairs, international security and defence is seldom denied openly and appears as a corollary to the more or less sincere acknowledgement that the member states, even the big ones, taken separately do not carry enough weight on the world scene – as another current saying goes with little consistency with the previous one of re-nationalisation. Moreover European public opinion has predominantly shown substantial support for a more active role by the Union in the world, although consistency is once more limited when such support finds itself associated with reluctance to shoulder diplomatic action with military or broader security commitments and expenditure.

It is in this light that that the prospects of an enhanced role by the European Union with its current size and borders and in the new international context must be assessed - if they exist. The compromise agreement grudgingly reached in 2007 was a substantial step back vis-à-vis the draft Constitutional Treaty initially devised by the European Convention (a more democratic forum, incidentally, than a diplomatic conference), but the Lisbon Treaty, in which it was translated, has been nevertheless seen as a framework for the EU institutions to resume progress, particularly in the field of external action, for which a few more tools are being made available. The external challenges that such international action face and the internal constraints will be discussed successively, followed by a suggested policy strategy and a succinct analysis of the tools provided for by the Treaty.

1. The international context

One important reason for Europe being more exposed to international responsibilities is that the United States is less in control of both the general situation and potential crises than it was a decade or two ago. The past administration has left behind a number of legacies that weigh heavily on the present one. Three are of direct relevance to the transatlantic relationship more than others. The first is the encouragement given to nationalism in general, and more specifically on our continent, when promoting bilateral security agreements with countries of the so-called 'New Europe' and thus eliciting age-old attitudes and feelings that came out as an obstacle to the draft Constitutional Treaty and later to the Lisbon Treaty. The second is that much of the fallout from the G.W. Bush administration's policies in third areas is significantly greater for Europe than it is for America: of the many possible examples, I shall only mention the Middle-Eastern frustrations that help infiltration of immigrants by fundamentalist Islamic terrorism and the exacerbation of relations with an increasingly nationalistic Russia, such as to make it an even more difficult interlocutor than it possibly would have been. The third negative legacy concerns the weakening of the multilateral system, either of general competence (the UN) or of a sectoral one (e.g. the Kyoto Protocol or the International Criminal Court), that remains a European priority, at least in principle.

At the end of 2008 the geo-strategic context featured an extreme variety of threats and conflict modes, from the various civil wars underway despite US presence (as in Iraq and Afghanistan) or possibly in gestation (as in Pakistan) to cases of hostility among states, from the continuing nuclear proliferation challenges (by Iran and North Korea) to the revived tensions between the US and Russia. The diffuse threat of terrorism complemented all that, with its various motivations (ethnic, national or religious) and manifestations (from guerrilla warfare on the edges of military conflict to attacks exclusively targeting civilians, be they Muslim or Western, through the ever more common resort to suicide fanatics). Some of these crises seemed to be on the brink of a status shift from unresolved to irresolvable, and not only in the Middle East. Add to that the abysmal state of the American image around the globe, particularly in the Muslim world, but also elsewhere (with only two exceptions, Israel and India, not without significance).

Paradoxically, this state of affairs, which in some respects went somewhat close to American impotence, came as result of a two-decade period of solitude of the United States at very top of the global power hierarchy after the end of the cold war and the ensuing sense of omnipotence, which made the comparison with Rome at the apex of its empire so popular among pundits and commentators and, at the same time, so superficial - as I argued in my essay "The US Hegemony and the Roman Analogy", back in 2002 (Merlini, 2002).

In the eyes of most Europeans, the new administration, besides the extraordinary initial popularity of President Obama, has started on the right foot as far as foreign policy is concerned. The new commitment to international institutions, the suggested 'resetting' of relations with Moscow, the open hand offered to antagonistic powers such as Iran and Syria, the less unconditional support for Israel, etcetera, all have brought the guidelines of the US action internationally closer to the European preferences. More importantly the Obama-Biden-Clinton team seems consistently more inclined towards transatlantic cooperation, counting on European support and sharing of decisions than their predecessors were.

This does not reduce the requirements for a more active and coherent European contribution to crisis prevention and management in the framework of the historically reduced Western influence, let alone dominance. It rather makes it more imperative. At the same time, the substantial foreign policy turn taken by the new administration since its inception is unlikely to bring about visible fruits in resolving the various above-mentioned critical situations in a short time. If anyone had any illusions in this respect, there have been people in Tehran, Jerusalem, Moscow and elsewhere who care to dispel them. Thus the risk is that of substituting the past conflict of orientations between the sides of the Atlantic with a conflict of expectations. The Europeans, who are under severe budgetary and political constraints domestically, tend to wait for the outcome of the US foreign policy changes and see whether they will improve those many critical situations that are proliferating in the broad arc that surrounds Europe from the East. The Americans now expect prompt and sizable European cooperation in order to help such a positive outcome to come about, lest to be disappointed and take unilateral approaches back into consideration.

The above complex picture of actual or potential geo-political instability has in fact been building up over the last two decades or more, while until the summer of 2007 the geo-economic picture had been consistently rosy and stable, despite a number of warnings voiced here and there. Then came the subprime mortgage crisis to trigger a recession, which is being discussed in other chapters of this collection of essays. Suffice it here to express two considerations. First: ways to reduce the impact of the global economic slowdown and to allow each country to come out of it sooner rather than later have taken priority attention by all governments, while the critical hot spots do not allow for much distraction. And second: the global distribution of power will likely look different, once the recession is over, to an extent that is not easy to predict at this stage, while the conflicts and instabilities of the 'wider' Middle-Eastern area seem to be only marginally affected by the contingent global economic troubles, as they spring out of roots that are predominantly local, historical, ethnic and religious.

It is in the light of all this that attention is now turned to the other players on the international scene, and in particular to those that, contrary to the United States, still ranking first but declining, rank second or third but are rising, such as China and India, or have declined already (and more than the US), such as Russia, which however still ranks as a major power both because of the past legacy (nuclear weapons) and current leverage (oil and gas). All these powers basically hold ambivalent views about the situation - or at least this is the way it looks to us in the West. On the one hand, they are aware that their current status has been the result of a long-lasting economic expansion, mostly driven by the West and marked by a high degree of global interdependence. The recent downturn, which has rapidly spread from the West to significantly slow down their growth, has come as a confirmation of global interdependence. Now, geo-political instability may entail additional obstacles to the global recovery, for one reason or another.

On the other hand, the Chinese are not insensitive to the relative decline of US power in the world, as their thinking remains well attuned to balance of power, the dynamics of which appear to them to suggest a return to a *grandeur* lost for centuries (see Hu Jintao's confident prediction to D'Alema); nor indeed are the Russians, whose nostalgia of a past superpower status has more recent points of reference. Furthermore, both countries detect with some satisfaction the dilemmas facing Western policies, and primarily that of the US, torn between the imperatives of fighting against terrorism and insurgency on the one hand, and the legacy of supporting democracy and human rights on the other. In this respect the Obama administration seems inclined to resort more to diplomacy than to ideology, along the preferences of most capitals on this side of the Atlantic. China is for Europe a very important partner, although more exclusively for economic reasons than is true for the US. Russia is an even more important partner, since geo-strategic motivations combine with economic ones, as a consequence of geographical proximity.

India was able to reach a nuclear agreement with the G.W. Bush administration, which was broadly deemed negative for the global non-proliferation regime, but which was to take the country out of the pariah status it had suffered. Hence the high ranking of the US in Indian public opinion, similar to the situation in Israel, as mentioned above. Moreover, Indian nationalists were not disconsolate at the problems experienced by the privileged relationship between the US and Pakistan, their hated arch-rival. They did not win, however, in the last elections, to the relief of everyone, beginning with President Obama. A civil war in Pakistan, with the Taliban involved and the control of a nuclear arsenal possibly at stake, is a great regional concern hardly compatible with India's aspirations to resume economic growth and consequent broad power status.

Such a potential chain reaction in the South-Asian region affects Europe in two respects. India is also an important economic partner, although not as much so as China. Several European countries are engaged in Afghanistan, not so much because of the size of the interests they have there but because of the solidarity they felt for America after 9/11 and now because the future of NATO, and more broadly the credibility of the West, may be at stake. Consequently the potential fall-out of failure in

Afghanistan, let alone of an eventual Pakistani explosion (whatever meaning this word may one day acquire) is of great concern to them. However the leverage that even the major European states, let alone the EU, have there is not remotely comparable with that of the US. Hence, there appears a lack of adequate commitment in the eyes of some Americans.

If we come to those critical situations that are high on the transatlantic agenda and are at the same time geographically closer to Europe, we find that the very proximity to the EU space becomes a decisive factor. Cases in point are of course Turkey, Georgia and Ukraine. They are seen by the United States as 'border countries', in the sense that the former is key in the West's relationship with Islam, and the latter two are key with respect to Russia,. As a consequence the Americans believe that Europe should continue in the longstanding and successful process of expanding its area of intrinsic security and contemplate the inclusion also of these countries sooner or later, in the conviction that the prospect will have a stabilising effect by itself both regionally and domestically.

The Europeans find themselves in a bind. Most of them think they have given enough in terms of inclusion, the cost of which has been higher and higher, and tend to consider these cases - as several others around them - as the object of their enhanced foreign policy, which however is lacking. Even the intermediate step of including Georgia and Ukraine into NATO, by the way, is seen with hostility, not so much because of the Russian sensitivities, as many in the US suspect, but because the alliance would end up being in serious jeopardy. Moreover, if further EU enlargement has to be contemplated, other candidates, such as the Balkan countries, seem to enjoy geographical priority and they are difficult enough.

Different from what happens in relatively distant areas such Asia or even the Middle East, the policy choices the Europeans make concerning their 'near abroad' carry a more decisive weight, but such weight is often connected with the perimeter of the common institutions rather than with the existence of a common foreign policy. It may also be revealing that as far as the external action in the economic domain is concerned, the EU's response to the recent global recession has been unsatisfactory in terms of cohesion, but the crisis did generate a new application to join, that of Iceland.

2. The Union's Internal Context

Let us now turn our attention to within the EU and try to shed some light on the obstacles preventing the shaping and implementation of a foreign policy sufficiently active and common. First, nationalism has to be mentioned, which has been seen as rising throughout the continent. Among the 27 member states, various expressions and claims emerge on a daily basis, including in the new members, egged on – as mentioned earlier – by the two Bush presidencies. But even a country such as the Netherlands, once a founding father and Europe's champion, became inward-looking as shown by the referendum on the Constitutional Treaty in 2004. In Belgium, another traditionally pro-European country, there are two strands of nationalisms that risk breaking up the country, its limited size notwithstanding. We focus here however on two of the more important and possibly paradigmatic cases, that of the United Kingdom and Poland.

British nationalism is aristocratic and decadent, born of a great history made up of victories – some more those of others than its own – which have led to the UK's current formal status as a great power. But there have been defeats as well, in some cases cleverly concealed, which led to the demise of an Empire that once spanned from ocean to ocean. External to Europe, Great Britain tends to take from integration what suits its needs, with English pragmatism, and to throw spanners in the works of the rest, to hinder progress when it is deemed to infringe on its sovereignty. While it takes advantage of the past enshrined in its permanent seat on the UN Security Council, it keenly views its role as the closest, although rarely rewarded ally of the only superpower left. But it has tried also to be forward-looking, with its flagship stance on the new seas of globalisation, where the slower and more timorous ships of the rest of Europe's fleet follow in its wake. That made the UK even more affected by the economic downturn and its currency more vulnerable without the euro shield. The partly consequential dramatic weakening of the Brown government and the likelihood of an eventual return of the conservatives to 10 Downing St, with several euro-sceptics among them, suggest that this nationalism and the related obstacles to European integration and joint action outside are here to stay.

Polish nationalism, conversely, is less sophisticated and the product of a history of defeats, often heroic, nurtured by a culture that is prevalently romantic or religious or both. Located at the heart of the old continent, Poland has forever been squeezed between major powers that have treated it harshly - occasionally with the support, within the country, of authoritarian, or religious or simply naïf circles. Too often Poland looks at its past where it finds fodder for its frustrations and recriminations, both domestic and international, under which it seems inclined to bury the generous and forward-looking political class that accompanied the return to democracy and the accession to the EU. The change sanctioned by the 2007 elections was a positive development, however. With time Poland, which has resented the global recession less than the other Eastern countries, will move closer to Europe, thanks also to lavish EU funding of agriculture and infrastructure, the benefits of which public opinion has begun to acknowledge. By the way, the experience of various previous accessions shows that even culturally, assimilating participation in the integrated system takes time. In the field of external action, EU relations with Russia, a country that understandably touches on the nerves of the Polish, have been under constant pressure from Warsaw and will remain a test case.

After two countries at the periphery of the Union, let us turn to two countries at its heart, beginning with France under the now consolidated leadership of the new President, whose international activism has already been hinted at. One however should not be misled by it. In fact, despite the Gaullist heritage Sarkozy claims to be faithful to, his main role has been so far one of reducing the very French specificity the Général was so proud to have brought about. The return to the military structure of NATO is probably the most evident example. As far as Europe is concerned, Sarkò has to deal with the legacy of his predecessor, who wrought irreparable harm to French leadership in it, from the Nice Summit to the call of a referendum that for all practical purposes *"a tué dans l'oeuf"*, as the French say for killing at the start, the Union's Constitutional option. The 2004 rejection of the Constitutional Treaty was certainly very negative for the Union, but France's future position in Europe may also bear its mark in the long run.

Something similar had happened exactly half a century earlier, with the Assemblée Nationale's "non" to the European Defence Community, which not only killed the European army at its start, but also prevented the founding of a community devised along French lines, modelled on its institutions, that would have spoken French. Germany at the time was one step down the ladder and the UK one step off the European system as it was taking shape then. Later, with the Common Market, the Community and subsequently the Union came to rely to a large extent on the Franco-

German reconciliation then *entente*, joined first by Italy and Benelux, and later by the subsequent entrants, including the UK. Over fifty years, in the management of this so-called 'axis', Germany has basically stood for European integration (and Atlantic solidarity) while France alternated playing the other pole, and giving more or less free rein to its national autonomy. Meanwhile, the Germans have fully come up that one step down, and the British have, at least partly, come across that step off, and this has changed France's relative position. Perhaps voters in the French referendum were not fully aware of this new situation.

Time will tell the long-term consequences of 2004, but I would tend to think that Paris will have problems maintaining the Paris-Berlin axis with the same division of labour as previously. In 2006, I wrote in an article that the foreign policy of united Germany, the Union's largest member state, "is moving on a biga, the Roman two-horse chariot, where one horse is European, and the other stands for the aspiration to become a de facto great power, even without the de jure sanction of a permanent seat on the Security Council" (Merlini, 2006, p. 1120). The Germans have now more choice when it comes to deciding which horse to prod. The French, conversely, while obviously still decisive, will have less leeway. It may be fitting such perception the care the current occupant of the Elysée has taken in mending relations with his partner on the other side of the Atlantic, to balance its loss of weight vis-à-vis his partner on the side of the Rhine.

Possibly the German response to the French "no" to the referendum that would have substantially reformed the institutions of the Union has come this year with the ruling of the federal Constitutional Court, by which the ratification of the Lisbon Treaty has been given a green light, but with an accompanying chorus of conditions and provisions that will make the future working of the Brussels machinery, let alone the famous "ever closer" integration more problematic. Among other things this applies to German participation in the development and conduct of common foreign and security policy actions, especially when a military component is involved, which is likely to happen frequently. Evaluations of the Karlsruhe court ruling are still under way, but the suggestion that it comes to express the rebirth of a German nationalism deserves some consideration.

The description above of the context inside the Union is meant to help us identify the national obstacles that stand in the way of Europe having an active foreign policy. The absence of a common identity, it is said, comes as a further drawback. Hence it might be appropriate to ask a preliminary question: Does the EU today identify with Europe? Geographically and in terms of image, the question has to a large extent ceased to be one. As emphasised above, from the outside the Union is broadly perceived as a potential state entity covering the continent, so much so that it is surprising to foreigners that we, from the inside, should not feel the same. The fact is that politically and domestically the question still arises.

Internal advocates of autonomous national identities and interests are more vocal than ever. Their voices are heard on two levels, principally: a) in the defence of national interests within the Union's common institutions, the safeguard of which appears to be less of a priority (as if a zero sum game were favoured over a positive sum game); and b) in the pursuit of separate interests and preferences, proximities or distances vis-à-vis third parties, independently of, or in contradiction to, the stance prevailing among EU partners. "Les Etats restent au coeur du système international" said Sarkozy, fully mirroring in this case the teachings of De Gaulle.[3].

That view is widely shared. But it is not terribly new, one may say. An earlier expected return of the nation state to the heart of the international system occurred just after the end of the Cold War. Also at that time there was a widespread perception of weak systemic ties, as a consequence of the blocks' demise. While this meant to some that the Atlantic Alliance had lost its purpose and to others, on the contrary, that it needed to change into a political community, to many it simply spelled the return to full-fledged national sovereignty. European integration was supposed to be one of the casualties, being sidelined by the fall of the Iron Curtain and the consequent reunification of Germany. None of these scenarios has materialised: NATO has survived as a military alliance (its current problems not withstanding) and Europe has moved from the European Monetary System to the euro, and from a Community of 12 members to a Union of 27 (same).

Today the problem is that the strenuous defence of separate interests and preferences seems to have failed to a large extent to enhance the national standing of separate countries in the world, as we have seen earlier in this chapter, and the degree to which it has brought home sizable

---

[3] *Palais de l'Elysée*, 27 August 2007.

returns and specific gains is questionable. According to a number of opinion polls in the EU member states, not only does a broad albeit variable majority favour a common foreign policy, but both the general population and European elites are voicing fairly consistent, if not uniform, assessments and opinions on the issues of concern to them.[4]

Country-to-country differences remain, of course. A recent poll looks at those differences that can be identified according to the location of the considered country in Western or Central and Eastern Europe.[5] It has to be taken into account that, besides geography, the polled countries belonging to the former group (France, Germany, Italy, the Netherlands, Portugal, Spain and the UK) have been members of the EU for a longer time those of the latter (Bulgaria, Poland, Romania and Slovakia). Well, President Obama enjoys more favour and generates more expectations in the first group than in the second one. That may be not surprising, in so far as the situation was the opposite last year, when Bush was in the White House. More unexpected is the fact that concerns about Russia seem to be sizably lower in the neighbouring East than in the West.

Differences should not conceal similarities. Attitudes are in fact not that distant as to the question of desirability of EU leadership in world affairs: 76% in the Western part and 70% in Central and Eastern Europe. Both sets of data are substantially higher than those concerning the desirability of a US leadership: 56% and a meagre 44%, respectively. The result concerning the European Union fits with the preference of three out of four European respondents for a more active role of Brussels in the present global economic turmoil, but is in a striking contradiction with the low popularity of common institutions and the mounting 'euroscepticism' in most of the member states, including those traditionally in favour of European integration, such as Italy. One is brought to draw the conclusion that while the 'European project' is now on a decline, possibly irreversible, the 'need for Europe' seems to be on the rise. To borrow from the language currently used for the American wars in Asia, it may be said that a 'Union of choice' is being replaced by a 'Union of necessity' in the way Europeans perceive it.

---

[4] See for instance *Eurobarometer* surveys and subsequent *Transatlantic Trends.*

[5] See *Transatlantic Trends* (2009).

3. Suggested guidelines for a non-marginal common foreign policy

The dimension, the economic weight and the historical legacy of Europe, both as a collection of national states and as a common institutional body, are such as to make the array of problems to be confronted when relating with the rest of the world very ample indeed and full of challenges. Dealing with all of them is beyond the scope and space of this chapter. Attention is focused on the role and opportunities for the European Union in global multilateralism and broadly speaking in a world in which a number of systemic ties remain. The related political debate is the one between ambitions and capabilities. The related cultural debate is one between interests and values or between realism and idealism. The choice of the multilateralist approach is made in the assumption that the consequent priorities are the best outcome of both these debates, an assumption that I will try to demonstrate.

Praising multilateralism may sound like an 'idealistic' refrain somewhat passé these days, after the blows it suffered at the hands of Bush's unilateralism and in the face of the above-mentioned widespread 'realistic' assumption of the sovereign states dominating the world scene. Realism does not necessarily view institutions and multilateral agreements as flights from reality, but tends to assign them ancillary roles. The issue is whether that suffices in the current international system. My point here is that it does not. First of all, let us bear in mind that, despite the many setbacks, multilateralism made some progress during the last decade: take the case of the International Criminal Court or of the Kyoto Protocol, possibly, the first steps of the kind achieved without or against Washington's wish. Now the Obama administration seems inclined to resume constructively the dossiers of the global environment and of the international law.

Secondly, a multilateral system appears to be the most promising solution. It would be compatible on the one hand with the growing interdependence that stems from globalisation, both in its heyday and in the current economic slump, and on the other hand, with hierarchical multipolarism, given the large numbers of very different states in the world today. Multipolarism is not a strategy, but rather is a state of affairs. So is hierarchy, which is not quite vertical enough to allow for empire, but possibly not sufficiently horizontal either, so as to suggest a return to the balance of power of yore, whose historical record for generating international stability is not positive, anyway. Finally, multilateralism appears to be the most effective approach to address global problems with a high degree of transnationality, starting with global warming.

Betting on multilateralism continues to be in Europe's best interest. Out of necessity, first, because the option of Europe turning into a power that can stand in for a declining America, traditionally dear to the French,[6] simply isn't there. In fact, absent sufficiently strong 'systemic ties' between them, the Europeans are weaker and more exposed to contradictions between member states and the Union. But out of choice as well, i.e. out of the vision that in a world so extraordinarily composite (with states and international institutions, globalisation and localism, nuclear arms and fanatic terrorism, unbridled secularism and the return of religion, etc.) a new conceptual approach is required. The so-called 'post-modern' European governance system based on shared sovereignty may be a useful precedent to help to identify such a new approach. The EU does not harbour the ambition of projecting its power at large. The congenital lack of what one may call 'integrated chauvinism' and the irreversible constraints voluntarily accepted on continuing or resurgent nationalism by partly submitting national sovereignty to common institutions should be turned into an asset rather than a liability when dealing with the rest of the world. In other words, even if we adopt the realistic assertion that the world game is still largely a power game, the aforementioned European bet is tantamount to changing the rules of the game while playing according to them, for the time being.

Playing the game requires facing commitments and responsibilities. That is why the strategy advocated here is bound to be civil and armed at the same time. The residual influence of the cultural and social dimensions of the European way of life must not be neglected, while economic instruments such as aid, trade pressure and concessions, the single currency, etc., must be put to use. Then the capability to help build states by training people in the various branches of their institutional setup, must

---

[6] See for example Pascal Bruckner: "The time has come to relieve our older Anglo-Saxon sister from the heavy burden that is bearing down on her. In the face of the perils that loom (...) Europe must coordinate its own strategic capabilities and provide itself with the military power required to obviate ever more obvious American insufficiencies". See "Non contate sull'America", Sunday Edition of *Il Sole-24 ore*, 14 October 2007.

be enhanced. In other words, first and foremost, 'soft power'. However, effective international policy on the part of the Europeans should not hesitate to resort to the use of force – military or police manpower – in the framework of broader international institutions, insofar as possible, but also, whenever necessary, in lieu of or in addition to them.

The multilateralist method is therefore to be applied with conviction as well as pragmatism in order to pursue the primary goals of high-profile policies to further Europe's common interests. When looking for the necessary associates in this venture, attention obviously turns first to the United States, all the more so with the Obama administration. The current debate among the foreign policy community in Washington shows a substantial return to the traditional dialectics between idealism and realism, as illustrated also by some repositioning of think-tanks. Multilateralism is in the picture of both schools of thought, albeit in a different scale of priority.[7] Both schools contemplate transatlantic cooperation in dealing with either crisis situations (such as the wider Middle East) and systemic problems (such as global warming), although possibly in somewhat different terms, again. Hence the need for Europeans to interact with both.

An area of apparent overlapping between the two approaches is the idea of promoting a League of Democracies as a Western strategy, a proposal that may yet elicit bi-partisan support in the US. Caution is advisable here because it forces us to divide those countries whose cooperation is needed by the West between 'us' and 'them' (Where does that leave Egypt, for instance, or Saudi Arabia or Pakistan? What about Russia? or China?). Moreover, by advocating a sort of 'ideological multilateralism', we risk undermining institutional multilateralism (the UN, in particular) as well as functional multilateralism (the G8, G20 or whatever Gs, including the newly contemplated G2). The banner of democracy should be substituted with that of the rule of law. This means supporting and defending human rights, helping the adoption and the implementation of domestic laws that are compatible with them both in the established partner countries and in the failed states we are trying to put back on their feet. Electoral democracy is the last chapter in the process, as history teaches us. Rule of law also means further developing the systemic

---

[7] As an outstanding example of the multilateralist school, see Talbott (2009).

value of global justice, of properly legitimated rights of international institutions to interfere in unacceptable situations, and the like.

America is certainly not foreign either culturally or historically to this approach. Thus the partnership with the US in pursuing it has great potentials, besides being necessary. Things are more difficult with others. Let's limit ourselves to the main powers already mentioned. Europe's interdependence with China, India and Russia has been systemically growing and it may turn out to be even higher after the economic recession. Thus policies vis-à-vis these countries, whether initiated separately by member states or coordinated within the Union, are inevitably determined by the pursuit of interests involved in this interdependence. At the same time the limitations, conditions and ambiguities of these countries are well known when dealing with systemic solutions such as treaties or institutions and what has become fashionable to call global governance. In other words, their reliability as stakeholders in the global corporation is limited, to use business terminology. The effort to involve them should not be abandoned, however, beginning with culture (current multilateralism is to a large extent a Western concept that must adapted so that it can be shared by other civilisations) and ending with interests (multilateralism implies constraints for the West as well as for the rest of the world and it can provide stability to global interdependence).

Islam is an even more difficult interlocutor. There are Muslim countries and countries with a strong Muslim presence, often divided on all issues save for anti-Israeli rhetoric. In recent years there has been a decline in the power and influence formerly wielded by Arabs, to the benefit of the Shiites. Moreover fundamentalists often have the upper hand over secularists. Neither development is in Europe's best interest and its strategy should aim to reverse both. Hence a consistent initiative aiming to elicit regional multilateralism from the rubble of the Middle East could reflect positively on the strengthening of the Arabs and the secularists. Israel, had it preserved some of Shimon Peres' past vision, could perhaps understand that this would be in its best interest as well. For the time being, however, the Jewish state has chosen to fight almost exclusively for its own strength, including territorial expansion, relying on the spirit of the Bible and a lay, armed *Realpolitik*.

The Europeans should join what appears a new policy by the Obama administration aimed at helping Israel to redirect its role towards working for a secure and equitable order in the area. Not without ambiguities, they seem to be in favour of a regional arrangement but know that it is basically up to Washington to call the shots. That recognition should be reciprocated by the US accepting that their allies on this side of the Atlantic have a decisive word to say in dealing with Moscow and on the issue of whether or not to further expand NATO, let alone the EU.

4. The instruments for the EU to achieve a high-profile foreign policy

Finally, let us briefly recall the main provisions of the Lisbon Treaty (TEU) regarding Europe's foreign and security policy.[8]

Under Article 1, para. 3 of the TEU, "the Union shall replace and succeed the European Community" and "the EU shall have legal personality" (Article 47), which means it shall have the ability to negotiate and sign in its name international agreements of a binding nature for its institutions and member states.

A permanent President of the European Council, elected by qualified majority for a two-and-a-half year term that is renewable once, is contemplated (Article 15). The President's duties include ensuring the external representation of the Union for matters relative to the Common Foreign and Security Policy, alongside the High Representative (see below). The intent is obviously that of conferring the continuity and consistency not provided by the current six-month rotating presidency, especially in the field of external relations.

The other innovation is the High Representative for the Union in Foreign Affairs and Security Policy (Article 18), to take on the roles, competences and resources of the High Representative for CFSP and those of the Commissioner for External Relations (and therefore to have specific funding in the budget). Nominated by the European Council, ruling by qualified majority, with the agreement of the President of the Commission, he/she shall be entrusted with directing the Union's foreign, security and defence policy and with contributing, through his/her proposals, to its implementation in his/her capacity as representative of the External

---

[8] For these comments on CFSP and ESDP, I have availed myself of the analysis of the Lisbon Intergovernmental Conference drawn up by Michele Comelli (IAI), *Trattato di riforma e politica estera e di sicurezza europea: che cosa cambia?*, International Affairs Division, Italian Senate, October 2007.

Relations Council (now independent from the General Affairs Council) which he/she shall chair. His competences include coordinating the EU's existing policies and bodies, taking political initiative, implementing crisis management and external representation.

Finally there is the European External Action Service (Article 27) to be adopted by the Council, following a proposal by the High Representative. Made up of Council and Commission staff as well as staff on secondment from national diplomatic services, this unit shall operate in close cooperation with the latter, with possible conflicts of competence looming on the horizon. The Lisbon Treaty, for that matter, does not specify deliberately the organisation and operation of the Service, to be finalised by Council decision on the basis of proposals put forth by the future High Representative. What will also have to be decided is who will chair the Political and Security Committee (PSC, also known by its French acronym, COPS), an existing body in charge of monitoring international developments, formulating opinions for the Council and exercising political control and strategic direction in Union peacekeeping operations.

Let us turn to the Lisbon Treaty clauses pertaining to European Security and Defence Policies (ESDP).

1) There are, first of all, a number of solidarity-focused provisions, including reciprocal defence. This means that "if a member state is a victim of armed aggression on its territory, the other member states shall have towards it an obligation of aid and assistance by all the means in their power, in accordance with Article 51 of the UN Charter (Article 42, para. 3 of TEU). This text is similar to Article 5 of the North Atlantic Treaty, the 'compliance' with NATO obligations being for that matter explained a bit further down in the text. The obligation is extended to traditionally "neutral" countries, which showed gratitude by having the text specify that "this shall not prejudice the specific character of the Security and Defence policy of certain member states" (a good exercise of ambiguity). Another solidarity-focused provision of the Treaty on the Functioning of the European Union (TFU) mentions measures to be taken should a member state suffer a terrorist attack or a natural or man-made disaster. There is one caveat, however: the provision that states that action shall be joint and bring to bear all available means, including military, will not apply in the event of anti-terrorist operations outside the EU.

2) And then there is another provision (Article 42 TEU) that was actually implemented ahead of the failed ratification of the Constitutional

Treaty now replaced by the Lisbon Treaty. It refers to the European Defence Agency, set up as CFSP action in July 2004, in order to identify and if necessary implement all measures likely to strengthen the defence sector's industrial and technological base (the potentially larger part of the remit) and contribute to the definition of a European armaments policy.

3) Finally all provisions relative to Enhanced Cooperation have been taken on board almost in their entirety. The one single exception - not marginal - is that the exclusion of initiatives with military or defence sector implications has been removed. This is due to the fact that it is precisely in this sector that the Lisbon Treaty says that member states with adequate military capabilities and the desire to enter into more binding commitments in this field may set up among themselves a Permanent Structured Cooperation (Article 46), formally open to all, with the purpose of organising clusters of national and multinational forces, developing equipment programmes in the framework of the EDA, and achieving agreed spending and investment targets. In contrast to Enhanced Cooperation, which requires the participation of at least one-third of the member states, no floor has been set here. But more importantly, decisions are taken by qualified majority, which waives the general principle requiring unanimity in security and defence policy matters.

All these instruments, the potential impact of which is not negligible, have been tacked on to the existing base of those devised for the CFSP and the ESDP, both in terms of declarations, official procedures, common action, etc., and in terms of joint operations such as the several ongoing civilian operations and the one military (EUFOR Althea, in Bosnia).[9] These instruments have been used to implement what was called, in the introduction, the low-profile common foreign policy so far performed by the EU. In shifting from the Constitutional draft, the Lisbon Treaty has not undergone any major mutilation in this respect, if one discounts symbols - the flag, the 'foreign minister', etc. - ideal targets of nationalistic reservations.

Before closing, I would like to mention briefly the CFSP's younger sister, the European Neighbourhood Policy (ENP), which has mainly stayed under the Commission's jurisdiction. It is a little sister indeed, but not one to be underestimated, as it connects almost without separation with

[9] For a review and closer examination, see Bonvicini & Regelsberger (2007, p. 261).

the CFSP's more difficult challenges (Russia, the Middle East, Africa). Moreover it deals with illegal immigration, possibly the most difficult issue in the area of justice and home affairs, and with enlargement, i.e. the problem of the Union borders, the political relevance of which was discussed before. Thus ENP appears squeezed, almost asphyxiated, on the one side by the problem of Mediterranean cooperation including the hot issue of Palestine, and on the other by the problem of the inflow of migrants. A finally further enlargement looms over most attempts of the ENP to establish more or less special partnerships with this or that 'neighbour'.

In conclusion, once the remaining dominant unanimity rule is taken into account, the 'technical' limitations to the achievement of an ambitious foreign policy on the part of the Union remain in the Lisbon Treaty. These limitations do not pose insurmountable obstacles, however, if a strategy is adopted and the appropriate instruments to implement it are defined. Of course, all depends on the famous 'political will'.

References

Beck, U. (2004), *Das kosmopolitische Blick oder: Krieg ist Frieden*, Frankfurt aM: Suhrkamp Verlag.

Bonvicini, G. and E. Regelsberger (2007), "Growing without a strategy?", *The International Spectator*, Vol. 42, No. 2.

Comelli, M. (2007), *Trattato di riforma e politica estera e di sicurezza europea: che cosa cambia?*, International Affairs Division, Italian Senate, October.

D'Alema, M. (2007a), "Relancer l'Europe. Les responsabilités des gouvernements, les enjeux pour la Gauche", speech by Minister D'Alema at the Gauche Reformiste européenne Conference, Brussels, 12 February.

Kagan, R. (2002), "Power and Weakness: Why the United States and Europe see the world differently", *Policy Review*, No. 113, June/July.

Kagan, R. (2007), "End of Dreams, Return to History", *Policy Review*, No. 144, August/September.

Merlini, C. (2002), "The US Hegemony and the Roman Analogy", *The International Spectator*, Vol. 37, No. 3, July-September.

Merlini, C. (2006), "Un nuovo ruolo internazionale per l'Europa", in *Il Mulino*, No. 6.

Sarkozy, N. (2007), Speech of President N. Sarkozy at the Conference of Ambassadors, Paris, Palais de l'Elisée, 27 August.

Talbott, S. (2009), *The Great Experiment: The Story of Ancient Empires, Modern States, and the Quest for a Global Nation*, New York: Simon & Shuster.

Transatlantic Trends (2007 and 2009), German Marshall Fund of the United States (http://www.gmfus.org/trends/index.html).

8. The Enlargement of the European Union

Rocco A. Cangelosi & Ferdinando Salleo

The institutional standstill that followed the referendums in France and the Netherlands also shelved the enlargement of the European Union to the Western Balkans and Turkey, causing a temporary halt in a process that had completed a number of stages and aroused considerable expectations. The formal reason that brought the process to a halt was the pause for reflection Europe granted itself in order to re-consider its configuration and overcome the stumbling block of the interrupted ratification process.

1. European enlargement and vision

In addition to this standstill on the fate of the Treaty, the postponement of new admission procedures seems to be closely connected to the dilemmas that institutional review and enlargement policy have spawned for the Union and its members. The first dilemma hinges on what kind of Europe can realistically be built and managed with more members than the current 27, with new candidates that are unlike either the core Union countries or the elusive 'European average' – even more unlike those admitted in the so-called 10+2 enlargement of 2004 and 2007. The second dilemma, which stems from the first, relates to what kind of Europe can be proposed to candidates when accession negotiations resume. As European citizens show increasing awareness of future Union developments, public debate has been marked by a level of popular political participation that is higher than that regarding government decisions.

In fact, both conceptually and more importantly politically, the referendums brought home to European governments two long-avoided or talked-away truths. Firstly, as is particularly the case in foreign policy when the feared or real consequences for citizens of important political decisions are under consideration, the issue of admitting new member states to the Union confirmed the rule that sooner or later, governments have to face up to public opinion and the deep-rooted and often unexpressed feelings prevalent in any given country.

Similarly, debates on institutions and Union enlargement also show that to some extent the future of Europe is burdened by the anticipation of a looming, continually postponed 'hour of truth', which signals a need to emerge at long last from the ambiguities skilfully juggled by governments and diplomats alike. The continuing differences are basically between two schools of thought: the original vision of a political Europe and the much less innovative one of Europe-as-a-market, or a free trade area. Although borders have always been somewhat unclear, there has always been a great political and conceptual distance between the two major camps - integrationists and minimalists - not to mention the many undeclared intermediate positions.

Although attitudes to enlargement have often been dictated by special relations to this or that candidate country, or by alignment considerations, enlargement advocates have always had the minimalists on their side, whereas traditional supporters of integration and the political model have always viewed with considerable perplexity the potential consequences of dishomogeneity on the nature of the Europe they were building: there is, intuitively, a reverse relationship between the breadth of the European Community and the degree of integration between member states. Community, and subsequently Union enlargement has from the outset had two main terms of reference: on the one hand, completing the founding fathers' European design - political and institutional and not simply economic - and, on the other, attempting to achieve convergence and cohesion between diverse countries, proud of their history and jealous of their identity but willing to move rationally towards forms of shared sovereignty. These ideals dictated the principle according to which the deepening and widening of Europe should proceed in parallel. The principle is still to be found among the pre-requisites to European enlargement alongside the so-called 'criteria' for aspiring members. Although at first sight redolent of a political oxymoron, the close link between widening and deepening was designed and understood as a hendiadys, a two-for-one, as the belief that the two approaches would strengthen one another and make a robust and harmonious European construction possible.

Europe has gradually grown from its initial area, improperly termed 'Carolingian', to cover a vast region extending from the Atlantic to the Elbe and to Thessalonica. In the process it succeeded in digesting both a fair number of incongruities in its common institutions and significant legal, political and economic differences between members. The European Community's enlargement process was thus moving ahead according to an internal logic based on radically geo-political assumptions of 1989, when European scenarios and global balance were radically transformed by the collapse of the Berlin wall and the end of the cold war. The implosion of the Soviet Union revived an ancient idealistic drive for a Europe that was 'one and free', to be established in a continental area sharing freedom, democracy and progress. This political premise triggered a process which, despite a general awareness of the objective difficulties involved, drove the European Union towards the East and the Baltic Sea as soon as continental 're-unification' became possible, as signalled by the unification of Germany within a European and Atlantic process and the return to Europe of peoples who had been kept away from the heart of the civilisation to which they felt they belonged - first by century-old events and subsequently by Soviet domination.

The fact that countries subjected for almost 50 years to Soviet domination and the straitjacket of centrally-planned economies were actually able to restore representative democracy, the rule of law and the protection of human rights and market economics were to a large extent made possible by the support provided to their political and economic re-construction - first by the promise of membership, and subsequently by Europe's concrete assistance as they returned to the fold. But the experience was not equally positive for all concerned, which explains why further enlargement is a contentious political issue in both new and old member states, with criticism ranging from the rational to the visceral, from nostalgia for the greater cohesion of the past and contempt for the red tape and slowness of Brussels' officialdom, to the revival of ancestral diffidence vis-à-vis outsiders, and the nationalist and populist drives that have resurfaced on the extreme political fringes of various countries under new, often irrational and xenophobic guises.

2. Recent admissions and new candidates

With the successful admission of neighbouring countries from north-west Europe and the Mediterranean, the Union accepted into the fold European countries sufficiently similar to the founding members to be subsequently absorbed into the European institutions – at varying speeds and intensities according to the political, social and economic specificities of each new partner – but with an approach marked by realism and cooperation.[1] Coming from state-party regimes, command economies and state-controlled production systems, they found it a challenge to reconstruct civil societies, democratic and pluralist political systems with Western-style parties and unions, public jurisdiction and administration, human rights and environmental protection. Economically, they were as different from the rest of Europe as they were politically and socially. While the Union's surface area and population have grown by about one-third with the admission of Central and Eastern European countries, its GDP has increased by only about 5%, and per capita income in the enlarged Union has fallen by around 18%. These figures show that among the governments and public of the 'old' Union, the ethical and political aspirations that drove enlargement outweighed all considerations of national selfishness and accounts-based resentment. These resurfaced with a vengeance in the two referendums and are paradoxically also emerging in the more recently admitted member states with regard to new candidates.

Central and Eastern Europe presents a diverse and varied picture, in which commendable and laborious progress has not been linear. Initially the larger countries, with national income levels that stood at around 40% of European averages, recorded faster growth rates than the older Union members – and (with the exception of Hungary) also showed acceptable macroeconomic outcomes and positive structural adjustment, in conjunction however with high unemployment rates (above 15% in Poland and Slovakia) – and attracted significant flows of foreign direct investment (Dlouhy & Emmott, 2006).

While some new members achieved clear political and economic progress, the larger countries' initial economic progress was not matched by overall stability in the political structures of their recent democracies: in actual fact, the establishment of post-communist public order appears to have made both citizens and domestic political systems prone to widespread restlessness that has at times erupted into loud protests, rocking local political systems. Instability has already raised issues of

---

[1] See Nugent (2007) for the enlargement sequence.

governability in many of the Union's more recent members and if uncontained by systematic dialogue, may well worsen these countries' general and specific economic vulnerabilities and whittle down the comparative advantages (low labour costs, high levels of technical education, young executives) which the Central and Eastern European countries have so far used to boost exports and attract investment from other, offshore Union members. Today there are fears that the inflows of foreign currency that bolstered public accounts may dry up, leading to major financial imbalances.

Following the adaptation period heralded by the introduction of democratic institutions, signs of a revival of nationalism and populism are now visible in several countries, which can only be considered as a retreat from European ideals. By the same token, the fragilities and uncertainties of several Central and Eastern European countries may make it difficult for them to stay the course of the progressively stringent rules for economic and fiscal policy on which the development of the European process and convergence of member states hinge.

In other words, after a promising start, the EU's main new members' convergence with the mainstream is now faltering. The picture today is very different from that surrounding the entry of Central and Eastern European countries, due to the no doubt overly simplistic expectations of European public opinion and governments. The belief was that membership in the Union would stimulate a linear political, economic and social process with interdependent effects and beneficial outcomes for the various components of each new member's society. The process was actually posited somewhat abstractly as a kind of paradigm for forthcoming admissions - currently in abeyance - but evidence drawn from the experience of recently admitted members sheds doubt on its validity. Consequently, insofar as new candidates are similar to recently admitted members, decisions concerning their entry and the conditions to be attached to accession agreements will also be scrutinised on the basis of lessons learnt from the larger countries in the 2004 batch, filtering out external factors and the impact of the global economic situation in assessing their respective results and progress.

Although the various enlargement negotiations have so far been formally framed on the basis of considerations specific to each case, it is from a general political standpoint that Europe must contend with a series of decisions on enlargement that affect its whole edifice. In actual fact, as a result of the momentum built up with the 2004-07 big bang, the approach to future enlargements to the Western Balkans and Turkey has already been sketched out, despite underlying controversy, currently expressed in stronger terms and more openly than before. The generous idealism underpinning such decisions failed to take into account that recent experience has shown the need to base the process on a thorough assessment of actual circumstance; in addition, the Union's growing size has gradually begun to tell on its shaky structures, already in need of an overhaul if they are to provide effective governance for the current membership of 27. In any case, voters in current member states will need to be convinced of the desirability of further enlargements. In the meantime, momentum has clearly waned as the constitutional standstill has halted the enlargement process and forced Europeans to be more realistic in assessing the gist of the venture, i.e. which Europe do they want and what kind of geographical, economic, political, cultural and social configuration would best suit their goal. Conversely, should the minimalist approach win out, European construction will perhaps require adaptation to accommodate future enlargements.

3. The Western Balkans

Problems related to Europe's external relations and security are among the most pressing issues concerning the enlargements temporarily on hold. First and foremost among these is the stabilisation of the Balkan region, which occupies a geopolitical position of great strategic significance at the very border of the Union. The Western Balkans, which encompass Macedonia, Serbia, Albania, Montenegro, Bosnia-Herzegovina, Kosovo (the latter two having a hybrid state structure) and Croatia, which is close to concluding its own negotiations and is a different case, occupy a territory that is wedged deep into the Union and, as far as we are directly concerned, contiguous to Italy, from which it is separated by a narrow stretch of sea. There is no need to stress how important the stability, security and prosperity of this region is for Europe (and particularly for Italy). Mindful of the recent post-Yugoslav wars and their effect on Europe, one needs to be aware of how porous the borders separating the Western Balkans from the Union are - particularly with the free circulation of people that applies in the contiguous area of the Union under the Schengen agreement. We also need to be aware in general terms of the potential 'contagion' of political instability and insecurity that can, through metaphorical osmosis, transfer problems across borders just as stability can sometimes channel success. The Western Balkans are actually an historically and ethnically diverse region, made up of countries that have difficult relations with each other, most of which are small and unstable, imbued with nationalism - even sub-ethnic nationalism. They are still wounded by the memory of a recent bloody past and worried by the multi-ethnic make-up of the region and the national and religious minorities it has harboured for centuries - the Islamic presence is a case in point. Their institutions are often untested and their political structures fragile; there is no reliable rule of law or protection of civil rights, internal security is shaky and their economic dimensions are far from optimal. Their economies are perhaps not even viable because of fragmentation, as illustrated by inadequate, incomplete and un-integrated infrastructures. Finally, they have high unemployment and low per capita income, even compared with the rest of the Balkans.

The most important of the region's countries, Serbia, has also fallen prey to nationalism. It is economically backward, politically divided and in addition still entangled in a contentious relationship with the Tribunal established by the United Nations in The Hague to judge crimes committed in the post-Yugoslav war, which has been demanding that Belgrade hand over the Bosnian Serb criminals to be brought to justice. Most of all, it is in the throes of political upheaval at the idea of losing Kosovo, that 'cradle of the Serb nation', an inevitable territorial mutilation that it cannot bring itself to accept.

Bosnia - which to all intents and purposes is divided between a Serb 'republic' and a Croat-Muslim 'federation' - and Kosovo are still under international protection with a significant military and administrative European and NATO presence, which has so far prevented worst-case scenarios. Kosovo is also the focus of political disputes that led to protracted arguments within the United Nations on the prospects and terms of its separation from Serbia. The United States has recognised an independent Kosovo as did many - not all - European countries despite hesitation prompted both by fears of a chain reaction throughout the former Yugoslav region and by national minority restlessness in Romania, Slovakia and Hungary. Russia does not recognise Kosovo's independence, believing it will establish a precedent for restless nationalities within its own borders, particularly in Chechnya, and has hit back in the separatist regions of Georgia, i.e. Abkhazia and South Ossetia. In practice, Russia's veto has led to a deadlock that compelled the Kosovars to declare independence unilaterally. An international group of experts has drawn up a 'European' roadmap bringing Kosovo and the whole region closer to the Union, which includes guarantees of admission subject to the attainment of political, legal and economic goals and the protection of the Serb minority, but makes the prospect of entry into Europe an outcome applicable to the Balkan region as a whole, at the end of a long-term process.

Can Europe whole-heartedly welcome into its midst and absorb within an acceptable timeframe a group of peoples and societies so foreign, complex and dangerous and at the same time so close geographically? Will the citizens of the prosperous and distant North accept these new and, for them, incomprehensible and rowdy 'new Europeans'? Will it be possible to make room for them within common institutions geared to achieving the integration called for by the pro-Europeans, or should one devise some other compromise and pay the price in terms of European political cohesiveness and institutional progress? Will this not deal a final blow to the principle of deepening as a condition of widening? On the other hand, all governments are aware of the dangers that continuing instability in the Western Balkans poses for the Union's equilibrium and international role. They know that matters may worsen further if the Union rejects these countries and that there are in any event real risks of deterioration that may go as far as the re-eruption of only recently quelled local conflicts. The insecurity and political unrest of the 1990s, the horror of the post-Yugoslav wars, and the massacres and repressions committed at the Union's borders are still alive in our collective memory. Large segments of European public opinion as well as political leaders and decision-makers are now wondering what methods could be adopted, how much time would be required and what kind of Union status could be conceivable for these countries, and which compromise solutions could realistically be advanced without endangering the pursuit of Europe's grand design. The time factor that appears to dominate possible developments in the Western Balkans inherently and strongly defers the basic dilemmas of enlargement: it may actually turn into a factor for stability over and beyond current issues of Union development, as well as a major obstacle to much-needed clarification between two basic visions of Europe.

4. Turkey

Security of the Union's Eastern borders leads us to the complex issue of Turkey, NATO's Anatolian bulwark, abutting onto the Near and Middle East countries, the Caucasus and Central Asia, while directly bordering

Iran, Iraq and Syria. Looking at Turkey's geopolitical position recalls the opposing arguments that have always been advanced with regard to Ankara's entry into Europe. While it is natural for a political and military alliance to have a common border with potential adversaries, it is much less so for an innovative political and economic union, an integrated society designed with the special features and purpose the community of European peoples are committed to developing.

Several contradictions are inherent in Turkey's current political and cultural situation: a Muslim country with the history and tradition of a great power, with a capable establishment, Turkey has made considerable efforts to adapt to the Copenhagen criteria and implement the civil liberties, human rights and transparency provisions the Union requires its candidates to embody in their laws and everyday practice, although much remains to be done.

It is true that admitting Turkey would show the Islamic world that Europe is not an exclusively Christian club and is open to peoples of all religions and cultures. It is equally true that Turkey is also a political and cultural bulwark against radical Arab Islam and a concrete demonstration of the viability of a secular and democratic Muslim state, although its Kemalist secularism is guaranteed by the not particularly democratic supervision exercised by the military high command over Ankara's civilian power, which recent elections have clearly handed over to an Islam-inspired party. In addition, from a geopolitical standpoint, should the Union extend its borders to the Near East, the most unstable and turbulent area of the Mediterranean, it would find itself directly involved in the said area's endemic crises and regional conflicts, which are not just territorial and political, but also economic - relating as they do to energy and water supply - as well as ethnic and cultural. If Europe were to admit Turkey and extend to the conflicting states' borders, it would somehow become a party to matters there, and in so doing lose its ability to act as an intermediary and broker of agreements, a role it rightly aspires to and which in practice it has so far been denied.

Another point to bear in mind is the regional perspective as seen through Turkish eyes, even disregarding traditional 'pan-Turkic' aspirations towards Central Asia. Turkish pride often spills over into nationalism, as demonstrated by recurring and bitter arguments on the long-standing issue of the Armenian genocide perpetrated by the Ottomans and to date obstinately denied by Ankara. Furthermore, a much more topical issue, that of the Kurds, has recently acquired a higher profile in Turkey's international political and military stance, as well as in domestic policy, with threats of military intervention to destroy Kurdish terrorist bases located in the north-eastern provinces of Iraq (and actual raids took place), a prospect that has aroused deep concern in Washington as well, insofar as it could lead to Mesopotamian Balkanisation. For although Iraq's possible disintegration conversely highlights the relatively good performance of self-governing Iraqi Kurdistan, this in itself contains the seeds of destabilisation for south-eastern Turkey where a Kurdish population harbours hopes of an independent Kurdistan and can feel the attraction of the statehood their fellow Kurds, on the other side of the border, have been informally but effectively enjoying, counting as they do on a division of Iraq into three separate entities.

In any case, what with the institutional standstill, the postponement of negotiations on several 'chapters' for which criteria implementation was deemed inadequate by Brussels, followed by the recent re-opening of negotiations on three, as well as the very modest progress achieved in the Cyprus issue (still outstanding through the fault of both sides and of Europe itself imprudently admitting Nicosia to the Union prior to the re-unification of the island planned by the United Nations), Europe's relationship with Ankara is in a state of uncertainty marked by mutual recrimination. In both Europe and Turkey, those hostile to Turkey's accession to the Union - even played out over a lengthy process and postponed by a decade at least - have recently gained new strength.

Following the two referendums, as pointed out earlier, domestic political considerations have weighed in more heavily on all issues concerning the Union and in particular on enlargement: their impact is even stronger with regard to Turkey than it is for the Balkan candidates. There are renewed fears over the possible entry into Europe of 70 million Muslims and the integration of an economy which, although dynamic, remains very unbalanced; which has shown strong growth but is still far from the income levels prevailing in Europe, even compared to the 'ten' who entered in 2004 (but not Romania and Bulgaria); and which is saddled with high inflation and recurring financial imbalances. In addition to this Turkey would potentially elect the largest national representation in the European Parliament.

Furthermore, Sarkozy, who had already spoken out against Turkey's accession during the presidential campaign, has reiterated his grave doubts, which boil down to outright opposition, and are redolent of Chirac's earlier pledge to submit any treaty of accession to a referendum. Chancellor Merkel has expressed a strong preference for establishing a special relationship with Turkey rather than granting it membership. Conversely, London and other minimalist countries are in favour of admitting Turkey with the guarantees provided by a lengthy process and verifiable targets. All in all, several countries would appreciate alternatives to full Turkish membership, but Ankara has so far refused to entertain these possibilities.

5. The borders of Europe

On the whole, alongside recurring references to compatibility and convergence among economies, integration of tax and corporate regulations, standards extension and the adoption of broad European policies, discussions on enlargement are currently increasingly dominated by problems and questions that are essentially political, cultural and psychological. After two periods of geographical expansion, the first driven by geopolitical concerns with the pursuit of stability and balance in the Western part of the continent, and the second powered by the emotional and cultural thrust to recover Eastern Europe, the new accessions are now considered in light of Europe's own strategic interest and how it can realistically work towards the goals it has set itself. Bearing this in mind, discussions on the limits and borders of Europe, often deemed an exercise in pure speculation, appear increasingly meaningful. Europe's external borders and its identity, the Union's institutions and a common vision of its role in the world, internal compatibility among members and compliance with the duties, rights and values of a community of fates, all make up a set of interdependent issues that cut across both institutional and organisational dimensions and the issue of geographical make-up.

There is an understandable reluctance to discuss Europe's external borders in current terms, not only because Europe itself is extremely hard to define, beyond the borders traditionally plotted by geographers and historians, but also because there is a reluctance to draw lines that would exclude countries with which there are often deep and cooperative relations or cultural proximities. Another reason to refrain from defining frontiers is an awareness of the interdependence specific to today's globalised world, amid the decline in exclusive state sovereignty and jurisdiction, and the intrinsic porosity of contemporary borders.

From a political and cultural standpoint, any attempt to mark out an external border might seem to imply that Europe really wants to define itself by contrast to those beyond its borders, who are 'other', in a revival of the ancient Hellenic dichotomy between 'us' and 'them' (Gress, 2004). In economic terms, borders conjure up external tariffs and the restrictions that were ubiquitous until quite recently, feeding recurring bouts of protectionism, and that still pursue us from one trade round to the next. Finally, borders revoke the concept of security: a very clear point is made by laying down a border in the real sense of the word - a line where external defences, the walls protecting a given *demos* are traditionally placed. Nor should one overlook the sacred and almost timeless character extended to the concept of border by the political, cultural and also geographical shape given to Europe in 1648 by the Treaties of Westphalia, at the close of a series of conflicts that climaxed in the Thirty Years War and brought to an end a lengthy period in which sovereignties of various kinds and strengths had co-existed, overlapped and intersected.

On the other hand, can one really avoid an issue as basic as the definition of a clear external border, more grounded in recognisability and fellowship than in geography? However much trust one may have in the demiurgic nature of the *force des choses*, is it really thinkable to leave the definition of Europe's borders to unfurling events, external and random factors, or the slippery slope of Brussels bureaucracy when one knows how vague the original treaty was in limiting eligibility to Community membership to European countries - without however attaching the map? Today there is widespread popular demand for clear borders and the territorial definition of what is to become Europe: the question is not just where and how the European edifice will be completed, but also in which terms and with which features its boundaries will be established. In the end, the Union's enlargement policy will have to meet public demand: it is axiomatic that in a democracy government decisions have to be guided by due consideration for the attitude and will of the people.

Europe's external borders are first of all defined by two political benchmarks, the external and the internal. The external or 'foreign policy' benchmark corresponds to a comprehensive dimension covering Europe's security, the protection of its interests, the scope of its interventions and the foreign policy the Union wishes to uphold in a multi-polar scenario, as well as the political image it wishes to project in its relations with major entities such as states and intergovernmental organisations or the bodies and sometimes informal entities spawned by globalisation. Without entering into debates on soft and hard power and their relative effectiveness, or their recommended mix in the management of international relations, one should point out that Europe currently projects itself mainly through its political and social decisions. Europe's main features are a mature and participatory democracy, the rule of law and the upholding of civil liberties and human rights, tolerance and pluralism, the pursuit of prosperity combined with social justice, freedom of enterprise and trade, the defence of European security and a commitment to peace, the advocacy of multilateralism on the basis of agreed rules, a humanistic vision of relations between states and the belief that aid to poorer nations is a prerequisite for world stability and security.

Adequate political, economic and military resources will have to be made available to this end. Europe's political strength derives from the way in which it projects these values, as demonstrated by the attraction it exercises globally, something that is perhaps more clearly perceived by the outside world than it is within Europe, where debate is often glum, negative, 'declinist' and tainted with ideology and scepticism. Europe's international stance is in any case the frame within which its short-term goals are ordered: the pursuit of stability in contiguous European regions and security along its borders with areas of deep unrest. As stated earlier, future enlargement is linked to these goals.

The 'internal policy' benchmark hinges on the institutional issue and the inevitable adaptations its members, candidates, and the Union as a whole will need to accept in view of the legislative, political, cultural and value differences between candidate countries and the Union's core member states. This inevitably shifts the discussion back to the basic debate underpinning the whole European process, from the Treaties of Rome to enlargement, a debate featuring two opposing political views and focusing, in the final analysis, on Europe's very identity.

6. Europe's identity

In fact, looking beyond the slew of arguments and theories, what is at stake in Europe's political debate on institutions and enlargement is basically its very identity, insofar as external borders and identity are one and the same. This is an inescapable issue, not only because it is clearly defining for the overall European design, but also because principles of democracy and political caution require that it be put clearly to the peoples of Europe, regardless of whether accession treaty ratification is entrusted to parliaments or referendums.

One can easily argue that deliberate vagueness on issues of European identity was a decisive factor in the French and Dutch rejections, as pointed out in the interpretative controversies and *ex-post* rationalisations that followed the referendums. The controversies were fuelled by a number of biases, either genuinely felt to be important, or stemming from overly simplistic argumentation – inter alia because of a lack of communication on the part of national governments and Brussels – or from yet other controversies based on reasoning and arguments echoing ancient misunderstandings. Alongside reasons of a general nature – a disappointment with Europe voiced by those who seemed unable to recall the distressed circumstances of yesterday from their current position of prosperity largely ascribable to progress achieved by the whole continent, or growing hostility to the Commission's perceived over-regulation – one prominent and widespread feeling was so-called 'enlargement fatigue', a dwindling belief in the ideal, a lack of trust in the future, risk aversion and a set of fears linked to enlargement. Today, other member states have followed the French and the Dutch, months after the fact, in expressing anxiety at the idea of letting into their common home other poorer and politically unstable countries, economically weak and lacking in infrastructure. There is also dread of a massive inflow of immigration (the 'Polish plumber'), fear that new members will be granted priority access to structural funds that will end up being directed to their poorer regions, as well as lurking trade protectionism, ever suspicious of whoever manages to produce more competitively. And to that one must add a visible concern at the 'otherness' of Islamic values and the Muslim way of life, as compared with European traditions.

Beyond these specific reasons, the underlying cause for rejection seems to be a deep and widespread fear of what the Germans call *Entfremdung*, the loss of identity. For Europe, a voluntary union of different peoples and states that have decided to share a large part of their sovereignty, modern self-awareness does not equate identity with race or unifying ethnicity, any more than with geography, language or religion. Europe includes countries with a clear awareness of their identity but where a number of different languages are spoken, elsewhere languages and cultures spread beyond national borders, people share a language and a culture but not a religion, states have lost or gained vast territories and in the process suffered losses and taken in refugees or moved into new lands, and yet their identity has remained unchanged. These are all-important ingredients in a people's self-awareness and self-image, whether true or distorted by legend, and therefore an integral part of their self-perception (Barzun, 2000; Le Goff, 2003). Further basic components of identity are a common history and great and illustrious traditions, often tragic and weighty - with the seeds of war, misuse of power and disaster - to be prevented.

Since the Enlightenment, there has been a growing awareness that the keystone of social groups' 'republican' (Viroli, 2002) identity is their decision to live together, that conscious will of citizens, that 'everyday plebiscite' referred to by Ernest Renan and others, that state citizens have devised for themselves, the basic law of the country, the social contract and the institutional arrangement consciously and freely chosen by the people. In the case of Europe, where strong member state identities coexist with the Union's developing identity, the latter is particularly to be sought in the 'comun diritto' (or *acquis communautaire*) as expounded upon in this volume by Mazzini. As it develops it will increasingly be embodied in the Union's institutions, its shared freedoms and duties, the common principles and values around which the social contract and political institutions have been shaped as well as in the Charter of Fundamental Rights - which, despite having been legally sidetracked in Brussels, mainly because of the United Kingdom, is still referenced in the Treaty. The broader the range of human activity governed by common rules, the clearer the borders of Europe will become to its citizens and the outside world.

In this sense, the issue of enlargement and institutions intersect each other in such a way as to require that they be dealt with together. Intuitively one sees that the Union will in any case require a clear definition of its nature, its legal identity - the international personality of Europe has been retained in the Lisbon text - through its institutional arrangements and strategic goals, so that candidates can knowingly decide in what kind of regulatory and organisational context they wish to view their future. What is at stake is no longer simply accepting the *acquis communautaire*, but rather finding a position within a specific institutional system, internalising the consequences domestically, adapting laws and culture as required, signing on to the sharing of a number of areas of Westphalian sovereignty, and devolving allegiance for each of these to the Union or to the Union component candidate countries are able and willing to adopt. The societal paradigm deriving from this shall be based on a free and conscious choice, while purely instrumental accession aimed at obtaining short-term advantages or striving solely for prosperity would soon lead to dysfunctions that endanger the whole system.

Conversely, in deciding what type of Europe they want in the future, members will have to consider future enlargement and have a basic idea of the type of candidates they feel could be accommodated within their geopolitical and ideal vision of the Union. We know that this will not be an easy choice, considering the differences in approach upheld by minimalist, sovereigntist and integrationist member states, so far reconciled by deliberately reduced ambitions. It is also obvious that different countries have different attitudes to the outside world and there is widespread concern about the required ratifications. For this reason too, it would be better to avoid confronting European states and peoples with a stark choice between two extreme positions, in a take it or leave it alternative. Candidate countries will also need to choose what kind of Union to accede to or, put differently, which European identity they are willing and able to identify with, and what timeframe and procedures they realistically think they can commit to as candidates for accession, without running the risk of being rejected, be it only by a single member state refusing ratification.

In view of the current standstill, one wonders whether it was wise to put the cart before the horse and give rise to unwarranted expectations. One also wonders how much time we have left and how we should make use of it. More importantly, what kind of complex diplomatic activity will be required to prepare a resumption of enlargement while avoiding hasty decisions that might damage European construction? Such haste might lead to the possible rejection of countries drawn into ill-fated negotiations and end up creating areas hostile to Europe at our very borders – an outcome diametrically opposed to the original intentions of the Union's governments.

7. Enlargement in 2009

Whatever one's verdict on the Treaty of Lisbon, there is something of a temporary nature to it, as in all compromises with built-in obsolescence, because of the need to accommodate two visions of Europe that are increasingly at odds. It is impossible to tell whether, with time, Europeans will go for: 'one' European Union or several entities and bodies, concentric or partly overlapping, a Russian doll or a set of different levels or different 'densities'. Clearly if the Union were to be reduced to its lowest denominator, a free trade area that would at best lead to a single market, this would mean one kind of pact, whereas a more markedly integrationist model would entail something quite different. Concentric circles and different speeds would require yet another approach, and a variable geometry system or the hub and spoke model of enhanced structural cooperation would entail something else again. Not to mention the additional intricacies of opt-outs and other complex mechanisms. The enlargement policy will have to adapt to these unknown quantities.

Approaches to negotiations and negotiation methods have also undergone considerable changes following the European Council and in view of the Lisbon Treaty. Even though its political significance has been diminished by British reservations, in particular, and its terms of reference are not clearly defined, the 'long' European Council presidency will certainly play a leading role in the resumption of enlargement. Furthermore, the new text of Article 49 of the European Union Treaty states that in regard to eligibility criteria and procedures for accession to the European Union, reference shall be made to the values of the European Union and European states' commitment to promote them. New Article 49 has also been made to include a pre-existing provision whereby the European Parliament and national parliaments shall be informed of membership applications.

There is also a new mention of the accession criteria agreed by the European Council, as defined in Copenhagen in 1993 and modified in Madrid in 1995. These require the presence of stable institutions guaranteeing democracy, the rule of law, human rights, respect for minorities and their protection (the political criterion); the existence of a reliable market economy and the ability to cope with market forces and competitive pressure within the Union (the economic criterion); the need to accept obligations deriving from accession, and in particular the goals of political, economic and monetary union (the community *acquis* criterion). For accession negotiations to begin, the political criterion must be met. Amendment of the criteria by the European Council therefore requires unanimity. These changes will have an impact on the Union's very ability to define its own boundaries and in many respects will provide an implicit response to the call for clear border definition. Within the complex system of international relations, the type of interaction between the High Representative (the de facto Foreign Minister, who will also be Vice-President of the Commission) and the Commissioner responsible for enlargement remains to be seen. The matter is not simply one of form, as it raises the currently very sensitive issue of relations between Council and

Commission, where the balance has so far fluctuated over time depending on the personalities involved and the political positions prevailing in capitals, not to mention the need to adapt in terms of timeliness and geopolitical analysis to the complex relationship between foreign policy and new member admission.

8. After the Lisbon Treaty

Confidence in the ability of candidate countries and their citizens to move closer to the European Union and its political and economic standards seems to suggest that the intermediate stages of the process leading to full membership can be outlined. In order to manage enlargement realistically while avoiding the dual pitfalls of total closure - for which time has probably run out - and of a complete watering down of the European concept into a mere economic area, what is required is an approach that combines stringent compliance with the requirements for full membership in Europe on the part of candidates able and willing to do so, and the possibility of alternative flexible or partial models of participation in the life and activities of the European Union. These could include a vigorous 'neighbourhood' policy as well as initiatives under consideration for the Mediterranean area, an area of free circulation as well as open-ended enhanced cooperation or closed initiative-based groups, all of which, however, would be connected with the core institutional set-up.

Regarding cooperative relations with contiguous regions, the Mediterranean should be returned to its central place in European policies, which currently seem to lean increasingly towards the East and the Caucasus as a result of biased or short-term perspectives likely to involve Europe in areas far removed from its centre of gravity. After the failure of the Barcelona process, a strengthened Mediterranean policy requiring innovative fleshing out to overcome the predictable reservations of many members would restore some balance to Europe's geopolitical position and help the Union consolidate its interests in contiguous regions. The prospect of a structured Euro-Mediterranean organisation begs the question of whether this should entail an alternative status for some of the enlargement candidates so as to connect them in a stable but evolving manner to Europe.

Despite its many limitations, the Lisbon Treaty, which although simplified does preserve the essence of the Rome text, could signal an intention to move together towards greater integration, at least among the able and willing, as long as the good faith of its signatories is more robust than that of those who signed in Rome. For the time being it would appear that we have dispelled the prospect of a neo-sovereigntist victory - with its advocates not only in the East but in Paris as well - and avoided a resurgence of British minimalism.[2] The upcoming British elections will tell us more.

Interests may however yet splinter not only politically but also in terms of greater single market design. Without stronger institutional power, this market might become a wholesale battleground or the premise for an unregulated free-for-all; instead of a market-place coordinated by competition, a locus of substantive anomy that would only benefit the strongest. If that were to occur, launching a two-speed Europe would become the only solution for those who feel more integrated and effective policies need to be developed around the central core represented by the Eurogroup.[3]

---

[2] The positive aspect lies in the fact that the most significant aspects of the Constitutional Treaty have been retained: in particular, the legal personality of the Union, the Minister for Foreign Affairs (although the term used will continue to be High Representative), the European External Action Service, permanent structured cooperation in the defence sector, a stable European Council president, the Charter of Fundamental Rights (despite waivers for the UK), the extension of majority voting, voting modalities (dual majority as of 2014), the hierarchy of rules, the elimination of the 'pillar' system, the new policies.

[3] The negative aspects are first and foremost the definitive abandonment of the term Constitution, of the Union's symbols (flag, hymn, motto) and the various concessions granted to the Poles, the British and the Dutch in order to reach an agreement. Particularly regrettable is the removal from the text of the primacy of Community law and its transfer to a declaration by the Inter-governmental Conference to be attached to the Treaty; the decline in the Commission's powers of initiative following the strengthening of the principle of subsidiarity and the power granted to national parliaments to challenge Commission proposals, greater rigidity in conferring new competences to the Union and the possibility of renationalising common policies. Equally noteworthy: the opt-outs granted to the UK and Ireland in the judicial and home affairs sectors, and the special system whereby the Charter of Fundamental Rights will not be fully applicable with regard to the UK and Poland (although Poland's position might change as a result of recent elections there). The IGC also granted the UK the unprecedented possibility of opting out from the *acquis* of the so-called 'third pillar' if, after a

The common institutional system, Europe's main heritage, will in any case need to provide assurance against an *à la carte* Union, overseeing the special formulas worked out among members and protecting instead the overall grand design. In this perspective, the enlargement policy will to some extent be a litmus test of whether the minimalist outlook or the outlook supporting gradual political integration will prevail. Those institutions that stand at the cusp between membership and various forms of association and which coordinate and provide consistency to the system's various component parts will therefore require strengthening. How the Union moves towards an institutional arrangement that meets today's needs and allows for progress towards integration will in turn be influenced by whichever concept of enlargement prevails – not in abstract terms, but with specific political reference to current candidates and others that can realistically be considered as prospective partners in the European venture.

References

Barzun, J. (2000), *From Dawn to Decadence*, New York: Harper & Collins.

Dlouhy, V. and B. Emmott (2006), "The Vulnerable Success of Central and Eastern Europe", in *Gazeta Wyborcza*, Warsaw, 9 October.

Gress, D. (2004), *From Plato to NATO*, New York: The Free Press.

Le Goff, J. (2003), *L'Europe est-elle née au Moyen Age?*, Paris: Seuil.

Nugent, N. (ed.) (2007), *European Union Enlargement*, The European Union Series, Basingstoke: Palgrave Macmillan.

Viroli, M. (2002), *Republicanism*, New York: Hill and Wang.

---

transition period, the country were to decide against being subject to the power of the Commission and the Court of Justice in this area. Finally, following a French request, competition has been deleted from the list of Union goals and transferred to a protocol annexed to the Treaty. As far as voting procedures are concerned, the dual-majority system – again following Poland's request – will enter into force in 2014, with a transition period running to 2017 and with a strengthened safety net (the so-called Ioannina compromise, to be defined by an ad hoc decision, subject to amendment or revocation by European Council consensus decision).

9. EUROPEAN DEFENCE OR DEFENCE OF EUROPE?

ALESSANDRO PANSA

1. The institutions: A past of great hopes, a future with no illusions

Europe's commitment to defence and security dates back a long way and is also a recent phenomenon.[1]

It dates back a long way as the attempt to create a European Defence Community (EDC) arose in the 1950s in response to US pressure (*plus ça change…*), but was abandoned in 1954 when it failed to obtain ratification from the French Parliament.

It is also recent, however. Following lengthy discussions and the creation of institutions with little political and military importance, it was only in 1999 that the European Security and Defence Policy (ESDP) was created. Even now, European defence capabilities are still being implemented (some are still at the assessment stage).

The concept of European defence is closely linked to the issue of sovereignty, part of which must be ceded in any joint security initiative.

The failure of the EDC – perhaps a too ambitious project for its time – led to the abandonment of attempts to limit the sovereignty of countries and to create an 'organic' European structure using a problem-based approach, much favoured by Jean Monnet. Thus the issue of European defence was not discussed for a long period.

NATO was at that time responsible for European defence, based on the collective defence principle set out in Article 5 of the North Atlantic Treaty. After the EDC failed, the call by the Eisenhower administration for

[1] On this subject, see Missiroli & Pansa (2007).

a European defence angle was superseded by the creation, following a proposal by the UK, of a new organisation: the Western European Union (WEU). The WEU had little political and military importance, but it did create an agency for armaments cooperation, the Western European Armaments Group (WEAG).

The role of NATO has always generated a great deal of debate ever since President Charles de Gaulle's initiative in 1966 to withdraw France from NATO's integrated military command structure in peace time, in support of a European defence structure independent of NATO, while the UK remained loyal to the idea of a North Atlantic alliance. These actions gave rise to the complex situation that still influences European decisions today.

At the end of the Cold War, the changed international situation provided an opportunity to go down the path of a common security and defence policy; it was time to reorganise NATO, which until then had been based on the defence of European territory against the Soviet threat. Moreover, in 1991, the first Gulf War highlighted the inadequacy of European armed forces compared to the technological capabilities and projection of the United States, while the start of the war in the Balkans highlighted the issue of European intervention in crisis-hit areas. The need thus arose for European military capacity to enable it to intervene beyond its borders in support of humanitarian assistance.

The European Union's Maastricht Treaty in 1992 created the Common Foreign and Security Policy (CFSP) – the second pillar of the European Union – as well as the first draft of a defence policy. The CFSP represented a compromise between the positions of France, Germany and the UK. While France and Germany supported the need for a common policy, the UK did not want to create competition with NATO. The result was that the CFSP had many good intentions, limited instruments, but no military capability. The Treaty declared that the CFSP included "the eventual framing of a common defence policy which might in time lead to a common defence" (Article J4). The WEU, meanwhile, was responsible for defence.

To achieve a common defence, NATO had to become more European. The North Atlantic Council that was held in Berlin in June 1996 advocated the creation of a European security and defence identity within NATO. Agreement was reached on measures to grant planning capacity, military capability and the use of NATO commands in favour of the WEU for military missions of crisis management. President Jacques Chirac therefore decided on France's partial return to NATO's integrated military command. But controversy on the appointment of a European commander to the NATO command AFSOUTH in Naples[2] blocked France's definitive return and any hopes that the alliance would become more European.

The WEU therefore again formed the nucleus of a European 'armed wing'. The Amsterdam Treaty in 1997 provided for the incorporation of the WEU into the CFSP, the inclusion of the Petersberg missions (humanitarian and rescue, peace-keeping tasks and tasks of combat forces in crisis management including peace-making) and the possibility of reciprocal cooperation between member states in the armaments sector.

From this came the beginnings of multilateral cooperation in the armaments sector. In July 1998, France, Germany, Italy, the UK, Spain and Sweden signed a Letter of Intent with the aim of restructuring the aerospace and defence sector; while in September 1998, France, Germany, Italy and the UK founded the Organisation for Joint Armaments Cooperation (OCCAR) to manage joint industrial projects.

The arrival of Tony Blair in Downing Street in 1997 paved the way for a reconciliation with France and a more credible European defence policy, given that the new British prime minister seemed to be in favour of European integration, which he considered an unstoppable phenomenon.

The first step towards a European Security and Defence Policy was taken at the Franco-British summit at Saint Malo in December 1998, where it was proposed that the EU must have the capacity for autonomous action, backed up by military forces, in order to respond to international crises. The word "autonomous" was chosen as a compromise between the positions of France ("independent") and Britain ("complementary to NATO").

There was, however, agreement on one issue: Europe needed a strong, competitive industrial and technological defence base. The agreement between France and the UK was a necessary but not sufficient condition: external events also contributed to the creation of a defence policy.

---

[2] See Dassù & Menotti (1997).

1999 was a decisive year. NATO intervened in Kosovo in March, and the failure of the Rambouillet agreement again convinced Europeans that the capacity to use military intervention as well as diplomacy was needed. The aerial campaign once again showed how Europe as a whole was technologically inferior to the US.

The Cologne European Council meeting in June established the first principles of the ESDP, incorporating the decisions taken in April at the North Atlantic Council in Washington, which – as previously established for the WEU in Berlin in 1996 – extended access to NATO capacity by the Union for autonomous European[3] missions according to the formula subsequently renamed the 'Berlin Plus'.

Concrete objectives for autonomous capacity were established at the Helsinki European Council meeting in December 1999: the Helsinki Headline Goal required member states to make 60,000 personnel available for Petersberg missions by 2003.

The ESDP inherited the WEU's crisis management systems. In October, as stipulated by the Amsterdam Treaty (Article J8), Javier Solana was appointed Secretary-General of the Council and High Representative of the EU for the CFSP. He also became Secretary-General of the WEU. It was decided that the WEU would cease its activities by July 2001 and transfer to the European Union its functions and organisations, with the exception of the WEAG, which would remain active for the time being.

This development began to meet with early success: in the 'Force catalogue' – prepared at the conference on military deployment in November 2000 – some 100,000 men, well in excess of the stipulated 60,000, were made available by the member states for the Helsinki objectives. In December 2000, the French Presidency approved the Treaty of Nice, and defined the Berlin Plus agreements and the politico-military structures of the ESDP. The Capabilities Improvement Conference of November 2001 instituted a European Capability Action Plan (ECAP) to bridge the gaps in military capacity, thereby rationalising member states' defence programmes.

---

[3] *Washington Summit Communiqué*, NAC-S(99) 64 of 24 April 1999 (available on the website www.nato.int).

The year 2003 was critical for the ESDP. In January the first mission (the European Union Police Mission, or EUPM, in Bosnia-Herzegovina) was launched, while the start of the first military mission (Concordia in Macedonia) in March was made possible by the implementation of the entire package of Berlin Plus agreements via a framework agreement contained in an exchange of correspondence with NATO. However, in order to respect the civilian nature of the organisation and avoid controversy between member states, most of the ESDP's missions are still non-military, such as police missions or the restoration of the rule of law.[4]

The European Council of December 2003, which ended the six-month term of the Italian Presidency, was a decisive moment for the future of the ESDP, which saw the adoption of the European security strategy, "A secure Europe in a better world", drafted by the Solana administration. This represented a genuine strategic conception of the identification of scenarios, threats, objectives and concepts for the ESDP.

It is opportune to note that this Council is mainly associated with the breakdown in negotiations to finalise the Constitutional Treaty. The unsuccessful attempts to implement the treaty have parallels with the EDC. As is well known, the treaty was redrafted by the European Convention (Convention on the Future of Europe) and amended by the member states at the Intergovernmental Conference but was not approved, as anticipated, by the December Council. It was then adopted in June 2004, only to be rejected by the French and Dutch referenda in 2005. Following a period of reflection of around two years, a new Reform Treaty was signed in Lisbon in December 2007. The Treaty of Lisbon will come into force in December 2009.

The Treaty of Lisbon envisages the convergence of national defence policies: member states no longer have the objective of developing a common military capacity, but must make their national military capabilities available to the European Union (Article 28A). The Treaty is strongly inter-governmental; national security, in particular, is considered to be the exclusive responsibility of individual countries.

---

[4] See Alcaro (2006). For an up-to-date list of ESDP missions, see the Council's website (www.consilium.eu).

The Treaty of Lisbon seems to accord a greater role to NATO at the expense of autonomous defence. NATO is still the bedrock of a common defence for the allied countries. The Berlin Plus agreements are the pillar of cooperation between NATO and the EU, and the Union's best tool for implementing a common defence and contributing to the restructuring of NATO.

The Treaty of Lisbon preserves the main provisions of the ESDP stipulated by the Constitutional Treaty, which are currently being implemented by means of permanent structured partnerships such as battle groups (tactical groups) and the European Defence Agency.

The idea of battle groups was first proposed in February 2004 by the British, French and Germans as a package of autonomous multinational forces of around 1,500 men to lead out-of-theatre military missions at the request of the UN. Battle groups became operational in January 2007, and the concept has been incorporated into the 2010 Headline Goal, the current objective for military capabilities.

The European Defence Agency (EDA) – established by a Joint Action of the Council of Ministers on 12 July 2004 – is tasked with supporting member states in their efforts to improve European defence capabilities to bridge any gaps identified by ECAP; to promote research and technology, and to harmonise European purchasing, armaments policy and military procurement. The Agency took over all the activities of the WEAG, which ceased operations in 2005. It also liaises with OCCAR.

Is the Treaty of Lisbon a step backwards compared to previous decisions? From a decision-making and legislative point of view, this is undoubtedly the case. It talks about a common defence and 'sharing' security initiatives.

But it looks like a compromise – perhaps the only one possible – between countries that have gradually developed differing perceptions of the role, and even the 'essence', of Europe. It may be the only way forward at a time when Europe seems less likely to be able to 'lead' Europe than in the 1990s.

However, initiatives such as the creation of the European Defence Agency are one of the positive results in recent years on the issue of defence. As we will go on to see, this Agency can effectively be considered the fulcrum around which a common military capacity can be built.

The Agency attempted to create a European defence procurement market - using the 2005 procurement code of conduct - thereby increasing competition and improving transparency in European procurement.[5] The Agency acts to improve the defence industrial and technological base, both by preparing projects and strategies for research and technology and through funding programmes, such as the Joint Investment Programme on Force Protection, which is currently the only major joint programme. Many of the initiatives proposed in the EDA's documents remain on paper.

The European Commission has now issued an interpretative Communication on Article 296 of the Commission's paper[6] - intended to reduce the number of restrictions on competition that member states apply in the sector, under the article - and in December 2007, published the anticipated Communication on the defence package, the effects of which have still to be seen.

The EU is finding its way again, but the European defence industry must develop the military and technological capacity required.

2. The industry: Oligopoly, foreign policy and internationalisation

Where and how does the European defence industry fit in the political and institutional context that we have described? Does it have a future, whether as a vital component of security policies or as an important part of Europe's economic and industrial landscape? And if it does, under what conditions?

To answer these questions, we have to first of all understand what we are talking about: we should clarify immediately that the term 'European industry' is an expression more of hope than of reality, as otherwise we would talk about the 'industry of European countries'. An industry that has the characteristics of an oligopoly: 70% of defence systems worldwide (which represent 1.2% of global GDP, or just over €400 billion in 2006) are produced by the ten largest industrial groups, which operate in an environment that is at the same time both cooperative and competitive,

---

[5] The initial impetus came from the EU's Green Paper, "Defence Procurement" published by the European Commission, COM(2004) 608 def., 23 September 2004.

[6] European Commission, European Commission Interpretative Communication on the application of Article 296 of the EC paper on defence procurement SEC(2006) 1554; SEC(2006) 1555; COM/2006/0779 (definitive), 7 December 2006.

especially in Europe. Companies work together to develop technology and products, but compete when marketing them.

Like all oligopolies, the defence sector has high barriers to entry. These can be technological (acquiring expertise is a long and complex process); financial (huge resources are required to develop, manufacture and market products); and political/regulatory, since the authorisation procedures, necessary to operate and to export, and contract negotiations require extended timescales, as well as costly skills and resources. In addition, the more powerful members of the oligopoly adopt strategies to prevent new businesses entering the market (including acquisitions) or assuming important roles and positions, which can lead to changes in the rules of the game, and force the incumbents to review their manufacturing and investment decisions. There are many such examples in the defence industry.

Barriers to exit are equally significant. These are also financial in character (adequate returns on investment in the sector are only realised in the medium to long term) but also political/regulatory: a manufacturer of products relating to national security - financed by public funding over many years - is not in a position to exit the industry without incurring costs. Similarly, it is inconceivable that a company's shareholding structure would be changed without formal and/or informal checks being undertaken by the public administration.

The relationship with the public administration does not end there. Since the end of the 19th century, the energy and defence sectors have continually been the most important, listened-to and influential partners of the governments of industrialised countries. But, while in the past, government decisions and budgetary policies influenced industry, the comparatively recent globalisation of production and the growing informational asymmetry associated with increasing technological complexity (which we will discuss later) mean that the sector is less influenced by political decisions and more able to influence them. This is particularly important for Europe, where industry can influence the decision at either national or EU level.

The relationship with the public administration does not end there.

The relationship between industry, defence and industrial foreign policy is equally important for the future of the EU.

The use of companies as a foreign policy tool by the governments of large countries is well-known. Moreover, a strong, cohesive industrial structure is clearly a powerful international policy tool. Medium-sized countries with a significant industrial base are a very interesting case. Foreign policy in these countries is, of course, based on compliance with treaties, the management of partnerships and participation in international initiatives: but it consists to a large extent of safeguarding the international economic and industrial interests of its companies - so much so that the foreign policy of these countries could be described as "made by multinationals, backed to the hilt by their governments".[7]

The body of interests to be safeguarded thus becomes crucial, and the foreign policy of a country will vary according to the industrial nature of its economy, and its international influence and role. The more technologically advanced a country's industry is and the greater its international influence, the more the country's industrial foreign policy is (or should be) geared towards its companies in an attempt to influence the technological standards of other economies, thereby having a lasting influence not only on the production system of other industrialised countries, but also more generally on the development model. This creates a virtuous circle between the technological development process, and a country's industrial policy and foreign policy.

In this context, the importance of the defence industry lies as much in its technological content as in the fact that its activity relates to a sector that retains its own decision-making and technological models of production systems, especially defence and foreign policy, long-term decisions and models that could only be abandoned at great cost.

The defence industry is therefore a crucial element of a country's industrial foreign policy; but it is equally important for the development of production systems in advanced economies, given its contribution to a country's technological assets. The ratio between R&D activity and revenues in the industry is around 8%. Although not the biggest investor in relative terms, the pharmaceutical industry is the only one that invests more heavily than defence in absolute terms.[8] This shows the importance of

---

[7] See De Cecco (1998).

[8] In the sense that sectors with a higher ratio between R&D and sales revenues post lower revenues in absolute terms than the defence industry.

the absolute value of investment in research by defence companies, an importance that is increasing due to the growing significance of dual-use technology that has both military and civilian applications.

Moreover, there is a technology gap of 10 to 20 years biased towards the West compared to defence systems developed in the rest of the world. Some commentators maintain for example that Chinese military technology is 20-30 years behind that of Europe and the US.[9] Such a gap, together with the low price elasticity of high-tech goods, makes defence-industry products one of possibly the few areas where, in the long term, Western economies enjoy a clear competitive advantage in exports compared to the aggressive production and marketing of emerging economies.

The future influence and role of Europe's security industry will also depend on its ability to successfully ride out the 'denationalisation' of the sector at various levels (technological, commercial, manufacturing and shareholding), a process involving many factors: some exogenous and others largely endogenous. Exogenous factors include the spread of technology and changes in global demand for military equipment, while trends in European military procurement policies would fall into the latter category.

Up until the fairly recent past, the development of military technology took place in locations and under conditions that allowed limits to be placed on its use and forced innovation in the civilian field to take a secondary role to that in the defence sector. The expansion of scientific and technological expertise, the significant investment in technology in civil industries (e.g. semiconductors, telecommunications, bio-engineering and bio-genetics) and the increase in the skills base in many countries - due both to the relocation process in some important sectors and the training of new classes of technicians and scientists - set in motion the gradual spread of military technology and a growing fusion of military and civil technology. The much-feted concept of 'dual technology' is a clear admission that military technology is no longer circumscribed knowledge.

Running alongside the 'internationalisation' of know-how is the growing importance of changing global demand for military products. Estimates agree on the growth of the latter, with some analysts putting the

[9] See Bitzinger (2005) and also Stokes (1999).

real annual rate at 1.5-2% over the long term (from now until 2035-40). But the main boost to growth in demand will come not from Europe or the US but from two other groups of countries. The first is made up of the oil-producing nations (in the Middle East and Asia) that have to balance a growing perception of geo-political instability with substantial trade surpluses generated by high oil prices. The second group comprises the three big non-Western economies: Russia, India and China. Budgets for defence equipment are growing at more than double the rate in these countries than in Europe and the US. Clearly, they are trying to secure Western industrial technology through supply contracts, the acquisition of shareholdings and the creation of joint companies.

The situation is therefore changing rather quickly. The defence industry will never be global in terms of product standardisation or the structure and localisation of activity: the technology and goods it develops are considered too sensitive to be produced and marketed in the same way to all clients. But the sector has rapidly evolved towards a 'multi-domestic' model, in which although there are still significant restrictions on the circulation of technology and other limits on production standardisation, companies derive an increasingly large share of orders from overseas customers and tend to localise (if not transfer) some of their operations to commercially attractive economies (i.e. to countries with large defence systems budgets), which also have the appropriate infrastructure and high-quality human resources.

The defence industry is thus experiencing significant and rapid growth in competition (a word that was virtually unknown in that sector until a few years ago) with companies facing pressure on prices, margins and financial structures. In order to compete effectively, companies must first obtain economies of scale and scope in the use of their manufacturing base and technology (the home-oriented policies of the 19th century, known as the *piede di casa,* still have some importance, despite globalisation). Secondly, they must secure adequate access to the capital markets required to finance strategic and industrial projects, which owing to their size and technological content, are becoming increasingly costly. Such opportunities are not open to European industry.

3. Europe: Cooperation, inefficiency and nationalism

Many commentators maintain that European investment in defence systems is insufficient, and there are probably good reasons to believe this.

Europe as a whole has the largest budget for investment in defence systems in the world after the US (over €60 billion in 2008), but the industry is not able to take full advantage of this due to the limited integration of the procurement activities of the individual countries, which still make the decisions and hold the purse-strings. In reality, the maintenance of cost centres that are both limited in their financial capabilities and largely independent from each other accentuates the effects of the relatively scarce resources. The Centre for Defence Economics at the University of York estimates that if the investment decisions of the six main EU countries were integrated, savings of around €6 billion a year, or 13.5% of Europe's total budget for 2005, could be achieved: it would be as if Germany doubled its investment in one fell swoop. It is by no means certain that the problem could be solved through multilateral programmes, if it is true, as the Swedish defence minister maintains, that defence programmes managed by more than three countries are generally less efficient.[10] Estimates put efficiency losses associated with the different procurement systems and the product differentiation required in multilateral programmes at around 23% of output cost when two parties are involved in procurement. The figure jumps to 30% when there are three. This is due both to the different configurations required for the same product by individual countries and the varied remuneration systems of production companies. The UK, for example, uses 'cost plus' criteria aimed at minimising the business risk borne by the contractor, which in turn will have fairly low profit margins, after allocating a share of the profits to the client. Conversely, continental European countries generally use 'fixed price' methods of remuneration, which can theoretically lead to higher income for contractors in return for a greater assumption of risk.

The disadvantages of the lack of integration (or the economic advantages of a possible greater integration) therefore seem obvious. First and foremost, it would lead to a more efficient use of financial resources. The average return on invested capital for European companies is around 12%, which is higher than their cost of capital (8.5%) but lower than that of their US competitors, whose average return is 16% and cost of capital around 8%. This gap is partly due to the fact that US companies are able to take relatively greater advantage of existing economies of scale in the

[10] See Pansa (2002).

industry and partly because they do not have to find complex and costly corporate structural solutions or accept sometimes inefficient compromises in production structures in order to manage the funds of several countries relating to specific programmes.

Moreover, the relatively limited return on assets means that it is less efficient for European companies to obtain funding from the financial markets. In reality, this fundamental springboard for development is not generally accessible to many European defence companies, as their shareholder structures do not allow them to raise large amounts of risk capital on the market. This is often the norm with government-owned or family-run companies, but is even more specific to French companies (the cornerstone of any likely reorganisation of European industry), which are bound by a shareholder structure chiefly designed to prevent them from being taken over.

The integration of both procurement and industrial activity is a vital element for any European ambitions regarding defence policies. It goes without saying that this could not be efficiently undertaken without the integration of the armed forces. But such integration could only occur if the technology required for defence products could be made available to all. What's more, over and above the incentives arising from the actions of companies (the integration of which have facilitated greater progress than any policy since 2002), the effective completion of such a process is highly political. As such, developments are not always linear, but subject to political and regulatory resistance.[11]

While it is true that the industry today seems more proactive than policy in pushing for integration – and that due in no small measure to the combination of technological advances and the discipline imposed by the financial markets on listed companies – it has not always been this way. In the 1990s, European policy stimulated the integration and restructuring of an industry that to all intents and purposes was still self-sufficient: the Franco-British Joint Declaration on European Defence in Saint-Malo (December 1998) and the declaration of the European Council in Helsinki (December 1999) seemed to have ratified the Europeanisation of EU countries' military capabilities that would have inevitable repercussions on

[11] For an analysis of the mechanisms that determine these processes, see Eliassen & Sitter (2002).

industry. It seemed as if Europe was about to launch that virtuous circle of *"active foreign policy – public investment – manufacturing and technological expertise"*, which until then had only worked in the United States. An active foreign policy requires the public administration to plough huge investment into the defence sector, investment that will fuel the growth of a country's technological expertise, enabling it to strengthen itself against other countries, play a more important role on the international stage and therefore be more involved in international relations. This process did not take place.

4. Governments, institutions and investors: A changing role

If integration and restructuring initiatives today seem to be more in the hands of industry than politicians, this is not only due to political inertia, but also to structural developments that are rapidly changing the role of the players involved in the relationship between the defence industry, public administrations and financial markets in Europe. It is therefore opportune to reflect on possible future developments.

At first glance it might seem strange that European governments will see their role gradually diminish over the medium term. The main reasons for this are four-fold: the informational asymmetry stemming from increasingly complex technology and the risk of making decisions on the basis of an inadequate information set; the cost of this technology and the budgetary difficulties that individual European countries (including even France and the UK, the two biggest investors in defence systems) will face in financing its development; the gradual internationalisation of the market and the greater influence that foreign interests will have on companies' decision-making as a result; and the trend towards consolidation and bigger shareholder bases. In this case the adage "strength in union" is more appropriate than ever: the European Union could play a greater role to compensate for the diminishing influence of individual countries.

The military capabilities required for a joint defence policy cannot be built overnight. The starting point must of course be a joint technology base: this could be the role of the European Union. The decision to provide the European Defence Agency with sufficient funds to undertake the kind of work performed by the US Defense Advanced Research Projects Agency (DARPA) – responsible for identifying civil or military technologies that could be used for national security and promoting their development – would represent a significant turning point both in procurement (for the first time a supranational European body would operate alongside the procurement bodies of individual countries) and in respect of the EU's budget, which would have a new 'defence' category.

Beyond financial considerations, if the EU could influence investment and strategic decisions by directly allocating funds to defence-related activities, it would have a direct role in strengthening and restructuring the industry, and have bargaining power with member states.

So why is this not happening? It is not possible to identify a single reason for this umpteenth missed opportunity, but clearly legal and regulatory difficulties, European bureaucratic inertia and vested interests played their part. But the fact remains that if a defence category were effectively added to the EU's accounts and the EDA were to assume a role, this could have significant consequences both on the relative influence of individual European countries on defence policy (individual national budgets would become less important over time) and on arms procurement decision-making. The existence of a European institution with financial powers would require an increase in joint investment decisions, and the countries with the greatest propensity to spend would be partly affected by it. The UK and French approaches to defence industrial policy (which we will refer to later) show how difficult it would be for these countries, in reality and behind the public declarations, to accept the effective launch of a European arms procurement policy. Thus there is a risk that the Agency, far from becoming a driver for European technological development, would join the list of useless and expensive EU bodies.

There is, however, another initiative that could facilitate the integration of European defence and also significantly strengthen the industry. Moreover, it is directly linked to individual countries' budgets: the national accounting criteria currently established in Europe through Eurostat (and confirmed by a resolution in March 2006) includes defence systems investment in current expenditure. Apart from being questionable at a conceptual level (military aircraft, warships or cost control systems are not exactly comparable to photocopiers or service cars), it does not permit the costs of purchasing goods with a period of use not normally less than 15-20 years to be allocated to more than one financial year. Methods of accounting more appropriate to the nature of and criteria for the development, production and use of military vehicles, which often have fairly lengthy timescales and considerable research costs, could, and in our opinion should, be introduced. These different accounting systems would have a significant impact on both the cost borne by the public purse in any one year and the option to introduce funding systems for defence investment that would make it possible to fully exploit available procurement resources without recourse to creative accounting of dubious acceptability. Once again, this would assist the countries that have the most difficulty in increasing their budgets for military equipment, and hence the entire procurement system.

In recent years, private equity funds also seemed to be able to play a role in the European defence industry. These investors were supposed to bring a more scrupulous application of financial discipline and management criteria strictly geared towards the creation of value - an important element for an industry that still seems, on many fronts, to be much less efficient than a more business-like management would allow.

5. Industrial structures, control systems and the equity market

But here again, we believe that the equities market will play the lead role in the future of the European defence industry, regardless of its performance and its short- and medium-term trends. This might seem a strange and risky assertion, considering that until a few years ago, the majority of defence companies in EU countries were not listed and generally had no relationship with the capital markets, but we don't think it is.

In Europe, there are two fairly typical models - the UK and the French model. The UK model is extremely pragmatic and based essentially on three principles: collaboration between companies makes sense only to the extent that it enables them to develop and manufacture competitive defence systems; the state must remain outside companies' shareholding structures, or it would be inconceivable to talk about integration between European companies. In this scenario, the identity of the UK companies is relatively unimportant; it is much more important that they develop research, technology and products on UK territory. (One wonders, moreover, whether this British pragmatism hides not only an unwillingness to take part in European aggregation but also a desire to prevent this from happening and the EU having a greater influence than it does currently on procurement policy.) Conversely, the French approach, which we could call 'dominant autosegregation' or 'competitive autonomy', is based on a labyrinthine network of defence company shareholder structures, which seems to have been created to ensure that the state retains control of the companies and at the same time prevents them being taken over. French industry seems willing to participate only in mergers that allow it to gain control of foreign assets without sharing control of its own, and furthermore, does not allow overseas strategic investors to hold a significant stake in the capital of its own companies. This approach is not conducive to integration, especially since the French system is undoubtedly the cornerstone, in terms of size and technology, of virtually any restructuring or consolidation of European industry. The French attitude to maintain a strict control over its defence industry has recently increased, as a response to the financial and economic crisis.

The equities market plays an important role in both models: managing changes in ownership and management in the UK case, and ensuring sufficient liquidity for investment without jeopardising the shareholder structure in the French model. But only an expansion of this role could ensure a successful long-term future for European industry.

The structure of the industry does not require the government to be a shareholder in sector companies in order to control one of the country's vital resources, national security. The methods of assigning contracts (favouring companies that maintain or plough investment into the country), their financial structure, the availability of funds and public structures (or funding by the public sector) for the development of technology are also incentives to maintain and expand the national industrial base. The UK ministry of defence, for example, has adopted a definition of national defence industry on the basis of the place where the technology was developed, the site of the intellectual property, the location of new jobs and the destination of investment. This definition to a large extent excludes companies' ownership structure.[12]

Conversely, the distribution of most (if not all) of European defence companies' capital on the market - this is what is meant by the "greater role of the market" - could promote a different, more efficient and stronger industry structure, without diminishing the indirect control that the public administration has over them. This could lead to more efficient (albeit not necessarily more generous) financing of companies' growth, a strengthening of the financial discipline to which they are subject and a drive to implement streamlined processes of restructuring and integration.

---

[12] See UK Ministry of Defence (2002).

The effects of an expansion of the shareholding base would be seen both in companies' business structures and in their monitoring and control criteria.

From the first point of view, with stricter financial control stemming from an increase in 'public company' status, companies vie for leadership in their reference markets. In the defence sector, leadership can only be achieved through technological superiority and the ability to exploit economies of scale and associated economies of scope. By manufacturing goods with a high technology content, companies can effectively reduce the price elasticity of such goods, thereby increasing profit margins and the cash flow available for investment aimed at strengthening technological leadership, which enabled them to generate such investment in the first place. It is therefore likely that we are seeing a concentration of companies in those areas that allow better capital allocation alongside a gradual reduction of their activities in sectors where an allocation does not optimise the risk/return profile of the asset portfolio. Defence companies, in other words, will tend to "do fewer things" but will have greater influence in sectors in which they will maintain a presence.

The expansion of the shareholder base and the ability to take over companies would also root out at source the problem of the control of assets that, in today's climate, is a real concern for some European countries, and especially for the French industrial system. The absence of key shareholders would facilitate company mergers, triggering a process of greater integration between national procurement procedures, a process that, in order to be efficient and effective, also requires considerable political will. This would also benefit the managerial structure. Here too, increased competition in the leadership of companies could facilitate innovation and changes in a sector that is somewhat resistant to integration with other industries, and enable senior managers to be brought in from outside.

Put simply, European industry will be able to operate between four extremes: on the one hand consolidation versus specialisation; and on the other, tight control versus a more open and dynamic shareholder base. While different combinations of industrial and shareholder structure would theoretically be possible (including a powerful process of consolidation that is not only stable but completely 'closed'), it is likely (we might even say "to be hoped") that companies will become increasingly specialised, open their ownership structure and subsequently regroup by production sector or by technology, with a further expansion of the shareholder base.

Are there dangers inherent in this potential opening up of the market and reduction of power currently held by the controlling shareholders, which are often public or at least influenced by the will of the public administration? Is there not a risk in letting financial democracy determine the ownership structure of companies that develop and own technology that is important for the security of a country, and at least 10 to 20 years ahead of that of some countries, which harbour foreign policy ambitions and therefore have an interest in undertaking active defence policies?

We don't think so. Or rather, we think that if there is a risk, it's one worth taking, essentially for two reasons. The first is, strictly speaking, defensive: control of specific technologies - and increasingly the control of their use - is clearly important, but there are many formal and informal tools with which to achieve it, other than the rigidity of the ownership structure. We referred to this above. In this sense, proposals to institute procedures to limit the investment of important financial players from outside the EU do not seem appropriate. The change in the conditions of financial democracy - one of the key competitive advantages of Western economies - which would enable this, would go in tandem with an approach that would maintain the status quo in the defence industry, which is structurally inefficient (too nationalistic and fragmented) and unstable in terms of shareholder base.

The second reason is more prophetic. Perhaps only the transfer of defence companies' control mechanisms to the market can usher in a phase of definitive industry reorganisation (following that which occurred at the beginning of the century), encouraging fundamental integration, which would create companies of a sufficient size, asset base and technological expertise to achieve a position of leadership, and foster the launch of pan-European defence policies.

Finally, in this environment, the role of the sovereign wealth funds as a potential shareholders of some defence or, more general, high-tech companies could be considered more an opportunity than a risk. These institutions have until now showed more an interest towards financial returns of their investments (actually very limited in the most recent periods) than the intention to play a more "political role" in the companies where they are shareholders. Their role as providers of capital as well as of business opportunities in their home countries could well be compatible, through an adequate system of regulations and corporate governance provisions, with either the protection of the technology or the independence of the companies.

References

Alcaro, R. (ed.) (2006), *Le Missioni PESD Operazioni, strutture, capacità* (EDSP Missions: Operations, systems, capabilities), IAI Research Department of the Italian Senate, No. 49, July.

Bitzinger, M. (2005), "The PRCs Defense Industry: Reform without Improvement", *China Brief*, Vol. V, No. 6, 15 March.

Dassù, M. and R. Menotti (1997), "The Ratification of NATO Enlargement – The Case of Italy", proceedings of the Conference on NATO Enlargement: The National Debates over Ratification, 7 October.

De Cecco, M. (1998), *L'oro di Europa. Monete, economia e politica nei nuovi scenari mondiali* (Europe's gold), Roma: Donzelli.

Eliassen, K.A. and N. Sitter (2002), *Between Regulation and Competition: Hard and Soft Resistance to Europeanisation in the Financial Services and Defence Sector*, Centre for European and Asian Studies, Norwegian School of Management, Oslo, June.

Missiroli, A. and A. Pansa (2007), *L'Europa della difesa*, Genoa: Il Melangolo.

Pansa, A. (2002), *European Defence Procurement and Industrial Policy: The case for Sweden*, Norwegian School of Management.

Stokes, M.A. (1999), *China's Strategic Modernization: Implications for the United States*, Strategic Studies Institute, U.S. Army War College.

UK Ministry of Defence (2002), *Defence Industrial Policy*, Ministry of Defence Policy Paper No. 5, October.

10. EUROPE AND GLOBAL ECONOMIC GOVERNANCE AFTER THE CRISIS

PIER CARLO PADOAN

Even before the global crisis, all long-term scenarios confirmed that over the next 15 to 20 years, Europe's relative economic weight would shrink as that of new emerging economies – China, India, Russia, Brazil (the so-called BRICS) rose. The crisis has done nothing to alter this scenario, but it has made clear that the global economy is suffering from a governance gap.

The crisis itself is proof of this statement, and is the result of both market and policy failure. The international macroeconomic aspect of such a twin failure is reflected in the inability to address the global payment imbalances that have accumulated over a decade or so, (also) in the belief that markets could finance such widening imbalances, thanks to their resilience and efficiency. The post-crisis reconstruction requires a serious reconsideration of how to deal with global macroeconomic imbalances, now and in the future, and how to maintain the global economy on a balanced and sustainable growth path through cooperation among all major players, including the large emerging economies. To this effect, in addition to macroeconomic governance, trade and capital market openness and stability are essential prerequisites for a stronger global governance, as has been stated repeatedly by the G8 and G20 summits. Is Europe willing and able to contribute actively to meeting this challenge?

1. The breakdown of Bretton Woods II and beyond

Most crises are drivers of change because they often lead to the breakdown of key mechanisms and institutions and create the need for new ones. The crisis that started in the US subprime mortgage market is the most severe in eight decades and is also truly global. When it ends, the international economy will never be the same again.

The crisis has destroyed the fundamentals of the so-called 'Bretton Woods II model' (BWII) on which global growth has been based for the past decade or so. In the BWII world, excess savings in emerging economies, including oil-producing countries, were reinvested in the centre of the system, as the US economy was considered the 'safe haven' par excellence. The crisis has destroyed the credibility of the centre and, with it, the main engine of growth and the financing of growth. It is highly unrealistic, not to say unthinkable, that in the foreseeable future the main engine of global growth will still be US household demand, fuelled by sophisticated but opaque financial instruments.

Growth will resume after the global recession but it will most likely be a structurally lower growth. More importantly, global growth will be driven by several engines rather than by a single engine, and each of these engines will be individually less powerful than the one that has collapsed, as well as being partially disconnected from the others. Household demand in the US will be partly replaced by American exports driven by a weaker dollar, and also by the still powerful US productivity engine. It remains to be seen if US investment and innovation will be able to generate, at least in part, a productivity cycle as long and intense as the one that lay behind the 'new economy' of the 1990s.

One key question is whether the BRICS will move into the driver's seat of the world economy and become global engines of growth. As mentioned above, long-term projections see China and India (although much less so) as the top economies 20 to 30 years from now. But most of these projections extrapolate into the future a scenario that may no longer be there; a relatively stable world economy in which global markets are open, economic integration continues to progress and there is no major crisis. For this scenario to materialise, the post-BWII economy will have to be based on two pillars – more domestic demand in emerging economies and more 'investment integration' globally.

Concerning the first pillar, emerging economies both large and small will, sooner or later, have to face the challenge of their own internal transformations as domestic demand will have to be given more space and export-led growth will be less relevant. This transformation will need to be accompanied by high and sustained growth rates; necessary conditions for these countries to raise the standard of living of a large part of their populations who still live below the poverty line. Needless to say, such a transformation will be even more demanding politically than economically.

The 'investment integration' pillar will have to offer a major contribution to global growth. In BWII excess investment in the US led to America's growing current account deficit, while excess savings led to the accumulation of international reserves in many emerging Asian economies and in oil-producing countries. The scenario that worries countries like China is the risk that their reserves will lose value because of the US dollar's depreciation and/or capital losses in the US treasury market. The request for reform of the international monetary system and the creation of reserve currencies as alternatives to the dollar - something increasingly suggested by top Chinese officials - reflects this very real concern.

But this is only part of the story. A look at gross rather than net capital flows shows that in BWII, while China exports capital that is invested in US financial markets, it also imports capital from the US and elsewhere that adds to its physical, knowledge, and human capital resources. China has become a fast-growing base for international R&D and a key component of global value and innovation chains, which could not have taken place without a massive inflow of capital from the world's advanced economies. Much the same can be said of India and a number of other Asian economies. A more sophisticated interpretation of the BWII growth model therefore suggests that the massive investment of Chinese reserves in US Treasury bills is a way of providing 'collateral' so as to attract the levels of investment from American and other multinational companies in China, which are essential to sustaining its high per capita GDP growth. This interpretation also underpins the idea that China sees its own best interest in the long-term profitability of its invested resources, not in short-term gains. Of course, this works both ways, as China increasingly values long-term capital outflows, as can be seen in the increasingly important role of its Sovereign Wealth Funds. These, in China as in other emerging economies, are instrumental in directing huge reserves towards long-term investment and thus boosting the long-term growth rate.

A sustained long-term growth rate of the Chinese and other Asian economies is fully consistent with a post-BWII model, where stronger growth in emerging Asia would compensate for lower growth in the US, especially if increased productivity growth in China is accompanied by a gradual slackening of the propensity to save. This largely reflects structural rather than short-term factors as the high-saving propensity of Chinese households reflects the need to counter the absence of social protection. And the high-saving propensity of companies reflects the inadequacy of

China's domestic financial sector, which has led to high levels of retained profits.

What about Europe? During the BWII years Europe was a slow-growth economy, which could grow even more slowly in the future. The massive use of fiscal measures to deal with the last financial emergency and with the recession loosening fiscal disciplines, the sustainability of long-term debt will be made more difficult still, as is also the case in the US. More flexibility in the application of the EU's Stability and Growth Pact is welcome and needed, but there is a risk that the credibility it has earned over the past decade could evaporate. On the other hand, a long-term European growth strategy based on a revamped and 'green' Single Market, as well as the Lisbon Agenda for competitiveness, has yet to be implemented to any large extent. Such a strategy could benefit greatly from a more open global investment regime encouraging both inward and outward long term capital flows.

In a post-BWII scenario, we could and should see smaller global imbalances, and smaller current account deficits and surpluses in the US and China respectively, but we might also see larger gross capital flows between the world's main economic regions. These flows would transfer both physical and knowledge capital and thus drive productivity growth on a global scale. This would be all the more so if climate-related and green technologies were transferred much more than they are at present. But to be really effective, these gross flows would have to be complemented by flows of goods and services, whose role in a knowledge-driven economy is essential. Open markets will be more important than ever.

What international institutions will we need to support a post-BWII world? The post-crisis response led by the G20 includes a commitment to major reform of the IMF and a strengthening of the Financial Stability Board (formerly the Financial Stability Forum). The IMF has received substantial additional resources, and its governance is to be reformed to give more room to the emerging economies. It will also carry out, together with the FSB, the enhanced monitoring of systemic stability. The FSB is leading the reform of the regulation and supervision of the financial system, even though it remains to be seen whether this will lead to a truly global framework. But this may not be enough. If not, the BWII system will have to rely, even more so than in the past, on open markets for both trade and investment, which will also require stronger global governance and stronger institutions.

A stronger post-BWII world is in the interests of Europe. How can Europe contribute to the post-BWII world, and what role should Europe play in reformed international institutions?

2. Keeping markets open in investment and trade

The post-BWII world should be based on more open economies and on stronger long-term capital flows. For this to happen we need a 'global investment regime' based on shared regulation and standards related to investment activity so as to complement the FSB's sound 'financial regime' and the IMF's stable 'macroeconomic regime'. Investment will go where there is a transparent relationship with governments and where the cost of doing business is low, where sound corporate governance prevails, where there is no corruption, where reliable and possibly cheap skills are available, where a level playing field does not discriminate against foreign companies, where competition policy lowers barriers to entry and supports innovation and where a free flow of goods and services complements investment flows.

But such a regime does not yet exist globally, and an agreement between all major economies, both developed and emerging, on these points still needs to be established. Such a regime would require an institutional framework to update and monitor rules and standards that are shared by all the major players. From this point of view, what is needed for the post-BWII world is an enlarged and reinforced OECD, for the OECD is the only international organisation that brings together all the expertise needed for a global investment regime to operate effectively, whether alone or in collaboration with other international organisations. The present-day OECD would clearly have to expand its membership to all major emerging economies so that a new regime can be built on a shared view of the post-BWII world. Europe should act forcefully to expand the role and membership of the OECD.

Let us turn to trade. At the time of writing, we still do not know what will happen to the Doha Development Round and whether multilateral trade negotiations will be successfully concluded. Whatever the outcome, it is generally acknowledged that over the next few years trade relations will be dominated by a proliferation of bilateral and regional agreements known as PTAs, or preferential trade agreements. To date, over 200 of these have been signed, of which many share a common feature – a focus on those areas that have remained outside the mandate of multilateral negotiations, i.e. services, intellectual property rights, investment, competition policy. In a context where both growth and competitiveness are increasingly based on innovation and the dissemination of knowledge, as well as the development of global value chains through relocation and outsourcing, these areas define the terms of global competition. In other words, whatever the fate of the Doha Round, both Europe and other countries will have to define policies to support growth on the basis of preferential agreements while leaving open, and possibly strengthening, the prospects for a multilateral agreement.

In recent years the European Union has been, at least in part, an agenda-setter in international trade; if and when it chooses to do so, its impact as a single entity is by far greater than the sum of its parts.[1] Europe's single voice on trade has prevailed, also in the presence of different national preferences linked to different national specialisations (on agriculture, textiles, advanced services, etc.) and different approaches to the organisation of national welfare systems. In multilateral negotiations Europe is a member of the G4 along with the United States, India and Brazil, i.e. a member of the group that during the critical phases of the Doha Development Round attempted to hammer out an agreement.

Global trade architecture today bears a significant European mark, as does the architecture of regional agreements, and Europe's commitment to a gradual opening of markets remains intact (regardless of the CAP). Should global imbalances not be settled adequately, one cannot however rule out Europe displaying some propensity to protectionism too, especially in conjunction with lasting euro appreciation and as an ill-advised response to the request for security that is currently being expressed by European citizens who are fearful of globalisation.

Europe has defined its own strategy for a trading system where PTAs prevail. In December 2006, the European Commission launched its 'Global Europe' Communication, which defines guidelines for the Union's trade policy in a framework of proliferating regional and preferential agreements, where topics not taken up by the Doha Round are going to become increasingly significant. The document clearly defines European philosophy in this context:

---

[1] See Lamy (2004).

> Our core argument is that rejection of protectionism at home must be accompanied by activism in creating open markets and fair conditions for trade abroad. (...) There are two core elements in pursuing this agenda: stronger engagement with major emerging economies and regions; and a sharper focus on barriers to trade behind the border. (European Commission, 2006, p. 6).

The message is clear and the line adopted echoes the 'strategic trade policy' principle that emerged in the eighties, when non-tariff barriers and market access policies became increasingly relevant.[2]

What remains to be seen is how this strategy will be implemented, and whether it will indeed lead to more openness and integration. Among the many possible future scenarios, the one in which this strategy is used to consolidate transatlantic integration, especially in the field of market access regulation, and where a shared vision of competition policy helps define technical standards, would clearly yield such a 'critical mass' of harmonisation as to become a standard-setter for all international trade relations. Moreover this strategy could be used more closely to involve new players in international governance.

This is all the more important in the framework of the response to the global crisis. The protectionist responses to the crisis that were feared have been very limited or non-existent. As we move forward in a protracted slow growth scenario, however, and with massive unemployment ahead, pressures for protection may be on the rise and it should be Europe's role and interest to resist them. But in order to resist protectionism effectively a convincing growth strategy must be designed and implemented.

3. Europe and the United States as 'global regulators'?

Open capital markets require stability. The response to the financial crisis has triggered a massive action to reform financial market regulations on a global scale. Yet, in spite of significant efforts led by the Financial Stability Board and supported by the G20, it is highly unlikely that at the end of the process we will see the rise of a single global regulatory and supervisory system.

---

[2] See discussion in Guerrieri & Padoan (1988).

In principle one should expect that moves towards this scenario could be led by a joint US European initiative. The United States and Europe together account for 40% of the world's GDP but they generate 80% of all regulation. Their converging on the definition of standards and institutional architecture would decisively impact world market regulation. Considering the role increasingly played by investment from emerging economies, financial and otherwise, defining a global regulatory framework would be key to supporting a multilateral framework and resisting the temptation of protectionism in investment. Is this in Europe's interest and capacity?

As noted by Becht & Da Silva (2007), the 27-member state European Union boasts the largest banking sector, the largest insurance industry and the largest payments system in the world. It also has the largest private market for fixed rate securities, and its derivatives and equity markets are comparable to those of the US. Despite this, Europe's influence as a major player in financial system regulation remains limited. In this field, as in that of monetary relations, Europe's voice appears to be weak and fragmented. In this area too, unexploited externalities require a single regulatory policy.

The technical difficulties involved in defining joint regulatory standards should not be underestimated, especially in light of the fact that regulation is per se a complex endeavour that concerns a variety of different fields, ranging from investor protection to technical standards, market supervision, and combating financial crime. But, as pointed out, Europe would have the 'critical mass' not only to identify common standards but also to gain their acceptance as global standards, all the more so if these standards were shared with the United States.[3] At the same time, a regulatory framework developed at the behest of the world's leading economic areas would be the most effective antidote to the (possible) political and 'non-market' use of resources controlled by SWFs. It would be a major contribution to the establishment of a sound 'investment pillar'.

Before the outbreak of the crisis, what was standing in the way of deeper cooperation between the US and Europe in this area was, on the EU side, the inability of European countries to overcome national visions, define European interests and policies, and to identify common rules for

---

[3] One limited but instructive example concerns accounting standards. European standards in this field are in the process of becoming global (see Veron, 2007).

the European market. Faced with this problem Europe's response has been: harmonisation where possible and mutual recognition, otherwise. But even mutual recognition, tantamount to a multiplicity of bilateral agreements, is not a workable solution if it is not supported by efficient implementation and enforcement, putting all participating countries on an equal footing. Despite a push to complete a European financial market under the Financial Sector Action Plan, gaps and redundancies still remain in the governance of Europe's financial stability, with over 80 agencies involved in financial market supervision and regulation. This is an obvious case of inefficiency that increases compliance costs for intermediaries.

Despite all these limitations, financial market integration has been moving on. Through a market-led process, a 'European bias' has slowly emerged in EU financial markets following the introduction of the euro and the subsequent removal of exchange rate risks, not to mention regulatory harmonisation and product-market integration. Intra-European Union cross-border capital flows have increased significantly. London has become the inter-bank market hub and this has, inter alia, elicited ever more UK investor interest in the euro. Finally, eurozone intermediaries are funding investment in the new member states.

Even before the crisis the general context was tending to push towards greater integration and increased uniformity in regulatory systems. New players emerging, not only in trade but increasingly in financing and investment, would have speeded up the identification of a shared European interest in participating, alongside the US and new members, in the definition of a regulatory framework tailored to the demands of globalisation.

The crisis has changed the scenario dramatically, accelerating it but at the same time showing the limits of European action. As a response to the crisis both the US and Europe have launched ambitious reforms of financial regulation and supervision within the G20 process. While these reform processes are independent, they do present a number of similarities, as well as inevitable differences.[4]

---

[4] For a more detailed analysis, see Masciandaro & Quintyn (2009) who also show how, in the decade before the crisis, EU regulatory retro at the national level has proceeded but moved towards increasing divergence.

Both reform blueprints present proposals that are based on very similar if not identical principles: stronger bank capital requirements, less pro-cyclicality, more control over rating agencies, a more relevant role of the concept of 'fair value' in accounting procedures, 'parallel' market institutions such as hedge funds and private equity have to be made more transparent and subject to regulation, OTC derivatives should be intermediated through clearing systems, managers' compensation must be tied to long-term performance, more effective crisis resolution mechanisms must be put in place, fragmentation in regulatory architecture must be reduced and central banks must be given more power in surveillance while a stronger role must be played by the Basel Committee, the Financial Stability Board and the IMF.

There are, however, also significant differences. Starting from the role assigned to central banks. The Federal Reserve has full responsibility of surveillance of the financial firms, both banks and non-banks, which have systemic relevance and can affect the stability of the system. The European Central Bank is assigned the more limited role of 'hosting', coordinating and chairing the European Systematic Risk Council (ESRC) which is made up of the members of the ESCB (European System of Central banks), the European Commission, and the chairs of the three authorities set up following the recommendations of the Lamfalussy report: the European Banking Authority (EUA), the European Insurance Authority (EIA) and the European Security Authority. The ESRC will have only macro-prudential responsibility looking at the system's overall stability, while micro prudential oversight will remain with the single national authorities. It will only be able to issue recommendations related to systemic aspects of stability. Its governing power will be limited to say the least. The US has also created an authority to oversee surveillance, the Financial Service Oversight Council, which includes the Fed, the US Treasury and other surveillance authorities. The Secretary of the Treasury will have a coordination role of both macro and micro surveillance.

In case of financial turbulence the different degrees of coordination could well prove essential. It is true that at the peak of the financial crisis Europeans showed an exceptional degree of coordination in facing the emergency. However, this *ad hoc* response required exceptional circumstances and can hardly be taken as a model for more effective governance.

A third difference is related to the creation of an agency for consumer protection in the US, the Consumer Financial Protection Agency, which will oversee products and processes in the credit, savings and payment system segments.

Finally, it is important to note that in neither of the two jurisdictions do we see a full consolidation of surveillance structures. The European System of Financial Supervision, which includes EBA, EIA and ESA, as well as the national surveillance authorities, is only a network of decentralised structures. Daily surveillance will remain with national authorities that are closer to the intermediaries. The EU-level agencies will act as standard setters and coordinate their implementation. The US will maintain six authorities in addition to the Fed and Treasury (the SEC, the National Bank Supervisor, the Commodity Futures Trading Commission the Federal Deposit Insurance Corporation and the Federal Housing Finance Agency).

To conclude, while both strategies fall short of full reform and take with them considerable institutional inertia, the European strategy suffers more deeply from such inertia, and we are long way from a truly European system of surveillance, which goes along with a still largely incomplete financial market integration. This suggests that in post-BWII there will still be regulatory differences among jurisdictions, and arbitrage. In short, a reformed US financial system will most probably prove to be the best option for global capital flows, looking, as in the past, for profitable and politically reliable investment opportunities.

4. Macroeconomic governance

Macroeconomic relations are different from trade relations but similar to financial regulation, with European presence largely devolved to individual states. There are four EU member states in the G8, but it would be hard to contend that the G8's agenda is clearly set by the Europeans. A similar yet even stronger case can be made for the G20. Attempts at reform of macroeconomic governance have been launched in the recent past. In trying to deal with global imbalances, and in the context of its Medium-Term Strategy review, the IMF has introduced an informal consultative group made up of the US, Japan, the eurozone, Saudi Arabia and China, i.e. all the major players in global imbalances, including those who are not G8 members.

Ever since the issue of global imbalances came to the fore, the International Monetary Fund has supported a coordinated adjustment strategy which, in line with official G7 statements, provided for a cut in public deficits and an increase in private savings in the US, more exchange-rate flexibility in Asia (and especially in China), structural reform in Europe and Japan to increase growth potential and more spending and absorption capacity in oil-producing countries. The IMF in this context was to implement more effective surveillance, both multilateral and bilateral, in individual countries,[5] with particular focus on those where performance has systemic implications. The crisis has shown that this initial attempt was not successful. At the time of writing, the G20 has called for a more coordinated and long-term oriented surveillance mechanism to ensure balanced and sustained global growth, where the IMF should play a leading role.

It is too early to say if the proposal will be implemented and if it will be effective. It is difficult to deny that, if more effective coordination among key players, including Europe, does not take place, the issue of managing payment imbalances and global growth will be addressed within US-China bilateral relations, with Europe (or rather, the eurozone) adopting an attitude of (benign?) neglect.

The time is also ripe for a rethink of the relationships between major currencies, as is necessary in a post-BWII scenario. Changing this relationship requires both flexibility and orderly burden-sharing in the adjustment and transition to a new monetary regime. Several measures are on the table that would, for instance, link the Chinese yuan to a basket of currencies, or identify 'target zones' or allow for the Chinese exchange rate to be fully flexible and even promote the role of the yuan as a global currency. Whatever the solution, the crux of the matter is that the eurozone should define its position much more clearly and uphold it in multilateral and bilateral fora. Europe's limited voice in this respect runs the risk of being interpreted as a lack of interest or worse still, as passivity in the face of events. All of this also suggests that Europe, or at least the eurozone,

---

5 This is the thrust of a recent revision in the IMF's terms of reference for surveillance, under which the Fund is explicitly entrusted with monitoring exchange rate regimes.

should opt as soon as possible for single representation in international financial institutions and in unofficial groupings (such as the 'G' summits).

Both the IMF and the World Bank are governed by boards on which 24 members sit with different share holdings, representing 185 countries. The United States has the single largest share, with a little over 17%. Taken together member states of the European Union have a larger share than the US. France, Germany and the UK represent a single country constituency each. The other European Union member states are distributed over six other constituencies, and in several cases also hold the executive director positions. The Fund and Bank boards operate on a consensus basis. This means that what happens upstream, most often in the framework of the G7/G8 for the advanced economies and the G11 for emerging economies (including China), and possibly in the G20 from now on, is of essential importance in establishing consensus. Although they do not have an absolute majority, historically G7 countries have had a predominant position in the decision-making process. In recent years, European countries have also developed a coordination method, in Brussels and in Washington, on the basis of which some of their board decisions are taken jointly. Interaction between the G7 and the European coordination group is complex, sometimes fraught, and at times European members of the G7 have upheld positions different from those of other EU governments.

A single EU, or at least eurozone, representation in international financial institutions would increase Europe's clout in global governance while at the same time improving global governance by enhancing the involvement and accountability of new emerging economies. A single EU (or eurozone) representation, if set on the same level of the US, would command more authority than the current sum of EU representatives[6] while at the same time making space available for a larger share of emerging economies. But there is more to this. Europe is currently faced with a paradox. Computing Europe's weight as a 'swing-voter', one can conclude[7] that if Europe were to speak as one voice, it would carry the vote

---

[6] Adding the current shares held by individual EU member states yields a figure of about 30%, but if eurozone countries were to go for single representation, the sum of their shares would have to be corrected for intra-zone trade, which is currently taken into account. See Bini Smaghi (2006).

[7] Ibid. (2006).

in practically all cases. But, and therein lies the paradox, Europe has so far proved largely incapable of using its economic and political clout in global governance, precisely because it has spoken with multiple voices.

Why hasn't Europe taken the decisive step towards single representation? Two possible explanations can be offered, which are partly complementary: different preferences and dysfunctional governance. Differences in national macroeconomic policy preferences would stand in the way of European countries arriving at joint positions in international fora just as different trade policy preferences would weaken EU positions in WTO negotiations. This assumption is not very convincing if we think to the euro, which implies a single monetary policy, regardless of the fact that a single monetary policy may at times yield differing outcomes in different eurozone member states. One could argue that having single IMF representation would imply speaking with one voice, also regarding fiscal issues, a field that has remained the purview of individual member states. But this is not a fully convincing argument either. On the one hand the Stability and Growth Pact requires fiscal policy convergence and shared policy criteria for all countries. On the other, through surveillance the IMF is already assessing the euro area's fiscal policy both in terms of internal consistency and operation, and in terms of global macroeconomic impact.

This leads us to the dysfunctional governance or decision-making inefficiency assumption.[8] Regarding macroeconomic relations, this describes EU countries' difficulties in identifying an internal decision-making mechanism that would yield joint positions in international fora. Put differently, there is no point in setting up single representation with the IMF if the executive director for Europe is not given clear and timely guidance by his or her authorities (while executive directors for individual European countries do receive such guidance from their capitals). Up to now there has been no such handing over of sovereignty and many European governments remain opposed to concrete steps that might lead to single representation. The reason this is not happening is simple. Moving to single representation would involve redistributing power within the European countries group. The larger countries would need to relinquish part of the clout they currently wield including in G groups, whereas smaller countries (who are not G7 members and are therefore fearful of

---

[8] See Pisani-Ferry (2005).

losing even more visibility and voice) are even more fearful of ceding power to larger countries.

Pressure for single representation (or rather, single voice) is nevertheless increasing. This stems first of all from the changes that have occurred globally. Shifts in economic power and the move to regional or bilateral governance models have reduced the clout of individual European countries, none of which can aspire to global player status. Pressure comes equally from the fact that single eurozone representation in financial institutions would free up space to increase the shares assigned to new emerging economies, thereby allowing for their increased involvement and consequently for more balanced international relations governance, which would facilitate the reform of the said institutions. Such a goal should be in the European Union's interest. Asian countries, including China, would carry more weight but also more responsibility as shareholders. And it would be easier to involve China in multilateral solutions, including those aiming to correct global imbalances, if responsibility for their management were more equitably shared. The response to the financial crisis has significantly added to this pressure.[9] While it is still too early to see how the process will evolve it is important to note that pressure for a single Europe voice is very strong from countries outside Europe, most notably the US, with the purpose of giving more voice to emerging economies.

Pressure, thirdly, stems from the role of the euro. The single currency's weight as a key currency is on the rise, regardless of what monetary union member states may wish. The euro is increasingly being used as an invoicing currency for trade among and between third party

---

[9] The G20 document on IMF reform states: "G20 members should call for meaningful reform to bring the Fund's governance structure in line with the realities of today's global economy in order to strengthen the Fund's legitimacy and effectiveness. In London, G20 Leaders agreed that emerging and developing economies, including the poorest, should have greater voice and representation. (...) The Fund's governance structures - specifically the Executive Board and the IMFC - should reflect the realities of today's global economy. (.....) A smaller, more streamlined Board has the potential to increase Board effectiveness." Accordingly, G20 members might support returning the number of Board seats to the 20 envisaged in the IMF Articles, *while preserving the number of chairs held by emerging market and developing countries* (italics added) , as one measure to improve the contribution of such countries to IMF Board decision-making.

countries, as a denominator for financial transactions, as a reserve currency held by third party countries. Finally, this is instrumental to making the euro area increasingly attractive as a location for foreign investment, all the more so with the setting up of SWFs by emerging economies. This raises the issue of defining a common policy regarding both macroeconomic relations and the supervision of financial markets, consistent with the establishment of a strong investment pillar in post-BWII.

Fourthly and finally, pressure is coming from the EU's enlargement. This provides not only for new member states adopting the euro, but it also implies that 'euro-isation' phenomena will proliferate more or less explicitly in countries wishing to join the Union or somehow coming under its economic influence. This strengthens the need for a 'key currency' policy that has repercussions on relations with other currency zones.

5. Conclusions

Globalisation implies growing interconnection between markets and growing policy interdependence: in trade, in investment, in the supervision and regulation of international financial markets, and in monetary relations. The global crisis has brought to light significant governance failures in most if not all such policy areas. So a durable response to the crisis and a return to sustainable and balanced growth requires stronger global governance. This, in turn, requires agreement and shared responsibilities of all major players, including emerging economies, and a new role for Europe. In Europe, competition and trade policies have been entrusted to the European Commission, Financial market policy has so far mainly been dealt with nationally, and macroeconomic policy comes under the jurisdiction of the Eurogroup Finance Ministers. The global financial crisis has produced a dramatic acceleration in global governance. Europe can take advantage of the crisis response to strengthen its voice in international fora and contribute to a more balanced global economy: an objective that should be in Europe's firm interest. If this opportunity is missed there might be a loss of European influence in international economic relations over the long term. Europe's influence is, in any case, set to decline further as the relative weight of individual European countries also declines, in addition to that of the EU as a whole. Contributing to shape a global investment regime, speaking in a single voice in monetary and financial matters, in addition to trade policy issues, would not only provide Europe with more clout, but would also force the

Europeans to devote more energy to figuring out where their interests lie in the global system, and what can be done to further them.

Despite the institutional and substantive differences in different policy areas, Europe's difficulties in identifying a common and effective economic policy harken back to a common trait that stems from the very principle at the root of its recent history. Europe's economic policy was devised as a mechanism to achieve a common goal, in terms of growth and welfare through increased internal integration. And this continues to obtain as Europe's policy takes on an external dimension, as is the case with trade policy. This mechanism assigns a central role to national preferences and works best when such preferences can converge in the definition of a 'European preference'. But that is precisely the point. If in the post-war years a European preference could be defined, keeping in mind internal goals such as peace among member states and economic welfare, Europe's preferences must necessarily be defined differently in the new global environment.

References

Becht, M. and L. Da Silva (2007) "External financial markets policy. Europe is a global regulator?", in A. Sapir (ed.), *Fragmented Power: Europe and the Global Economy*, Brussels: Bruegel Books.

Bini Smaghi, L. (2006), "IMF Governance and the Political Economy of a Consolidated European Seat", in E. Truman (ed.), *Reforming the IMF in the XXIst Century*, Institute for International Economics, Washington, D.C.

European Commission (2006), Communication on Global Europe: Competing in the world, Brussels, December.

Guerrieri, P. and P.C. Padoan (1988), *Libero scambio, protezionismo e concorrenza internazionale*, Bologna: Il Mulino.

Lamy, P. (2004), *Trade Policy in the Prodi Commission: An Assessment*, November (http://trade-info.cec.eu.int/doclib/docs/2004/november/tradoc_120087.pdf).

Masciandaro, D. and M. Quintyn (2009), *Reforming Financial Supervision and the Role of Central Banks: a Review of the Global Trends Causes and Effects (1998-2008)*, CEPR Policy Insight No. 30, Centre for Economic Policy Research, London, February.

Pisani-Ferry, J. (2005), "The Accidental Player: The EU and the Global Economy", prepared for a lecture at the Indian Council for Research on International Economic Relations, Delhi, 25 November.

Veron, N. (2007), *The Global Accounting Experiment,* Brussels: Bruegel Blueprints No. 2.

PART III

THE INSTITUTIONAL FRAMEWORK

11. From a Community based on the Rule of Law to the European Union as a Community of Rights

Mario P. Chiti

1. A community based on the rule of law

Outside institutional and legal circles, few are aware of one of the more relevant and forward-looking definitions once given to the European Economic Community (EEC): "a community based on the rule of law". Its author, the first President of the European Commission, Walter Hallstein, mentioning it in a 1965 debate at the European Parliament, intended to apply the gist of the *RechtsStaatsPrinzip* to the recently established European public authority. At the same time, he also wanted to underscore the fundamental and unprecedented role played by law, the keystone of the EEC, thus characterised in a totally original fashion as compared with states and the international organisations that had come before it. The Community did not then have, nor does it have today, its own power of coercion; as summed up by Jean-Victor Louis (1989) in a groundbreaking study of Europe's legal system, "the law it develops is its only force".

The idea of a community based on the rule of law was one that underpinned the constitutional case law of the Court of Justice throughout the 1960s. It later took hold in explicit terms in the ruling for *Parti ecologiste "Les Verts" v. European Parliament* (case 294/83, 23 April 1986) and became a constant connotation for all European Community/EU institutions in subsequent case law.

Forty years later, Biagio de Giovanni (2002), in order to explain "Europe's ambiguous power", referred to "the law, laws, and then rights, and the connected principle of the humanity of man". Similarly, Tommaso Padoa-Schioppa – at the time not yet burdened by government office –

published a 2001 collection of essays under the title *Europa forza gentile* in homage to Scotsman David Hume, who first introduced the concept of gentle force, and with a view to defining the European Union as a public authority exclusively based on voluntary acceptance, the sharing of a novel "supranational sovereignty" and the renouncing of coercion.

The road travelled over the 50 years since the first Rome Treaty - preceded by the essential although to date unknown threading of European integration through the European Coal and Steel Community, a genuine supranational organisation despite its mission-oriented mandate - would indeed have been to Hume's liking and to that of his Enlightenment contemporaries. It has led to an outcome involving a claim to a single legal space, centred on freedom, security and justice, to be implemented through a united Europe (a fundamental goal for the Treaty on European Union (TEU), Art. 2.1). In just a few years, this outcome has attracted in an apparently irreversible way states long governed by dictators or shaken by democratic crises, or left for a number of decades on the far side of Europe's wall.

Clearly, the European integration process has been neither linear nor constant. On the contrary, it has had its moments of stasis and very genuine crises (especially in the wake of the 2004 Constitutional Treaty), and has constantly evaded the rigid framework of institutions and principles.

Despite these limitations - or better yet, *features*, as there appears to be no benchmark for the EU's development, a truly unprecedented experience - Hallstein's insight has certainly been proven true, and the community based on the rule of law has played the role of a 'gentle force' and does so to this day.

How did this come to pass with no bill of rights, without Community or Union primary law having anything resembling a catalogue of rights? How do things stand today, and what is likely to occur now that the Lisbon Treaty has entered into force? Such are the questions this chapter intends to address, however briefly.

The interpretation offered here - and explained in the following sections - is that the features of the European Community (EC) and then the EU, along with the specific constitutional traditions of European states, have had direct consequences for individuals' fundamental rights. Regarding the nature of the EC, its qualification as a community based on the rule of law not only implies that its institutions and member states are subject to judicial review on the compliance of their laws and regulations with the basic constitutional charter that is the Treaty, but also that individuals' rights (and obligations, obviously) may under certain conditions directly derive from this same source. Individuals come directly under the new legal system, as subjects thereof, and this makes the system stand apart from all other international legal systems. The EC of course operates in a context of highly 'constitutionalised' European states - especially following the dramatic events of the Second World War - where fundamental rights are seen as an inalienable constitutional heritage, early on (from 1950) transmuted into a shared heritage through the Council of Europe's European Convention on Human Rights (ECHR).

An inherent characteristic of the EC/EU system is that individuals can assert rights directly and immediately, starting clearly with fundamental rights, vis-à-vis their respective states (the judges of which are obliged to apply relevant EC law) and European institutions. As the Court of Justice summed up in its most recent ruling in this field (case C-305/05, *Belgian Bar Associations v. Council of Ministers,* 26 June 2007), "fundamental rights form an integral part of the general principles of law whose observance the Court ensures, drawing inspiration from the constitutional traditions common to the Member States and in particular the Rome Convention".

2. Issues posited in the original 1957 EEC Treaty

The 1957 EEC Treaty assiduously avoided any reference to fundamental rights and liberties, in accordance with functionalist criteria that sought to achieve as much as possible in concrete terms without strong institutional or political premises, whose time was deemed not yet to have come.

This same Treaty nevertheless provided for the economic liberties essential to the emergence of the single market (establishment, circulation, etc.), which were soon to be viewed by the Court of Justice as genuine constitutional freedoms.

In addition to these functional freedoms required for the common market, the Court of Justice set out to mark the absolute originality of the EEC (destined to increase further with the later shift to the EC and the subsequent establishment of the EU) through the case law it developed in the early 1960s. Notable in this respect is the Court's claim (in case 26/62, *Van Gend & Loos v. Netherlands Inland Revenue Administration,* 5 February 1963) that not only states but also their citizens are the subjects of Community law, and that the Community system is more than just an agreement setting up reciprocal obligations among contracting member states, because of the direct repercussions on Community subjects.

The individuals mentioned by the Community judges cannot but have rights with respect to the Community, in addition to those they have with respect to member states. This stance was taken with the knowledge that the ever-growing sphere of Community law leads to legal situations regarding individuals and that these individuals may invoke the principle of direct effect (another original creation of the Court of Justice) in order to have such situations appropriately taken into consideration by national judges.

With economic liberties equated with fundamental rights and an increasing number of rights deriving from Community law (considered in the broader acceptance specific to European law, as legal situations entailing benefits), the new legal system could no longer avoid re-positing the issue of fundamental rights, as had the constitutions of the last two centuries in various states.

The method adopted by the Court of Justice for the definition of "general principles of Community law" followed this same orientation - and one cannot overstress the fundamental role played by the institution in the development of the legal grounding for European integration, unparalleled in any known legal system. This method centred initially on the identification of legal traditions common to member states. Clearly, in identifying such general principles - source law with cogent legal force - in the legality principle, the finality of law, equality and other principles as well, the Court was moving progressively closer to the issue of fundamental rights. These were indeed an essential part of the common constitutional traditions of member states, furthermore asserted by the Council of Europe's ECHR, to which all EU member states had acceded.

It was therefore not unexpected that the Court of Justice should state, as of 1969, in *Erich Stauder v City of Ulm* (case 29/69, 12 November 1969), that "the fundamental human rights [are] enshrined in the general principles of Community law and protected by the Court". As of a subsequent ruling, in *Internationale Handelsgesellschaft mbH v Einfuhr- und Vorratsstelle für Getreide und Futtermittel* (case 11/70, 17 December 1970), this position became a constant in the case law of the Court of Justice.

As pointed out by Federico Mancini (1989), "reading in Community law an unwritten Bill of Rights thus constitutes the most incisive of the Court's contributions to the development of a Constitution for Europe".

The Court was not solely interested in the development of individuals' rights, however, knowing that an essential aspect of its innovative case law concerned the 'communitarisation' of a significant part of national constitutional law, while stressing the 'primacy' of European law and of the integration process of national and European legal systems. This is already evident in the abovementioned *Internationale Handelsgesellschaft* ruling, which reads "that the protection of fundamental rights, whilst inspired by the constitutional traditions common to the member states, must be ensured within the framework of the structure and objectives of the Community". Otherwise, recourse to the legal rules or concepts of national law "would have an adverse effect on the uniformity and efficacy of Community law".

3. Developments subsequent to the 1992 EU Treaty

With the establishment of the EU in 1992, fundamental rights (inevitably one could say) were to find acknowledgement in the Maastricht Treaty. After the Preamble's confirmation of the "attachment to the principles of…respect for human rights and fundamental freedoms and of the rule of law", Art. F (now TEU Art. 6) asserts that the EU is based on the aforementioned principles.

But with the shift in the appraoch to the issue of fundamental rights away from one essentially based on case law and towards a constitutionalisation of these same rights in the EU Treaty, problems deriving from their triple dimension (national, EU and ECHR) were to come to the fore, along with issues of enforcement. One should bear in mind that so far, the EU has not acceded to the ECHR, partly because of the Court of Justice (which stated in opinion 2/94 that there was no jurisdiction for accession to the ECHR, an expression of a different international legal system). In addition, fundamental rights are acknowledged as part of the "general principles of Community law", with a specific location in the sources of the legal system, and member states' constitutional courts have been reluctant to renounce their authority over the protection of fundamental rights (recent rulings 348 and 349/2007 of the Italian Constitutional Court are a case in point, as analysed in greater detail below).

The solution found to these problems was the convening of a Convention, a special ad hoc body, unprecedented in European law, the very name of which was redolent of a glorious constitutional past.

Although not yet imbued with the significant distance vis-à-vis the 'intergovernmental method' that was to be the hallmark, soon after, of the Convention that in 2003 produced the Treaty establishing a Constitution for Europe, this first Convention worked quite autonomously from member states and produced a text of considerable significance.

The Charter of Fundamental Rights of the European Union signed in Nice in 2000 – although controversial and on some counts, such as its final "general provisions", unconvincing – bears witness to the evolution of a number of 'first generation' rights: the right to engage in work is supplemented by the right to seek employment and to pursue a freely chosen occupation (Art. 15). The Charter also formalises rights that have emerged in recent decades (such as the protection of personal data, in Art. 8; the rights of the child, in Art. 24; and the rights of the elderly, in Art. 25), and reasserts original rights, such as rights vis-à-vis public administrations (Art. 41, on the right to good administration), that give substance to EU citizenship.

The atypical nature of the Charter drafting process was mirrored by an equally atypical adoption, eschewing the forms provided for by the Treaties, with an unprecedented "proclamation" on the part of the European Parliament, the Commission and the Council in December 2000. After the negative epilogue of the 2004 Constitutional Treaty, a number of formal changes were introduced and in November 2007, the revised Charter was adopted by a huge majority in the European Parliament. In another atypical development, it was then once again "proclaimed" in the Plenary Hall of the European Parliament by the Presidents of the Parliament, the Council and the Commission.

As expected, the Charter's originality – as a constitutional seal appended to the new EU – elicited resistance and reactions. Indeed, no specific value was ascribed to it and its insertion into the 2004 Constitutional Treaty, of which it formed Part II, contributed to the subsequent crisis.

In spite of these difficulties, one could easily foresee that the Nice Charter was to represent an irreversible outcome, and a part of the Community *acquis*. It may not be binding, but advocates-general have often referred to it with a view to substantiating their conclusions; court judges have deemed it to be 'a source of inspiration'; national courts have on occasion made reference to it to corroborate their rulings; and the Italian

Constitutional Court has acknowledged its interpretative significance (ruling no. 349/2007).

4. Roles played by the Council of Europe and the European Convention on Human Rights

In parallel with developments in the EU, the role played by the European Court of Human Rights, designed to guarantee the rights addressed by the ECHR, has considerably strengthened.

Following the 1994-99 reforms, the Strasbourg Court has become more accessible to individuals and the range of issues it addresses has broadened. The outcome of this has been particularly significant with respect to states that have acceded to the ECHR, but on many points they are still far from full compliance. The case of Italy is especially telling: over recent years it has been 'obliged' to reform Art. 111 of its Constitution on 'fair trial', introduce subsequent legislative innovations (such as law no. 12/2006) and change its stance radically on property rights and expropriation. (This last matter has for the time being been concluded with the 29 March 2006 Scordino ruling of the Strasbourg Court and Constitutional Court ruling nos. 348 and 349/2007.)

The ECHR appears to be a wedge driven between the Nice Charter and national constitutions. As regards EU law, the issue is not so much one of differing approaches (although that is partly the case) but rather the role played by the Strasbourg Court, and its crowding out of the Court of Justice. The latter's case law attempts to combine the outcomes of the former with its own, autonomous approach, but the end-product is not always convincing. In any event, the Court of Justice has to consider the Strasbourg Court's case law as a given, insofar as the latter has sole jurisdiction over interpretation of the ECHR.

More significant problems emerge in conjunction with national legislation. The Italian case is typical in this respect, as a number of glaring asymmetries have appeared, despite efforts to demonstrate that the ECHR is substantively in line with corresponding national provisions. The most obvious example is that of property rights and expropriation powers, where various segments of Italian legislation – on many occasions deemed compatible with Art. 42 of the constitution – have appeared to conflict with property guarantees provided for in the ECHR (in Art. 6 and in Art. 1 of the 1952 Additional Protocol). To put it briefly, while the constitutional rule on property also expounds on its 'social function' and authorises various adaptations regarding modes of acquisition and use, the ECHR - as interpreted by the Strasbourg Court - does not allow for fragmented protection of property rights.

Yet the relevance (and primacy) of the ECHR is not matched, in the Italian legal system, by a formal role, and the ECHR was inserted into the system through a regular adaptation law, as is the case with all international treaties. Although the ECHR addresses issues that are objectively constitutional (fundamental rights, for instance), until the reform of the Constitution's Art. 117.1, one simply could not raise serious questions about the specificity of the ECHR in comparison with other international obligations. Only recently have some judges, in order to acknowledge the primacy of the ECHR, attempted to stretch general rules through the construct (of Community origin and specific solely to that system) of a disapplication of domestic law conflicting with the ECHR's provisions. Still, the means chosen do not hold water legally, insofar as ECHR's rules cannot be characterised as having 'useful effect'.

5. The 2007 Treaty and the recent Treaty of Lisbon

Luckily the system is now moving towards clarification of its more significant points under the combined impact of European and domestic factors.

As regards the EU, the Lisbon Treaty includes - in the section modifying the Treaty on European Union - a number of provisions that clearly set out the new centrality of the rights issue. A second paragraph has been added to the Preamble, according to which from the inheritance of Europe "have developed the universal values of the inviolable and inalienable rights of the human person, freedom, democracy, equality and the rule of law".

Then comes a definite clarification that the Charter of Fundamental Rights of the European Union "shall have the same legal value as the Treaties" (Art. 6, replacing TEU Art. 6). The Charter thus remains an autonomous text with respect to the two new Treaties - thereby accommodating a mainly British request, aimed at attenuating the constitutional form of the new EU Treaty. But this may well have a paradoxically positive effect, insofar as it positions the Charter as something that comes before and stands aside from the TEU, similar in that regard to the Bill of Rights in the constitutional system of the US.

Other elements of clarification concern the EU's commitment to accede to the ECHR (Art. 6.2, new) and the (re)-positing of fundamental rights guaranteed by the ECHR within the general principles of EU law (Art. 6.3, new).

All issues have not been solved by the Lisbon Treaty (the enforcement of rights and the role of the Court of Justice, in particular) and others have emerged (the peculiar in/out position granted to the UK and Poland, for instance). Even so, European observers are used to compromise solutions and the new Treaty in any event includes a number of innovative provisions.

6. The Constitutional Court in Italy and Europe's international obligations

With ratification and the entry into force of the Lisbon Treaty through a political and institutional process that was less daunting - on paper - than the one for the 2004 Constitutional Treaty, the most topical and controversial issue for Italian law has to do with the reciprocal interplay of constitutional rights and those rights guaranteed by the ECHR, in light of the aforementioned reform of Art. 117.1 of the Italian Constitution.

The issue was finally addressed frontally by the Constitutional Court in its rulings of 2007 (nos. 348 and 349), the significance of which are inversely proportional to their media coverage (discounting the conclusions regarding expropriation, on which the debate was based), almost as if fundamental rights were a topic so arcane as to be reserved to the most exclusive of sects.

The two rulings in question are complex, inter alia because the general disquisition regarding the scope of Art. 117.1 was entrusted to two separate rapporteurs who used similar, but not identical arguments. The rulings are addressed here from the sole point of view of their general implications.

The Constitutional Court put forth the following main arguments:

a) At the time of the ruling, the legal system underpinning the ECHR was still legally distinct from that of the EU (the Court was nonetheless well aware of the imminent absorption by the EU of the issue of fundamental rights).

b) The ECHR is legally particular compared with other international agreements, if only for its uniform guarantee of all fundamental rights.

c) The relationship between the ECHR and national legal systems remains "robustly governed by each national legal system".

d) The reform of Art. 117.1 finally fills the gap and "connects, from its systemic position within the Constitution, to the framework of principles that even previously guaranteed compliance, at the primary level, with a number of international obligations taken on by the State".

e) The new provision establishes a flexible reference to the ECHR, operating as an interposed rule.

f) The European Court of Human Rights retains jurisdiction in terms of the centralised interpretation of the ECHR, but in the last resort it shall behoove the Constitutional Court to check that rules specified in the ECHR, and referred to on occasion, do indeed provide a degree of fundamental rights' protection at least equivalent to that provided by the Italian Constitution.

Legal arguments are shared on a variety of points, such as the erroneous use made by some Italian judges of disapplication regarding domestic laws, and the originality of the new Art. 117.1 compared with Art. 10 and other 'internationally-geared' provisions contained in the Constitution. Overall, however, these arguments give the feeling that the legal system of the ECHR has been viewed as a variant of international law that may well be significant, but has been qualified as a mere 'interposed rule' with respect to the constitution. The specific features of the ECHR, both per se and in light of the use that EU law makes of them, should have led to the ECHR being slotted in differently from what is the rule for other international obligations. And the same can be said of the power the Constitutional Court has retained in terms of "checking that the appropriate balance is struck between the need to guarantee compliance with international obligations as set out in the Constitution and that of ensuring that so doing entails no *vulnus* for the Constitution proper".

On the whole, these two rulings leave one with the sense that after having digested the position taken by the Court of Justice on EU law – painfully, and only partially at that, as evidenced by the issue of legal system unitarity – the Constitutional Court decided to retain, as a matter of principle, a 'defensive' role with respect to rights grounded in the Constitution. It did so notwithstanding that it will in the end have to accept the conclusions of the Strasbourg Court, even on issues where the two approaches are objectively different. Expropriation, which prompted the two above-mentioned rulings, illustrates the point.

7. Pending issues

That being stated, there are still a number of unresolved issues and applicative difficulties within EU law. In the context of the new EU Treaty (as modified by the Lisbon Treaty), fundamental rights derive from both the Charter and the ECHR, while also being the product of member states' shared constitutional traditions. As regards the organisation of source law, the rights guaranteed by the ECHR and those deriving from common constitutional traditions are equally part of Union law, as general principles.

The ensuing model is not blindingly clear. Actually, now that the revision process has come to a close, on the one hand fundamental rights provided for in the Charter shall have constitutional rank (the Charter having been given the same legal value as the Treaties, as noted earlier), while on the other, rights guaranteed by the ECHR or derived from common constitutional traditions shall be deemed 'general principles', and therefore not have constitutional rank.

Furthermore, the acknowledgement of the legal value of the Charter is surrounded by a number of cautionary statements - probably too many. Among them is the Protocol on the application of the Charter to Poland and the UK, which states that "whereas the Charter reaffirms the rights, freedoms, and principles recognised in the Union and makes these rights more visible, [it] *does not create new rights or principles*" (emphasis added). Yet, a number of rights contemplated therein are absolutely novel.

8. Protecting rights - The EU's basic remit

However significant these pending problems may be, clearly no legal system has developed a system entirely based on the rule of law and guaranteed fundamental rights on a par with the EU. More specifically, freedom, democracy and the solidarity made possible by a social market economy have become, in just a few decades, such a given and appreciated fact of life for EU citizens that they are now viewed as 'natural', rather than as the positive outcome of a far-reaching policy. And yet nothing is as constructed and deliberate as this main connotation of the EU.

The 'rule of law' and fundamental rights thus play a dual role: within the EU legal system they represent the system's basic grounding, developing the premises for EU citizens' new sense of belonging; externally, they act as a driver both for countries interested in joining the Union and for those who enter into relations with the EU.

EU citizens now need to become aware that the EU is more than any other a system of actually functional and guaranteed freedoms. European identity has to be based on this pillar, which the Union itself has built, rather than on the dubious legacy of the past (that European inheritance that was the focus of so many arguments in 2004, on the occasion of the Constitutional Treaty).

As noted above, externally the EU exercises its drive through the gradual extension - always the product of 'gentle force', never that of coercion - of democracy and common security. Thanks to the peculiarity of a European space that was not predefined, the EEC originally founded by six member states has extended in stages to its current 27 members, delineating for each and every one far-reaching adaptations. The impact of the EU goes well beyond its changing borders, positively influencing states interested in joining (from Turkey to the Balkans) as well as states linked to it through specific trade relations. The EU is hence becoming a 'beacon of liberty' for the world at large.

It was therefore essential that in the ratification process of the new Lisbon Treaty, regardless of how formally centred it may have been on the role of national parliaments, that European public opinion (the most informed and sophisticated there is worldwide) was made aware of the crucial role of rights and the rule of law. A new 'European citizenship' will not come into being through complex institutional and economic mechanisms, but through the effectiveness of a system where "law determines power, and power does not determine law" (Pöttering, 2007).

References

de Giovanni, B. (2002), *L'ambigua potenza dell'Europa*, Napoli: Guida.

Louis, J.V. (1989), *L'ordinamento giuridico comunitario*, Commissione delle Comunità europee, Bruxelles-Luxembourg.

Mancini, F. (1989), "The Making of a Constitution for Europe", *Common Market Law Review*, Vol. 26, winter.

Padoa-Schioppa, T. (2001), *Europa, forza gentile*, Bologna: Il Mulino.

Pöttering, H.-G. (2007), *Discorso al Parlamento europeo in occasione dell'approvazione definitiva della Carta dei diritti*, November.

12. DEMOCRACY IN THE EUROPEAN UNION

*STEFANO MICOSSI**

Up until the early 1990s, the European Union's popularity with its citizens had been on the rise, despite a lack of active involvement in European affairs; subsequently, it appeared to drop radically. The Maastricht Treaty ratification had to overcome widespread resistance from various quarters: public opinion, national parliaments, the German Constitutional Court. The impasse in the 15 years of negotiations on institutions that followed the Maastricht Treaty projected an image of paralysed decision-making. A new wave of discontent and anti-integration sentiment has followed the accession of 12 new member states in 2005-07. The rejection of the Constitutional Treaty in the French and Dutch referendums in 2005 and the difficult ratification of the subsequent Lisbon Treaty in 2008-09 have appeared to confirm the detachment of public opinion in Europe from the institutions of the Union. The 'permissive consensus' that had until then entrusted European elites with developing integration seems to have evaporated. To some, this foreshadowed a collapse of the Union and a return to intergovernmental forms of cooperation.

According to many observers, the reason lay in a lack of democracy: in the dual sense that common policies had diverged from voters' preferences (*output* legitimacy) and that decision-making mechanisms appeared to lack the basic requirements of transparency, accountability and democratic involvement (*input* legitimacy). The issue of democracy has taken on greater prominence since the Maastricht Treaty, which set up the Union and extended its scope to monetary affairs as well as to two new

---

* The author wishes to thank Carlo Bastasin, Sabino Cassese, Giandomenico Majone and Gian Luigi Tosato for their useful comments, and Fabrizia Peirce for invaluable research assistance.

political 'pillars' for foreign policy and internal security: areas that had until then been the jealously guarded prerogatives of member states, under national parliamentary control.

In the 15 years since Maastricht, however, integration has moved forward at a fast clip, with enlargement to ten new member states and the achievement of monetary union. Major progress has also been made under the so-called 'second pillar', with strong support from public opinion: the Amsterdam, Nice and Lisbon Treaties have extended application of the Community method of decision-making to matters of border control, civil and criminal justice and law enforcement affairs; Europol has been made a European agency. Finally, despite a drawn-out slowdown in growth, the past decade has witnessed the full implementation of the Financial Services Action Plan (FSAP) and the approval of the services Directive, which covers on a residual basis all economic activities not yet liberalised under internal market legislation.

Two years down the road from the disastrous referendums in France and the Netherlands, member states have reached, with the Lisbon Treaty, an agreement on institutions that upholds the main innovations laid out in the Constitutional Treaty - albeit without the 'signs and symbols' of a constitution, which were strongly opposed by public opinion in quite a few member states - and basically settles political issues left pending, after Maastricht, in the operation of common institutions. The Treaty has thus specified the allocation of competences between the Union and the member states, the balance of powers between the Council, the Commission and the European Parliament, as well as rebalanced, within the Council, the voting weights of large and small countries. It has also put an end to the rotating Presidency of the European Council, strengthened the powers of the High Representative for the Common Foreign and Security Policy and vastly increased the number of topics subject to majority voting.

Thus, it appears that feelings of paralysis in decision-making may be widespread in the media and public opinion alike, but they are not confirmed by fact. Nor has the pace of decision-making been slowed by the accession of new member states, although some complain about the increased complexity of Council decision-making.

Public opinion support for European institutions plummeted after Maastricht, but has recovered somewhat since the middle of the 1990s: as shown in Figure 1, up until 2008 over 50% of respondents to a Eurobarometer survey continued to view participation in the Union as positive (although a drop in support below 50% is expected due to the current deep economic crisis, which is feeding disillusionment with the Union's ability to respond effectively). Opinion polls also show that among national and Community institutions, the European Parliament continues to enjoy considerable prestige, although declining voter participation in European elections might seem suggest the contrary.

*Figure 1. Public opinion on participation in the EU**

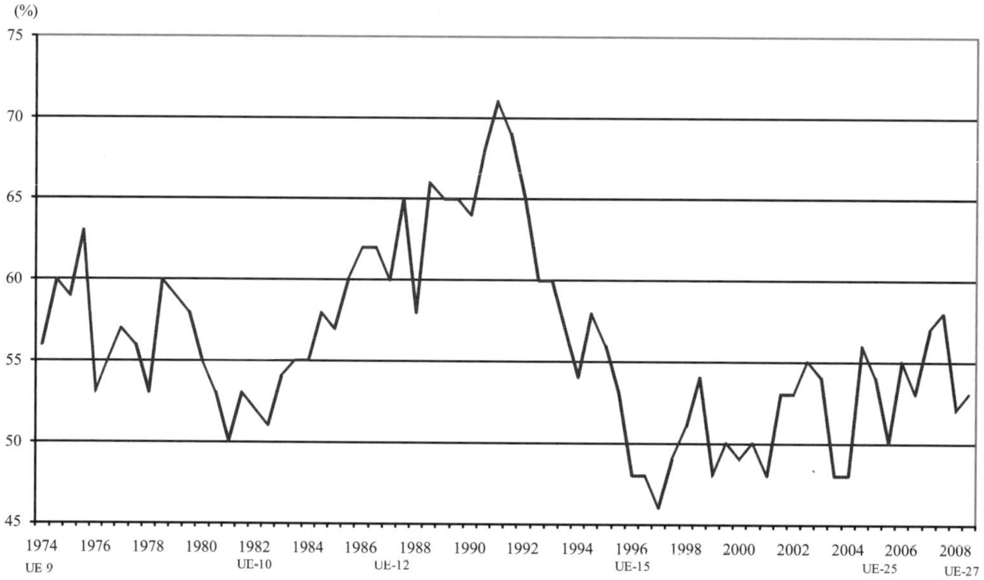

* % of positive answers to the question: "Do you think that your country's membership of the European Union is a good thing?

Source: Eurobarometer.

That said, the issue of democracy is perhaps better addressed in terms of adjusting a political system that has very considerably extended its scope and thus requires a corresponding extension in the scope of its democratic controls; but the lack of democracy does not appear to be the main cause of a crisis that, as will be argued, may well have stemmed more from the weakness of governments than from the opposition of the governed. Nor should one expect an extension in the scope of democratic controls to solve all of European society's pending problems, from unemployment to immigration, exclusion and security, in a world where the pace of change is controlled neither by individual states nor by the European Union.[1]

1. The need for democratic legitimisation

The Union is a peculiar polity, without the powers of coercion and linkage to a geographical territory typical of nation states; its powers are spread out over a number of institutions and procedures, each of which has its own legitimisation mechanisms (Lord & Magnette, 2004). These powers have been bestowed by the member states, which have democratic institutions and control the Union's activity through the European Council of Heads of State and of Government and the Council of Ministers. One must therefore first of all seek to clarify what is meant by the requests for more legitimisation channels.

The original design of the European Communities' competences and decision-making mechanisms reflected a technocratic and functionalist approach, under which Europe's higher interests were embodied in the European Commission, a non-democratic body with exclusive powers of legislative initiative and entrusted with the impartial custodianship of the Treaties. The Council was the necessarily opaque forum for political compromise among the member states; direct democratic legitimisation was confined to the European Parliament, initially assigned weak consultative powers, but later endowed with full co-decision of legislative measures in most EU matters (including, after the Lisbon Treaty, the EU multi-annual financial perspectives and yearly budgets).

One problem has been that decisions on the extension of the Union's functions were hidden behind the veil of small incremental steps justified by functional requirements – a solution devised by Monnet to pursue the European construction following the rejection of the European Defence Community by the French National Assembly in 1954. This intrinsically undemocratic strategy was facilitated by the integration process's

---

[1] This clearly does not rule out that European policies may yet improve in this respect, lending greater consistency to member state policies and strengthening their efficiency through better coordination. On this, see for instance the Sapir Report, containing ambitious proposals to revise common economic policies (Sapir et al., 2004).

indeterminate finality, which allowed supporters of the political union concept to co-exist with those who simply wanted a large open market. The fall of the Berlin Wall added further uncertainty regarding borders, as vagueness prevailed as to where the enlargement process would stop (Majone, 2005).

Developments in the wake of the failed Constitutional Treaty referendums in France and the Netherlands have radically changed this picture. First of all, decisions on enlargement were shifted to the political/constitutional level as a number of countries decided that they will in the future submit all enlargement issues to popular referendum; moreover, in the Lisbon Treaty political discretion in decisions to admit new members will be constrained by the need to respect the so-called 'Copenhagen criteria' (Article 49 TEU).

More importantly, the Lisbon Treaty has somewhat set in stone the attribution principle. It has established member state residual jurisdiction in all matters not explicitly devolved to the Union (Articles 4 and 5 TEU) and - through new Protocols on the role of national parliaments in the European Union and the application of the principles of subsidiarity and proportionality - it has introduced political and judicial procedures to keep in check the Union's competences. The risk of jurisdiction 'creep', eluding democratic control, now appears to be very much a thing of the past. Furthermore, by removing the 'signs and symbols' of a constitution, the Lisbon Treaty has also removed indeterminate finality from the picture: it is now clear that the Union is not destined to become a state and that the current balance between federal and confederal dimensions is here to stay. Therefore, the Lisbon Treaty has removed a number of obvious flaws in the Union's democratic legitimisation.

Some have claimed that democratic legitimisation of Union decisions *is not possible*, as there is no *demos*, no common identity or sufficiently shared values to guide institutional and political action (Dahrendorf, 2001 and Schmitter, 2000). True, a weak common identity makes it difficult to refer back to a single popular support base; but it does not preclude the development of partial mechanisms legitimising individual decisions or decision-making processes; nor does it preclude forms of legitimisation linked to the output of common action, insofar as said action meets voters' needs that individual nation states are no longer in a position to satisfy.

The lack of demos is mirrored in the restrained use of majority voting: the extensive discussions and long negotiations required for achieving consensus legitimise decisions that would not be acceptable were they imposed by a majority of member states upon a minority of dissenting member states.

Moravcsik (2006), conversely, has claimed that further channels of democratic legitimisation *are not required*, for two main reasons. Firstly, he sees the European Union as the product of an intergovernmental agreement, embodied in the Treaties, that is "pragmatically efficient, normatively attractive and politically stable": a satisfactory negotiated equilibrium, periodically modified when the need arises, and otherwise reconfirmed, and that therefore reflects the requirements of participating states. Secondly, he maintains that increasing the opportunities to participate and make decisions does not necessarily generate more participation, nor does increased participation always generate more legitimisation. In fact, in his view, declining voter participation in elections to the European Parliament may confirm that the greater scope for democratic participation provided for by the Treaties has largely been unused; and where and when it has been used, this has been to express dissatisfaction with the domestic policies of national governments (a point also made by Bogdanor, 2007, Hicks, 1999 and Schmitter, 2000).

Moravcsik considers that this is due to the nature of the tasks undertaken by the Union, which at least originally were of a mainly technical nature, with low general political salience for most citizens: international trade, development assistance, agriculture, safety standards for manufactures and services.

This is a minority view, however. A majority of political scientists and constitutionalists conversely stress that the Union's institutions have now taken on an autonomous role, even vis-à-vis the member states, in defining the rights and political, economic and social conditions of individuals; they go on to assert that these powers cannot be taken back by the member states, inter alia, because of the unanimity requirement for Treaty revision; and precisely for this reason deem that the accumulation of powers in Union hands has already exceeded the threshold requiring autonomous safeguards against possible abuses (Schmitter, 2000; Lord, 2004; Lord & Harris, 2006 and Schmidt, 2006). Such possible abuses concern first and foremost the Council, insofar as it can elude national parliamentary control when ruling at the Union level.

Moreover, as has been mentioned, further expanding the Union's political agenda and activities through functionalist methods is no longer possible. Further political and institutional progress can only stem from deliberate decisions on the part of member states acting in full accountability vis-à-vis their public opinions and parliaments.

The co-existence within the Union of two distinct levels at which public institutions exercise their power - federal and confederal - generates an intrinsic need for corresponding democratic legitimisation mechanisms and channels, focusing on the one hand on member state representation in the Council, and, on the other, on citizen representation in the European Parliament. This dual representation has now been explicitly incorporated in the Lisbon Treaty (new Article 10, para. 2, TEU).

At the member state level, national parliaments and the public at large need to be informed of the decisions to be taken within European institutions and be able to influence the positions of their own national representatives to the Council. Separate control and legitimisation channels are also required at the Union level since its acts and decisions acquire autonomous value with respect to individual member states' inputs: because of the use of qualified majority voting in the Council, and the attendant need to reach compromise solutions that may partly sacrifice national interests; because of the constitutional weight of principles of primacy and direct effect of community legislation; and because of the role the Community judicial system can play in the defence of individuals' rights, even vis-à-vis the member states.

The revealed preference theorem that is at the root of Moravcsik's analysis of negotiated equilibrium among Union countries supports this conclusion. Over the last three decades there has been a constant increase in the Union participation and control mechanisms, through the European Parliament and national parliaments alike, which have supplanted and taken over the role initially played by organised economic interest groups. Various other channels have been opened that provide individuals with direct access to European institutions: examples include the European Ombudsman and the right to petition European institutions in one's mother tongue, introduced by the Maastricht Treaty, and broader rights for individuals to institute proceedings before the European Court of Justice.

The new Title II of the Treaty on European Union adopted in Lisbon, "Provisions on democratic principles", while carrying over from the previous Treaty provisions on citizenship, specifies new rules on the right of Union citizens to take part in its democratic life, including the right of legislative initiative (Art. 11, para. 4, TEU). This same section also contains detailed provisions regarding national parliament participation in the functioning of the Union (see Art. 12).

A mapping of decision-making procedures in the various areas of common action confirms a growing demand for democracy at Union level that has been met. The extension of qualified majority voting in new areas - which reduces the control exercised by individual member states over Council decisions - was always matched by an extension of European Parliament powers. This occurred with the Single Act, which applied majority voting to decisions regarding the internal market, subsequently leading, in the Maastricht Treaty, to the introduction of co-decisions between the Council and Parliament; it also occurred with the Lisbon Treaty when issues of immigration, justice and law enforcement came under Community jurisdiction and co-decision was made the normal decision procedure.

Similarly, the Commission's exclusive right of legislative initiative has mainly applied to 'negative' integration, i.e. decisions that remove barriers to the internal market (Majone, 2005), while in matters such as the coordination of economic policies or foreign and security policy, the initiative has remained in the hands of member states, safeguarding the prerogatives of national parliaments. The Lisbon Treaty has decided that in "specific cases provided for by treaties" procedures followed for the adoption of directives, regulations or decisions may waive Commission participation (Article 289, TFEU).

Nor do facts confirm low public opinion interest in Union decisions. Public debate on issues such as the EU Directive on services, the accession of Turkey or the mention of Christian values in the Preamble to the Constitutional Treaty elicited active involvement of intellectuals, political parties and large segments of European society.

2. Control and democratic legitimisation mechanisms

There is widespread feeling that the existing democratic control mechanisms within the Union are weak and inadequate; as mentioned above, criticism has focused both on the *input* into the decision-making dimension and the substance of decisions, or the *output* dimension. Let us look into the former first.

2.1 *Elections and referendums*

The main mechanism of democratic participation lies in popular voting in elections and referendums. As noted above, voter participation in elections to the European Parliament is not high, at under 50% of the electorate, and it dropped by about twenty percentage points between 1979, the first election, and 2004.[2] Furthermore, voter positions on European matters have appeared to strongly correlate with the popularity of national governments in office: so much so that some observers have characterised European elections as 'second-round' elections, used to send signals on domestic rather than European politics (Hicks, 1999 and Schmitter, 2000).

Low voter participation may however stem from reasons other than disaffection from Community institutions (Lord, 2004): it may for instance reflect the fact that these consultations have little impact on the general thrust of European affairs and the identity of those who will be chosen to govern. Alternatively, in a more positive view, low voter participation may reflect the basic consensus of leading political groups as to the general direction of European affairs: when positions advocated by parties and candidates appear to be sufficiently aligned with the preferences of the median voter, the incentive to go out and actually vote is reduced. In fact, the remoteness and complexity of European issues tends to generate concordant positions of national parties, with little role for the traditional left/right cleavages (see also Bastasin in this volume).

That said, the central issue remains the absence of a unified public space at the European level where it would feel relevant to express one's personal preferences. This weakness in the European political system is not going to be remedied overnight; it can only fade gradually with the emergence of European political parties and an increased perceived relevance of European issues in everyday life.

In fact, European political groupings have turned into stable organisations over recent years and have begun to focus their meetings on specific European issues, according to timelines linked to those of the

---

[2] Some observers have claimed however that decline in voter turnout largely reflects spurious statistical phenomena in voter demographics, in particular the accession of countries where voter turnout is traditionally lower; when data are corrected for such phenomena, the downward trend is less strong (Franklin, 2001).

European Council. In their comprehensive study of the voting behaviour of members of the European Parliament, Hix et al. (2007) conclude that "voting along supranational party lines gradually replaced voting along national party lines".

The process could be speeded up - based on the new powers bestowed on Parliament by the Lisbon Treaty - if national parties were to take the opportunity of European electoral campaigns to make explicit their preferences regarding the Union's budget and other Union policy issues; alas, this did not happen in the course of the June 2009 European elections.

Conversely, the idea that the President of the Commission should be elected directly by voters seems unconvincing: politicising the Commission would be incompatible with the Commission's function as arbiter of Treaty application and its exclusive power of legislative initiative, which also assumes a shared, non-partisan vision of the integration process. For the moment, no such radical change in the institutional equilibrium of the Union seems imminent.[3]

Equally unconvincing is the idea that the democratic gap could be bridged by resorting more frequently to referendums: the dangers inherent in the recourse to direct democracy for the settlement of complex issues are increased, in the case of European issues, precisely by the lack of *demos* and the absence of strong collective identification with European institutions.

2.2 *The role of national parliaments*

At the member state level, what matters is adequate control by national parliaments over the actions of governments and administrations within the Council, which constitutes an *indirect* channel of democratic control by citizens over Union decisions.

National parliaments play a central role in the approval of Treaty modifications, which constitute the Union's primary law; in many member states this approval comes under constitutional procedures. Similarly, decisions on the Union's financial resources require ratification under

---

[3] The increased powers granted to the European Parliament in the appointment of the President of the Commission do not contradict this statement, as the appointment also requires the agreement of the European Council and a broad consensus within both institutions.

national fiscal procedures since they imply funding by state budgets. Clearly, national parliaments' powers are greater for Council decisions adopted under the unanimity rule, where European Parliament involvement is weaker. Since such decisions have considerable political and institutional significance, powers of scrutiny are usually exercised with high degrees of incisiveness and often with active public opinion participation. Conversely, national parliament control is inevitably weaker over Council decisions regarding Union directives or policies where majority voting is the rule.

This is why some observers have claimed that transferring functions to the Union implies shifting the balance of powers towards executive powers, which can avail themselves of considerable discretion when negotiating compromises within the Council, as well as towards bureaucracies, which cooperate in the implementation of Community norms within Council Committees. Both sets of institutions, far removed from the public eye, can collude with the Commission and with segments of the organised interest community, according to vertical *filières* that can use the Union to bring about decisions that would not be feasible at national level (Chryssochoou, 2003 and Maurer et al., 2000).

Some member states - in particular Denmark and the United Kingdom - have addressed this issue by adopting tight procedures to provide guidance and oversight for government behaviour within European institutions, while in other cases parliamentary procedures appear less incisive and could be strengthened (Hicks, 1999 and Lord, 2004).

That said, majority voting within Council and co-decision with the European Parliament rule out rigidly binding mandates that would preclude all compromise; similarly, any direct intervention by national parliaments in European decision-making would surely entail decision-making paralysis (see Manzella elsewhere in this volume). Democratic control must therefore be resolved through the Union's mechanisms, that is, mainly via scrutiny by the European Parliament.

One noteworthy exception to this conclusion concerns the role of national parliaments in defending subsidiarity, as in the Treaty of Lisbon: violation of the subsidiarity principle would indeed amount to an infringement of member state prerogatives by Community institutions, which national parliaments are fully entitled to oppose. Should conflicts arise and not lend themselves to settlement, the European Court of Justice will have the last word.

2.3 *Control and democratic legitimisation at the Union level*

The Union is a peculiar polity where power is spread out over multiple centres and is exercised through various decision-making procedures – which currently number about thirty.[4] It features not only frequent dissociation of territorial and functional jurisdictions, but also variability in the criteria defining insiders and outsiders with respect to the exercise of its powers, both functionally and territorially (Schmitter, 2000). For this reason, as pointed out earlier, it has been described as a polity with undefined borders. The European Parliament, the main expression of popular will at the Union level, has up till now only fully intervened in decisions regarding the so-called first pillar, but this will change, as has been described, with the Lisbon Treaty.

In addition, debate on European issues tends to elude the left/right divides typical of national political systems and break up on a case-by-case basis into different member state and interest group coalitions: this does not favour linkages between national political debates and decisions to be taken at the European level. In fact, voting patterns in the European Parliament reflect motivations that can rarely be traced back to traditional political stances within member states; and national public debate on European issues tends to run along pro- and anti-European lines, which are also poorly correlated to traditional party divides (see Hicks, 1999 and Bastasin in this volume).

Finally, as noted by Majone (2005), the Union is not organised according to the division of powers paradigm typical of Western democracies, but according to a model where powers are shared among stakeholders, as in pre-modern European polities: member states, the European Parliament, Community technocrats, social groups standing for organised interests and even magistrates participate variously in decision-making and procedures, depending on the topic and the coordination problem to be resolved.

---

[4] See European Convention (2002), Final Report, European Convention Working Party IX on Simplification, CONV 424/02, 29 November 2002.

The two most emblematic illustrations of this model are the so-called 'Community decision method' and the 'networked' participation of organised interest groups in decision-making processes. Under the Community method, the Commission puts forth proposals for directives and decisions, Council and Parliament reach decisions together according to procedures that combine varying degrees of majority voting and consensus, depending on the intensity of national preferences. If the Commission does not agree to the amendments agreed by Council and Parliament, it may withdraw its proposal; absent such a text, Council and Parliament cannot reach a decision. In practice, each of the three bodies needs the other two to come to a decision.

In the exercise of its power of initiative, as in that of guardian of the Treaty, the Commission's function can perhaps best be understood not as a supra-national independent interpreter of shared public interests, as envisaged by its founding fathers, but as a technical power: in other words, the Commission can be seen more as an executive agency and a judge, than a government. And in fact, its powers are specifically defined by the treaties and in many cases are exercised on Council delegation of authority. With the extension of the Union's 'political' remit, there has been a constant increase in the Council's and Parliament's weight in decision-making, whereas the Commission's role has been limited to one of technical support and secretariat.

Nor is the Commission's power of initiative exercised as if it were absolute: in fact the Commission responds to requests from member states, organised interest groups and Parliament. Over the last few years, the balance of such influence has shifted significantly towards Parliament, which approves the Commission when it is appointed, may dismiss it with a vote of no-confidence and controls its budget.

As for networks, the Euro-polity has from the very onset bestowed a privileged status on associations representing organised economic interests at the European level; it has often encouraged and financed the setting up of such bodies. Over time, producer organisations were joined by trade unions, consumers, environmentalists and 'single issue' advocacy groups; many regions have set up representation offices in Brussels. These organisations have become the focal point for networked, extended communities of interests in the member states, which rely on the network to take part in Commission and Parliament consultation processes, publicly debating the merits of measures as they are being developed, and standing in on the drafting of legal provisions, to which they may contribute with their technical input.

Similar developments have targeted public administrations and agencies as well, following the Single Act. Within the Union, the application of common legislation is entrusted to the member states (Article 10 of the Treaty establishing the European Community). Qualified majority voting was introduced in the Council for internal market measures in parallel with the setting up of Council Committees made up of member state representatives and (as a rule) chaired by the Commission, entrusted with coordinating the application of common legislation. These Committees went on to become the hubs of national public administrations' specialised functional networks; through these, vast swathes of civil servants have become the voice of national interests within Community institutions and the voice of the Community within national bureaucracies. The European Parliament has gradually developed powers of scrutiny geared to their activities, thereby controlling the exercise of the powers delegated to them and politically impacting their work.

Regulatory agencies – set up to provide continuity and independence to the executive in fields such as competition, financial market supervision, food and environmental security (Majone, 1996) – have also established their specialised networks, the hubs of which are the committees of national regulators where officials define regulatory guidelines and review implementation issues. European Parliament involvement in this area has been considerably less, as independence from political interference is an essential rationale for such agencies.

This increasing number of networks has contributed in no small manner to the legitimisation of Community institutions vis-à-vis various constituencies, through widespread participation, the emergence of broader bases for consensus on Community institutions' legislation and decisions, and the introduction of counterweights to the various decision-making centres. To some extent, this may weaken the European Parliament's powers of guidance and control. But the increase in the number of legitimisation channels thus brought about does strengthen the Union (see Cassese, 2002 and elsewhere in this volume), in a complex transnational system where the development of channels of representation and communication between representatives and those they represent remains limited.

Potential conflict between various legitimisation channels in turn induces adjustments in the way the system operates, through a continuous process of 'constitutional deliberation', a salient feature of European institutions (Lord & Magnette, 2004 and Cassese in this volume). Public opinion regarding the impact of internal market common policies was thus taken on board as of the Amsterdam Treaty, through a revision of Article 95, which constitutes the main legal basis for internal market legislation, and the introduction of the new Article 16A on public services, which extended the scope of national public interest protection with respect to the application of common legislation.

An apparent blow to the democratic legitimacy of the Union has now come from the German Constitutional Court decision that has declared the compatibility of the Lisbon Treaty with the constitution,[5] but which has (re)asserted that the Union is not a federation, that sovereignty only lies with the member states and that the European Parliament cannot claim to represent European citizens, due to its skewed representation formula that favours small member states. In reality, these positions are not new, they were already stated in the decision that opened the way to ratification of the Maastricht Treaty, and they do not contradict the normal functioning of European decision-making. Their real significance lies in the enhanced safeguards that they posit for the possibility, opened by the Lisbon Treaty, to change decision-making procedures by unanimous deliberation of the European Council: the German Constitutional Court has indicated that any such decisions will have to be ratified by the national parliament – although it is not clear under what procedures, constitutional or ordinary. But such passage would in all likelihood have been inevitable anyway, since under the Lisbon Treaty any national parliament would be able to oppose such a change.

2.4 *Popular legitimisation and constitutionalism*

Mény (2002) has argued that popular dissatisfaction with democracy has increased because of the larger role played by 'constitutionalist' or 'non-majoritarian' mechanisms in the exercise of public powers; this concerns member states as much as the European Union. Over the last few decades

---

[5] Cf. Federal Constitutional Court , Judgment of 30 June 2009, (2 BvE 2/08, 2 BvE 5/08, 2 BvR 1010/08, 2 BvR 1022/08, 2 BvR 1259/08 und 2 BvR 182/09).

these independent powers have taken on particular significance in market regulation, through the setting up of independent agencies (Majone, 1996). The paramount example is monetary policy management that has been entrusted exclusively to central banks, thereby removing it from the sphere of possible inflationary manipulation by governments.

However, central banks and regulatory agencies were set up by parliaments, which defined their goals and instruments in the law; and in the exercise of their powers, they were typically made independent from the executive but not from parliamentary scrutiny. Their legitimisation is secured not only by their political and parliamentary mandate, but also by procedures defining how decisions must be taken for the protection of the collective and individual interests they are responsible for upholding (Lord & Magnette, 2004).

A significant aspect of European Union activity does indeed concern market regulation, with a view to removing barriers to free circulation and competition. When it comes to implementation, the Commission operates as an independent agency, sanctioning states and individuals for violations and obliging them to put an end to prohibited behaviour. Decisions may be corrected through appeals to the European Court of Justice, but as a rule not by national or Union political powers. Some have claimed that the European Central Bank (ECB) enjoys even greater independence than do national central banks, as neither the Council nor the European Parliament provides an actual political counterweight. The ECB's mandate is treaty-defined, and therefore can only be modified via a unanimous vote of the member states, whereas in most countries the central bank's mandate is defined by ordinary legislation.

The loss of political control can generate unpopularity - understandably, insofar as public opinion may not perceive the efficiency benefits in economic policy management linked to this 'constitutionalisation' (Eichengreen, 2007). Unpopularity may also stem from the very attitude of national governments, which sometimes have shown no hesitation in blaming the Union for unpopular policies they had voluntarily agreed to implement within the Council. Unpopularity can also feed on the rising intensity of forces for globalisation and technological change, as these reduce the effectiveness of traditional tools of economic management and income distribution (Dahrendorf, 2001; Scharpf, 1999 and Schmitter, 2000).

The most significant contribution in terms of restoring government and Union popularity would come from better designed economic policies, able to address the challenges of global markets, which is the topic of the following section.

3. Legitimisation through substantive Community action

Public institutions are established to meet needs that cannot be met through individual action and thereby require forms of *collective* action. The quality of collective action plays a significant, and in the long run, crucial role among legitimisation processes. This applies to the European Union's institutions as well: all the more so, as democratic legitimisation through decision-making processes is weaker there (Schmitter, 2000 and Scharpf, 1999).

Various authors have considered this to be a leading cause of Union unpopularity: they feel that integration policies reduce the latitude national policies may have to achieve redistribution goals, thereby contributing to a 'race to the bottom' in terms of public welfare and public services (e.g. Dahrendorf, 2001 and Scharpf, 1999). Mény (2002) underscores the Union's role in shifting the balance in economic policies in favour of market forces.

These conclusions call for some qualification. First of all, as pointed out earlier, the loss of control suffered by national policies has to be assigned to globalisation more than to specific action on the part of the Union; the Union, and the member states for that matter, can do nothing but adapt to processes that elude control by all governments. The criticism therefore concerns the operational difficulties encountered by democratic systems in general, and not only by European institutions. Examples include difficulties in responding adequately to economic insecurity or to national welfare system strains linked to population aging. Moreover, during slow-growth years, weak and irresolute national governments did not hesitate to blame Europe for events that stemmed from their inability to reach decisions, thereby feeding hostility towards European institutions.

It is also worth noting that many Union initiatives have constrained state action, but to the benefit of citizens: for instance, by strengthening the defence of consumer interests through competition policy or transparency and quality requirements in the provision of public services.

Finally, empirical evidence confirms convergence in the fundamental philosophy of macroeconomic policies, in the sense that neither monetary policy nor public deficits are considered very effective tools to bring about lasting improvements in growth and employment. The data, however, do not confirm the existence of a general constraint on national policies precluding the pursuit of autonomous goals of equity and solidarity.

Mosley (2004) has shown that pressure exerted by financial markets on governments with a view to having them reduce deficits is not related to the adoption of the single currency. In general, empirical evidence confirms that countries of very different state size and resulting tax burdens can persist side by side in an environment of integrated capital markets. In other words, different collective preferences in terms of public intervention need not be incompatible with integration and globalisation.

Similarly, a whole body of literature has identified sustainable unemployment benefit schemes as well as inefficient schemes, which are unsustainable in an open and integrated environment (Sapir, 2006). Insofar as they encourage risk-taking, efficient systems that insure against the risk of losing one's job can increase growth, rather than dampen it (Ferrera & Sacchi in this volume). Gros & Micossi (2006) have called for common labour market policies that would facilitate the integration of immigrants while limiting the impact of wage undercutting for nationals.

As a rule, responsibility for economic and social policies lies with the member states, and this should be acknowledged publicly. That said, a sharing out of tasks between the Union and member states that would assign the former responsibility only for 'negative integration' policies – i.e. establishing a common market and removing barriers to free movement – would be necessarily unpopular and untenable in the long run. This is why the identification of appropriate 'positive integration' policies, taking on board public opinion demands – for social cohesion, security, effective management of migration flows – remains a crucial element of legitimisation.

3.1 *Opening new areas for decision-making in the Union's policies*

The Lisbon Treaty has kept the name of the Treaty on European Union (TEU), while modifying that of the Treaty establishing the European Community, which will now be called the Treaty on the Functioning of the European Union (TFEU). The name change is substantive: many rules regarding the functioning of what was previously called the second and third pillar are now included in this second part.

More important, this partition could also foreshadow a distinction between fundamental and ordinary law, as already exists in many countries. This interpretation is confirmed by the simplified revision procedures applicable to the provisions "relative to the internal policies and actions of the Union" (cf. Article 48 of the Final Provisions of the Treaty on European Union). These procedures envisage that the Council shall decide treaty changes in those areas unanimously, after having consulted the European Parliament and the Commission. Convening an intergovernmental conference will no longer be required.

The issue is addressed in a more general context by Tosato in this volume. Suffice it to say that this change has potentially significant implications for the Union's democratic legitimisation: common policies can now be changed without challenging the institutional framework of the Union. The policies in question have indeed become just that: common policies, about which political differences may appear, according to traditional left/right lines or to new divides specific to the European public arena. In other words, new spaces have been opened for public debate and political action at Union level; if they are used, the Union's democratic legitimisation may become stronger.

With new tasks to undertake and new public spaces for political debate at a transnational level - that of democracy "beyond States", to quote Lord & Harris (2006) - the politicisation of the Union's institutions seems bound to take up greater scope. The process will however need to take into account the specificities of European construction, where many authorities have been established to guarantee the impartial implementation of common rules: in order to survive, there is a need to preserve the areas of impartiality, free of partisan political influences.

4. Conclusions

The European Union is not a state, so comparisons with state-type models of democratic legitimisation may well prove misleading. Nor is the discussion about intervening *ex novo* to introduce democratic accountability within an organisation which did not previously know it. The first direct election to the European Parliament took place close to 30 years ago; since then, the Union's institutional system has continued to evolve, establishing in the process significant areas for democratic participation and control.

Once the Union is recognised for what it is - an innovative polity, where power is shared by a large number of players, with many mechanisms for participation and wielding influence, constantly adapting its institutions to the requirements of its component parts - it becomes apparent that on the whole it complies with democratic legitimisation standards no worse than do member states (Mény, 2002), even if multiple, and potentially conflicting legitimisation channels and principles may confuse observers.

In the end, the Union will be strong in the eyes of public opinion and member states alike if it manages to come up with solutions to the challenges of globalisation, external and internal security, energy and the environment. In this respect, there is no reason why the difficulties encountered over the last decade should last, to the extent that they were a systemic consequence of poor Union functioning. On the contrary, we are perhaps reaching the end of a long and painful adjustment process to an exceptional series of real and financial shocks, generated by the fall of the Berlin Wall. Time will no doubt tell.

For the time being, what saliently needs to be kept in mind is that the member states and EU citizens, however mangled by crises and difficulties, continue to turn to the Union when seeking solutions to problems that cannot be solved nationally, and that there is an extraordinary proliferation of subjects and channels providing participation in European debates and decisions, in new and ever-changing ways.

Of course, this continuous adaptation process has not been without consequences for institutional balance. The founding fathers' initial idea of a supranational polity has been scaled down to accommodate a more realistic view of power attribution and sharing. With the extension of the Union's scope, and its increasing politicisation, the weight of the Council and the Parliament in decision-making has increased; the Commission has strengthened its technical prerogatives in matters of treaty implementation and enforcement, while its right of initiative has been curtailed.

Through this continuous adjustment process, the Union has continued to design new legitimisation solutions for multi-level and transnational political structures, which may well represent the future of democracy in a world of increasingly integrated manifold communities.

References

Bogdanor, V. (2007), *Legitimacy, Accountability and Democracy in the European Union*, A Federal Trust Report, Federal Trust for Education & Research, London, January.

Cassese, S. (2002), "Is there really a democratic deficit?", in *Institutional Reforms in the European Union – Memorandum for the Convention*, Europeos, Rome.

Chryssochoou, D.N. (2003), "EU Democracy and the Democratic Deficit", in M. Cini (ed.), *European Union Politics*, Oxford: Oxford University Press, chapter 23, pp. 366-381.

Dahrendorf, R. (2001), *Dopo la Democrazia*, Interview edited by A. Polito, Roma-Bari, Laterza.

Eichengreen, B. (2007), *The Breakup of the Euro Area*, NBER Working Paper No. 13393, National Bureau of Economic Research, Cambridge, MA, September.

European Convention (2002), Final Report, European Convention Working Party IX on Simplification, CONV 424/02, 29 November 2002.

Franklin, M. (2001), "How Structural Factors Cause Turnout Variation at European Parliament Elections", *European Union Politics*, Vol. 2, No. 3, pp. 309-329.

Gros, D. and S. Micossi (2006), *Crisis in the European Union: A Fresh Start*, CEPS Policy Brief No. 117, CEPS, Brussels.

Hicks, S. (1999), *The Political System of the European Union*, London: Macmillan.

Hix, S., A.G. Noury and G. Roland (2007), *Democratic Politics in the European Parliament*, Cambridge: Cambridge University Press.

Lord, C. (2004), *A Democratic Audit of the European Union*, Basingstoke: Palgrave Macmillan.

Lord, C. and E. Harris (2006), *Democracy in the New Europe*, Basingstoke: Palgrave Macmillan.

Lord, C. and P. Magnette (2004), "E Pluribus Unum? Creative Disagreement about Legitimacy in the EU", *Journal of Common Market Studies*, Vol. 42, No. 1, pp. 183-202.

Majone, G. (1996), *Regulating Europe*, London: Routledge.

Majone, G. (2005), *Dilemmas of European Integration – The Ambiguities and Pitfalls of Integration by Stealth*, Oxford: Oxford University Press.

Maurer, A., J. Mittag and W. Wessels (2000), "Theoretical Perspectives on Administrative Interaction in the European Union", in T. Christiansen and E. Kirchner (eds), *Committee Governance in the European Union*, Manchester: Manchester University Press.

Mény, I. (2002), "De la Démocratie en Europe: Old Concepts and New Challenges", *Journal of Common Market Studies*, Vol. 41, No. 1, pp. 1-13.

Moravcsik, A. (1998), *The Choice for Europe. Social Purpose and State Power from Messina to Maastricht*, London: UCL Press.

Moravcsik, A. (2006), "What Can We Learn from the Collapse of the European Constitutional Project? A Symposium", *Politische Vierteljahresschrift*, Vol. 47, No. 2, pp. 219-241.

Mosley, L. (2004), "Government-Financial Market Relations after EMU. New Currencies, New Constraints?", *European Union Politics*, Vol. 5, No. 2, pp. 181-209.

Sapir, A. (2006), "Globalisation and the Reform of European Social Models", *Journal of Common Market Studies*, June, pp. 369-389.

Sapir, A., P. Aghion, G. Bertola, M. Hellwig, J. Pisani-Fery, D. Rosati, J. Viñals and H. Wallace (2004), *An Agenda for a Growing Europe (The Sapir Report)*, Oxford: Oxford University Press.

Scharpf, F. (1999), *Governing in Europe: Effective and Democratic*, Oxford: Oxford University Press.

Schmidt, V. (2006), *Democracy in Europe – The EU and National Polities*, Oxford: Oxford University Press.

Schmitter, P.C. (2000), *How to Democratise the European Union ... and Why Bother?*, Oxford: Rowman & Littlefield Publishers, Inc.

13. TRAIL-BLAZING DEVELOPMENTS IN JUSTICE AND HOME AFFAIRS

GIACINTO DELLA CANANEA[*]

Ever since the collapse of the Soviet system, capitalist market economies have prevailed worldwide, based on economic institutions such as prices, markets and businesses. However, market economies require a number of corresponding legal tools, such as property, contracts and judicial protection of rights. They also require 'public goods', such as security and public order, defence and civil protection, which public institutions are expected to deliver.[1] The importance of such goods has become even more evident during the last 10 years, due to the growing awareness that individuals and groups may jeopardise the ability of states to produce and provide those 'goods' that are essential to an ordered society. In order to preserve this ultimate value - a legally unchallengeable goal,[2] regardless of the modalities of its achievement - a dual line of analysis must be developed, by identifying the terms of the problem and specifying the constructs required to work out a solution. The first of these lines is not addressed fully in this paper. Rather, the paper focuses on the achievements at the level of the European Union and on their future

* The author expresses his thanks to Sabino Cassese, Stefano Micossi and Gian Luigi Tosato for their comments on an earlier version of this chapter.

[1] The term 'public institutions' is used here in the broad sense, including both supranational agencies and sub-state-level authorities, such as territorial bodies (regions) as well as legal entities that are formally private but that exercise public functions.

[2] According to Ziller (2007, p. 55), "research to date shows that citizens of all Member States expect the Union to provide protection in those fields that are of direct relevance to their everyday lives", as is the case with justice and home affairs.

prospects. It briefly describes less recent developments, in order to concentrate on the more recent.

1. The problem: Losing control over territory and individuals

The starting point is that the authority once exercised by the institutions that are used by states to exercise authority over territory and people has been undermined and eroded, even where state organisation is efficient. There is not a single cause for this, but, rather a plurality of causes, which often interact with one another.[3]

Territorially defined jurisdiction. Criminal organisations increasingly operate transnationally. Criminals, goods (drugs, weapons, hazardous waste) and the proceeds of illegal activities move around the world unhindered, including among European countries whose borders are 'porous'. A further impact derives from the gradual increase - brought about by conflict and famine - in the number of immigrants who attempt to 'illegally' enter EU member states. Public institutions thus find it increasingly difficult to prohibit specific deeds or activities, even when they resort, under extreme circumstances, to the use of force.[4] Meanwhile, various groups (separatists, terrorists, religious fanatics) are mounting deliberate attacks on collective security. Thanks to modern technology, the availability of funding and easy access to military weapons, these groups are now in a position to inflict unprecedented damage on property, persons and law-abiding society. They are challenging the ability of specialised agencies to exercise functions of intelligence-gathering and policing, as territorial separation constrains what these agencies may do.

Failures in information-gathering. The responsiveness of state bureaucracy is not only constrained by national borders. The information available to such bodies is also limited and its processing is costly. It is therefore partial, at times distorted and often obsolete. When administrations in charge of intelligence-gathering or policing are poorly,

---

[3] The issues covered here have been the focus of much work. For a global view, see Peers (2008).

[4] In the sense that the hallmark of the state - according to Max Weber's well-known analysis - is its monopoly over the legitimate use of force, as opposed to the use of force per se (see Giannini, 1990, p. 224).

insufficiently or belatedly informed, decision-making is inevitably affected by these shortcomings. Expected outcomes cannot be delivered.

Discrepancies in focus and organisation. In addition to often not being in a position to fully exercise control over their territory and not having access to adequate information, state bureaucracies follow different approaches. Such differences to a large extent reflect political ideas, but depend also on national administrative styles. Consider, for example, the plurality of police force structures, as one finds in Italy.[5] Such asymmetries risk further eroding the ability of states to achieve territorial control. For example, if Spanish police forces go so far as to use extreme force in refusing entry to illegal migrants, while Italy and Greece let them in, this may be viewed as an incentive by migrants.

Insufficient cooperation. Although the need for more stable and prompt cooperation is now broadly acknowledged, many obstacles remain. Language is one, especially if vehicular languages, such as English, are not yet diffuse even between senior officers. Technology is another obstacle. Not only assuming information is not an easy task, but it may prove difficult to interpret it properly, especially if different technologies are in use. Last but not least, all state bodies are generally reluctant to accept external constraints, to coordinate the work they do in various areas with that of similar bodies in other countries, to take joint decisions. This is hardly surprising, however, when considering that only at the end of the first quarter of the 20th century did the United States set up a Federal Bureau to fight against crime.

These inadequacies lead to inefficiencies in the use of the inevitably scarce resources that states can muster in order to ensure the rule of law and protect the interests of the community they represent. Not only does this prevent the development of joint strategies, but it can even lead to the misuse of state powers. Moreover, often it is hard for them to reconcile security with safeguarding liberties and rights.

2. The European rescue of police powers?

In order to reduce the asymmetry vis-à-vis individuals and groups, the states cooperate in many forms. Governments and administrations

---

[5] For more on these discrepancies, see Cassese (1997).

increasingly engage in the exchange of information and assistance beyond what is required by their respective legislation, for example in the fight against terrorism. Sometimes, even the courts affirm their jurisdiction over events that have occurred elsewhere. The rulings of the British House of Lords, in a matter initiated by a Spanish magistrate regarding former Chilean dictator Augusto Pinochet, are only the best-known illustration of this development.[6] As far as the European arena is concerned, cooperation with regard to public order has taken on a variety of different forms that ultimately can be traced back to three paradigms. These paradigms are not logically linked to one another, nor are they sequentially connected, in the sense that one follows or is replaced by another. Rather, they have co-existed and to a considerable extent still do. The three are straight vanilla intergovernmental or 'voluntary' cooperation with or without multilateral agreements, cooperation among all EU member states and enhanced cooperation among some of the latter.

Up until the mid-1980s, intergovernmental cooperation took place entirely outside Community provisions. It covered a variety of different subjects: initially immigration and asylum rights, then terrorism and the fight against transnational crime. Cooperation implied adopting legally binding agreements or significant – albeit non-binding – texts such as conventions and recommendations. It also meant developing information exchange, and setting up structured counterpart panels of national experts. Other changes occurred during the years 1985-86. First, the European Single Act strengthened the constitutional status of individuals' freedom of movement whilst codifying the widening of the competences of the European Community. Second, the Schengen Agreement was enacted by a few countries (five of the six founding countries, with the initial exception of Italy). It aimed at eliminating internal border controls and strengthening controls at the external border level. The agreement was subsequently extended to other countries several years later, when they adapted their administrative systems. Eventually, the Community itself extended the scope of its own jurisdiction with a view to include this agreement within its institutional framework.

---

[6] See Volcansek & Stack (2005) and Bianchi & Naqvi (2004). See also Slaughter (2005) for the thesis that the global interaction between judges and administrators generated a new world order.

Ever since 1992, EU member states have been actively involved in the establishment of the Freedom, Security and Justice Area provided for by Article 2 of the Maastricht Treaty (TEU). As a result, the treaty covers a broad range of fields, including asylum and immigration policies, combating drug addiction and customs and police cooperation,[7] which regard the *compétences régaliennes*, a domain that states jealously retain. This explains the specificities of the action of the Union. First, its functions are carried out in a partially distinct legal and political environment, as it emerges by the 'third pillar' metaphor (the second being that of foreign and security policy). Second, decision-making procedures are based on unanimity, instead of majority-voting. Third, and also its final outcome, namely the acts differ from those of the EC, including common positions, conventions and other documents. Fourth, it was found that genuinely supranational institutions, such as the European Commission and the European Court of Justice, enjoy only a marginal role.[8]

3. An area of freedom, security and justice

At the end of the 20th century, a further constitutional change was introduced through the Amsterdam Treaty (1999). Various fields or sub-fields were shifted from the third to the first pillar: policing of external borders, asylum and immigration and judicial cooperation in civil cases, which is the focus of a recently adopted convention involving third-party countries such as Switzerland. For other fields, the role of the Community has been specified (Article 29 of the TEU).[9] The salient change is that public functions in the field of justice and home affairs are legally and not only politically determined by the goals and rules established by the European Union.[10] This does not mean, however, that the states concerned have renounced pursuing their own active policies in these fields. Rather, it implies that national authorities have to abide by common rules and decisions. Closer cooperation is thus made possible not only by the sounder

[7] See Monar (2003, p. 497) and also Delmas-Marty (1996).

[8] See Tosato (2000, p. 331).

[9] See Adam (1999, p. 225) and Alvarez (2005, p. 27).

[10] Drawing a line between the 'territory' concept (once considered an essential tenet of the state, on par with the 'people' and 'sovereignty') and that of 'area' is essential. For a political scientist's view, see Monar (2003, p. 497).

legal basis provided by the treaty, but also by the definition of new categories of legally binding acts. For example, framework decisions are binding as to their goal, as are directives, but with no direct effectiveness. These new instruments, together with 'Decisions', supplement common positions and conventions, the adoption of which is *recommended* to member states. The latter may enter into force in the adopting member states, unless otherwise specified, once at least half of all member states have indeed adopted them. No attempt has been made even partially to unify national legal systems: constitutional traditions proved far too different for that to be contemplated (the centrality of trial by jury in common law countries is but one of the most evident examples). If anything, this may emphasise the need for some measure of convergence among national parliaments, through the removal of structural obstacles.

Further progress has been made in recent years.[11] As regards organisational issues, several steps have been taken to strengthen the action of Europol, an agency set up in 1995 with a view to coordinating the operations of national administrations. The head of Europol is now authorised to enter into external agreements. A European judicial network has been put into place[12] - and acknowledged by the 2001 Nice Treaty - which has *Eurojust* at its centre. New networks have thus been added to pre-existing Community and national structures. At the same time, the principle of information availability has been stressed. This means that the information available to specific bodies in a given state must be provided to counterpart bodies in other states. A further requirement has been added: to the extent possible, information thus exchanged must be sent using modern technology. Even more important from a legal standpoint has been the replacement of traditional extradition procedures with the European

---

[11] This has been acknowledged, albeit critically, in a European Parliament Resolution on "Progress made by the EU in creating an area of freedom, security and justice", adopted 30 November 2006.

[12] Joint action No. 98/241/GAI. The Justice Ministries are clearly involved in a number of different cooperative projects, as evidenced by the fact that they participate in meetings of the following groups and committees: a) committee on Article 36, b) multidisciplinary group (justice and home affairs) on organised crime, c) horizontal group on narcotics, d) group on cooperation in criminal law proceedings and e) European judicial network group.

Arrest Warrant (EAW).[13] This is a streamlined procedure that the judiciary may use to obtain the handing over of convicts or suspects. For a number of explicitly listed crimes, this handing over is possible regardless of dual criminality considerations, provided that the maximum sentence to be incurred is at least three years. Thus, not only has cooperation between the states extended to the power to punish, but their legal systems now increasingly practice mutual recognition (as reiterated in TEC Articles 61 and 61 C, as modified by Treaty of Lisbon (hereafter, ToL) Article 64).

This approach, initially used to build the single market, presupposes and strengthens principles that are part of a shared constitutional heritage. At the very core of this heritage lies the principle of the legality of crimes and punishment. Interpreted in the light of mutual recognition, it allows for exceptions to the dual criminality rule. The basic assumption is that the high degree of confidence established among public institutions is such that the criminal law of any given country is deemed to constitute a valid legal basis for the exercise of legal proceedings in another. A second shared principle is that of equality and non-discrimination. This is safeguarded by the list of crimes published in the Framework Decision, which ensures legal certainty, at least to a certain extent. It does not, however, rule out there being different implementations in different countries. On the other hand, the Framework Decision admittedly does not aim to harmonise substantive criminal law in member states.[14] A third principle, which is usually referred to as *ne bis in idem*, prevents the possibility of sentencing someone twice for the same crime. According to the European Court of Justice, the rationale for this stems from the need to avoid having the same individuals taken to court for the same sets of facts in more than one member state, as this would impose an excessive limitation on their freedom of movement. Thus

---

[13] Framework Decision No. 20027584/GAI, of 13 June 2002. The uniform implementation of the framework decision was called into question following a ruling handed down by the German Constitutional Court in the *Darkanzali* case, which partially voided the national implementing regulation, stating that it conflicted with constitutional principles of the rule of law. Cases concerning Belgian and Polish constitutional courts are reviewed in Siegel (2008).

[14] European Court of Justice, 3 May 2007 ruling, Case C-303/05, *Advocaten voor de Wereld VZW v. Leden van de Ministerraad*. The convergence of criminal legislation is granted *if necessary* under new TEC Article 61, while recourse to legislative procedures can only lead to *minimum rules* (Article 69 A).

defined, the principle applies not only to cases where individuals have been deemed not guilty as to substance, but also when the non-guilty ruling has been handed down for reasons relating to statutes of limitations.[15]

4. From the Laeken Declaration to the Lisbon Treaty

A further development in the definition of the Union's new constitutional framework was initiated in December 2002, at the European Council meeting in Laeken. On this occasion, member states expressed their intention to further strengthen their cooperation, including through the adoption of new institutional provisions. A revision process of both the Treaty of Rome and the Treaty setting up the European Union thus begun and gave rise to the "Treaty establishing a Constitution for Europe", which clarified the functions of the EU, identified new instruments and corrected a number of rules relative to decision-making.[16] However, the Treaty was rejected by some countries (France and the Netherlands, following the failure of referendums) and eventually did not enter into force.

Following further negotiations, some of the more significant innovations agreed in 2003 were included in the Treaty entered into in Lisbon on 13 December 2007, which modified the constitutional rules of the European Union as well as those relative to its functioning. Provisions regulating Union jurisdiction in the fields under review have not been changed. The legal principles and goals to be pursued by public institutions have however been restated, and new principles introduced. All this will be considered from two points of view, which aim at identifying the more relevant changes introduced and shedding some light on the substantive logic that underpins them, respectively.

The first change concerns the Union's goals. The new treaty specifies that within the area of freedom, security and justice, the freedom of movement of persons shall be safeguarded, and the adoption of appropriate measures to ensure external border control, asylum, immigration, as well as the prevention and combating of crime (TEU

---

15 European Court of Justice, 28 September 2006 ruling, Case C-467/04, *G.F. Gasparini*.

16 See Ziller (2004).

Article 2, as modified by ToL Article 4), guaranteed. Responsibilities taken on vis-à-vis citizens and third-party nationals are significant: the Union is "to ensure a high level of security" (TEC Article 61, as modified by ToL Article 64).

The second change derives from the relinquishing of the three-pillar approach to the European Union's powers. This is further demonstrated by the fact that legal safeguards are to be provided for in the framework of administrative measures taken to prevent or combat terrorism, while directives are contemplated to facilitate cooperation between police and judicial authorities, in addition to the mutual recognition of judicial decisions (TEC Arts. 61 H and 69 A, as modified by ToL Article 64).

These developments do not imply that the specific features mentioned earlier with regard to decision-making procedures do not exist anymore. A number of changes to those rules have nevertheless been defined. Some are of a very general nature, and focus on the establishment of enhanced cooperation (§8). Others are more specific, and can be quite relevant: in order to protect the financial interests of the Union, including against crime, the Council may adopt regulations on a unanimous basis. In the absence of unanimity, however, a group of at least nine member states may request that the matter be referred to the European Council. If no consensus emerges within four months, and should the nine member states wish to proceed with enhanced cooperation, they shall notify Union institutions accordingly and "in such a case, the authorisation to proceed with enhanced cooperation (…) shall be deemed to be granted" (TEC Article 69E).

The essence of this new legal framework is characterised by two features. First, the task to strike an appropriate balance between authority and liberties is no longer the exclusive responsibility of the member states. It is shared with the EU. Second, however, the new legal framework allows national public institutions (governments, administrations, judiciary) to operate in a context that is clearly more favourable than that which prevails outside the EU. Such a legal framework does not preempt state jurisdiction, nor does it erode their legal - or political - responsibilities. In particular, coercive powers remain the province of national authorities even though the legal framework that determines the legitimacy of their use increasingly bears the mark of the European Union's rules and operations.[17] In other words, this new development has further stressed the fact that the Union has taken an increasingly administrative turn, and that progress has been far less marked in terms of political consolidation. Time will tell whether one dimension can develop independently of the other and if so, to what extent.

5. Issues of efficiency and safeguards

After this cursory review of the new legal framework, two different sets of questions may be considered. The first is whether interactions between new and old holders of authority, i.e. the European Union and its member states, are likely to offset the asymmetry that leaves private players in a disadvantageous situation, in particular transnational organised crime. Clearly, the ability to exercise control over private players cannot be assessed solely as a zero-sum game between public institutions. It may be more than that, or less. The issue, however, is whether cooperation within the EU limits the undermining of state bodies' powers. This issue must be reviewed separately from another, which is more frequently addressed in government studies. Improving the ability of government officials and government bodies and departments to reach and implement decisions beyond national borders may lead to a gradual qualitative and quantitative drop in the safeguards provided by public legislation.[18] There are different views as to the scope for strengthening such safeguards within states, as opposed to rebuilding them within European law. However, one point should be absolutely clear: not only are safeguards needed as regards the exercise of such powers, but also adequate forms of accountability, according to the principles of constitutional government.

On the first of these levels of analysis, that of public decision-making and implementation effectiveness, there are several obstacles. The very fact that decisions have to be reached with several member state governments implicitly entails a number of heavy burdens, which add on to the specific constraints and limitations that justice and home affairs departments have to contend with, and that have no EU equivalent. The Commission's ability

---

[17] For a convincing theoretical overview of these issues, see Diez-Picazo (2005, p. 133).

[18] See Weiler (1999).

to take initiative, to set the agenda of the EU or to mediate between specific interest groups and governments is far less developed than that of states. As regards international agreements, for instance, it can at best support the Presidency in the launching of negotiations.

Furthermore, the fact that the Community has not one, but a number of different decision modes (different types of majority, unanimity, consensus) ensures the prevalence of dialectics, and can be construed as positing efficiency in their use. Justice and home affairs decisions, however, remain bound by rules of unanimity. This is not necessarily a bad thing. Unanimity requirements may ward off overly hasty decisions that do not properly take into account specific interests and circumstances. This may lead to trade-offs and the emergence of comprehensive agreements among national governments, provided that the Commission acts as an efficient and impartial mediator. But unanimity may also jeopardise the adoption of indispensable decisions or at the very least, postpone them. A way out exist, anyway, with so-called 'bridge' provisions allowing for unanimity-based votes to rule on shifts to majority voting. This has however remained largely theoretical. As a result, many of the proposals put forth have proved difficult to translate into actual concrete decisions and action.[19]

If the Union's decision-making ability is thus constrained, that of individual member states appears even further weakened.[20] The accession of 14 new member states between 2005 and 2007 has extended freedom of movement to their citizens and eliminated internal borders. As always, this generates both opportunities and risks. The opportunities resulting from this extended freedom of movement can hardly be assessed. Nor is it possible to rule out the possibility that risks may yet materialise, in particular in the form of increased security gaps. Governments and parliaments may thus be tempted to move away from the high ground of cooperation or, at the very least, to add new conditions and limitations to

---

[19] On this point, criticism voiced in the European Parliament Resolution on "progress made by the EU in creating an area of freedom, security and justice" mentioned above, i.e. multiple legal bases, delays in the activation of 'bridges', lack of genuine democratic controls, has certainly retained its topicality – if one disregards some of the democratic deficit rhetoric.

[20] The nature of this paper does not allow me to address the distinctive features of negative and positive integration. See Stone Sweet (1998, p. 9).

existing cooperation schemes. Clearly, conditions and limitations may be imposed by national courts on EU legislation, as happened in the UK legislation with respect to the European Arrest Warrant. But this may also elicit further reaction from national politicians faced with what they feel is undue interference on the part of non-elected magistrates and the European law they uphold.

In the meantime, obstacles continue to preclude the full realisation of those 'values' on which the European Union is based. At the heart of such values lie the preservation of democracy and the rule of law, the protection of rights and fundamental freedoms (TEU Article 6). They have a two-fold meaning. Insofar as they are absolute prerequisites for Union accession, states that do not meet either of these criteria will not become members. Moreover, Community institutions are designed to promote and pursue these values through their work.[21] And yet, from the point of view of effectiveness, the relevant Treaty provisions contain a number of enduring inadequacies.

The most salient inadequacy regards mechanisms designed to ensure that policy-makers are accountable. National parliaments have very different levels of effectiveness in terms of the checks and balances they enforce vis-à-vis their individual governments. Moreover, they are ill-suited structurally to engage in checks or the supervision of decisions reached at the European level. This applies particularly to decisions taken by majority vote. As regards the European Parliament, it may well have general consultative jurisdiction, but this does not adequately offset the Council's right to reach binding decisions.[22]

More significant progress has been achieved with regard to judicial safeguards. The Court of Justice not only has jurisdiction over compliance with Community powers;[23] under TEU Article 35, the Court has 'consistent'

---

21 See von Bogdandy (2006). On issues of immigation and asylum, see an interesting clarification in Guild & Harlow (2001).

22 See Satta (2003, p. 254). For a general assessment of the various forms of accountability, see Peers (2005, p. 253).

23 Moreover, the Court has asserted jurisdiction in matters pertaining to infringement of Community powers in its 12 May 1998 ruling, Case C-170/96, *Commission v. Council*. It has furthermore ruled that framework decisions are binding in its 16 June 2005 ruling, Case C-105/03, *Pupino*. For a critique of the

powers, which include preliminary rulings regarding the validity and interpretation of framework decisions, decisions and relevant measures of implementation. The exercise of such power is optional, however, and subordinate to specific requests expressed by one or several member states. Accordingly, a potential wedge has been introduced among legal safeguards. The fact that most member states have so far agreed no doubt attenuates the problem, but the issue still remains. In addition, the jurisdiction of the Court does not include any review of the validity and proportionality of the measures taken for purposes of law enforcement and domestic security. An equally serious flaw concerns individuals' and groups' legal standing. In the framework of the EC, though these players have a less favourable position than Community institutions or member states, they have the right to challenge both decisions that are of direct relevance to themselves and regulations that contain concealed decisions. By contrast, in the field of justice and home affairs, a similar right does not exist.[24] For those who hold that legal remedies are by far more significant than solemn declarations of rights, since the former ensure the effectiveness of the latter, this shortcoming is more serious than the Charter of Fundamental Rights' lack of binding legal effects, let alone the fact that access to justice is included by the ECJ within the general principles of Community law that it draws from member states' shared constitutional traditions, as well as from the European Convention on Human Rights. The question thus arises whether EU courts are ready to show that they are aware of the need to uphold such principles even when law enforcement and collective security interests are at stake. While the first decisions taken by the lower court with regard to anti-terrorism measures raised serious concern, the ECJ has argued that the *noyeau dur* of fundamental rights must be protected even in such cases.[25]

---

allegedly inadequate innovations introduced by the Treaty of Amsterdam ("a missed opportunity"), see Guild & Peers (2001, p. 284).

[24] Court of First Instance, Case T-228/02, *Organisation des Modjahedins du peuple de l'Iran v. Council.*

[25] See CFI, Case T-315/01, *Kadi v. Council of Ministers and Commission* and ECJ, Joined Cases C-402/05 P and C-415/05, with comment by della Cananea (2009, p. 511).

6. Future Prospects: 'Choral' cooperation and trail-blazing initiative

The observations made thus far imply that inadequacies remain not only regarding specific checks and balances, but also with regard to the general structure of the system as well. Such inadequacies concern the ability to choose, decide and act, as well as the corresponding safeguards. Defining the way forward on the basis of this analysis, however, is not obvious. There may be some consensus among institutional and academic circles regarding the very existence of such inadequacies, but the way in which they might possibly be remedied elicits dissent. At the cost of somewhat oversimplifying the issue, two opposite positions may be identified.

The first of these positions coincides with the 'official' stance taken by the Union, as evidenced in particular by political documents produced by the Commission and the Parliament. Moving towards a more united Europe is a wish solemnly underscored by all national policy-makers, even regarding the two major areas where intergovernmental cooperation has prevailed over the so-called 'Community method'. In fact, member states often do not follow traditional avenues. They have often opted for specific solutions, but this has not appeared to alter the basic political choice (and the underlying mutual trust) of European leaders to proceed together towards a closer Union. Removing obstacles to trade and competition seems to have yielded, over the 50 years spanning the shift from 'common' to 'single' market, considerable benefits in terms of efficient resource allocation. Centralised currency management has further contributed to guaranteeing stability and protecting European economies from the turmoil of this last decade, despite the severity of the last financial crisis. According to this line of reasoning, choosing to move together towards ever-closer ties is by far the best way forward. Otherwise, further benefits of cooperation among member states may be at risk. Even current benefits could be jeopardised, should institutional issues become increasingly complex, unity increasingly frail and the public's understanding of these issues ever dimmer.

The opposite position underscores the advantages of differentiation – strengthened cooperation and *avant-garde* initiative.[26] The basic assumption

---

[26] For an analysis of enhanced cooperation, see Ehlermann (1997, pp. 51-90). An updated analysis of the logic of differentiated integration is to be found in Klliker

is that the institutional structure of the European Union may be singularly complex, and its processes at times lacking in transparency. However, nation states, simpler in their uniformity and centralisation, are not an adequate source of benchmarks. Empirical analysis provides some evidence. Consider Economic and Monetary Union. Economic theory does not single out unassailable potential pros and cons. Implications for national interests are perceived in different ways not only by national governments, but by public opinion as well. Choosing to differentiate accession paces and modalities has thus helped some countries improve their position, while others were granted the right to wait for better conditions or circumstances. Further proof of the value of this method is provided by the Schengen Treaty. Initially entered into by five member states, and thus positioned outside the purview of the European Community, the Treaty was later signed on to by other countries. It does not rule out exemptions, in special circumstances. Yet further proof is provided - should any be required - by the Prüm Treaty. Entered into on 27 May 2005 by five of the six founding member states, Austria and Spain, the instrument remains open to general accession. It aims at enhancing trans-border cooperation, to fight against terrorism, organised crime and illegal immigration. It permits a level of cooperation unthinkable until few years ago, including organising and exchanging information on DNA, fingerprints, introducing air-marshals and repatriating illegal immigrants. Cooperation between and among trail-blazing countries thus allows public authorities to take steps that are more effective. They can use confidential information, gradually made available to all those concerned, on the basis of bilateral relationships.[27]

Such positions should not, however, be regarded as conflicting, but as complementary. The complementarity stems, first, from the fact that the political and institutional paradigm of Europe cannot be the same as had been designed initially, under very different circumstances. So many sudden and unexpected events occurred: the collapse of the Communist

---

(2005). New rules applicable to enhanced or strengthened cooperation can now be found in TEC Section III, as modified by ToL Articles 277 and 278.

[27] See Brady (2005). There are further references to conventions entered into by member states in the field of judicial cooperation and law enforcement in Amato (2007, p. 229).

bloc, growing domestic opposition in Islamic countries, the proliferation of international terrorism. The initial framework must in addition be adapted to the changing nature of a polity that was adequate for the six founding countries, but already proved inadequate in 1995. It is still more inadequate after the last enlargement, including countries that are both different from one another and especially with regard to the founding member states. Believing that all Western European countries would immediately agree to French Foreign Minister Robert Schuman's project[28] was not a realistic proposal in 1952. Expecting all 27 member states to always agree on essential policy choices is not realistic today. Conversely, should a limited number of countries engage in various forms of innovation, they may hit upon different solutions and develop closer, albeit non-exclusive ties. There appear to be no legal or political obstacles thereto, insofar as basic government principles (such as the separation of powers or unitary administrative organisation) devised for states at the acme of their development do not apply to the European Union. Lawyers and political scientist are aware that the Schengen Treaty experience shows that states may embark on the high road of integration together, and yet do so at different paces and according to different modalities.[29] This line of reasoning can be taken one step further still, so as to assert that a number of valid reasons, both ideal and pragmatic, today call for a parallel deepening of Community method-based integration and consistent trail-blazing developments in justice and home affairs cooperation. Though one should not rule out, for that matter, the activation of decision-making processes deriving from the Community's traditional method.

7. Implications for checks and balances

The above-mentioned way forward – a combination of united progress and initiative by an *avant-garde* – has several implications, some of which

---

[28] See Monnet (1976).

[29] Denmark, the United Kingdom and Ireland do not fully take part in a set of decisions concerning justice and home affairs, or they take part under specific circumstances. Thus the United Kingdom and Ireland are not party to Schengen provisions relative to the freedom of movement of persons, external border controls and visa policy. At the Council level therefore, representatives of these countries do not vote.

require proper clarification. These relate both to safeguards, and to that other area of intergovernmental cooperation, i.e. the EU's Common Foreign and Security Policy.

What is required is both discretion and flexibility. Discretionary powers are necessary to assess the solutions best suited to preserve collective interests in the fields of enforcement and security. Flexibility is necessary in the selection of legal instruments and effects. Historically and logically, discretion and flexibility first appeared in the framework of states' public order functions for at least two reasons. The first of these is functional by nature. Preventing and punishing forms of behaviour that are a threat to collective interests assumes the ability to adapt and respond to trends and events that are only partly foreseeable and unlikely to fit into preordained models. The second reason is perhaps more important, from the point of view of the institutional framework. It has to do with jurisdiction and authority among the higher echelons of executive power, the exercise of which has to be contained by a number of specific doctrines, limits and controls.

The need for these checks and balances is particularly keen regarding interstate activities. The establishment of organisational and procedural agreements to acquire, process and share confidential information, regarding the more sensitive data available, can prove risky both to those receiving this information and to national governments, for reasons of comprehensive transparency. Developing special relationships among and between public administrations, beyond the scope of regular diplomacy, will strengthen government over parliament. New legal instruments such as the European Arrest Warrant undermine the traditional safeguards provided by ad hoc procedures devised to check that requirements for extradition are indeed met.

The range of institutional safeguards must therefore be extended in different ways. Should the British approach based on administrative and judiciary remedies (ombudsmen, tribunals and boards) prove overly informal - and the French, grounded in the assertion of Treaty-enshrined rights, overly formal - a median solution could usefully be sought out in two ways: through explicit reference to the European Convention of Human Rights, which is what Article 6 of the Treaty of Lisbon does. A further positive innovation would be a clear mandate to the Court of Justice to assess on a case-by-case basis the balance of interests thus achieved under the 'margin of appreciation' doctrine developed by the European

Court of Human Rights. This would both allow for rigor in terms of general principles, because of the reference to the norms of the ECHR, and provide flexibility. Additional and supplementary steps would then to be adopted, in particular regarding compensation to be provided to individuals and associations, not to mention the possibility of voiding legal instruments that have entailed said compensation claims.[30]

Although this would increase the level of safeguards provided to individuals and groups, one must not forget the more general requirement of reconciling flexibility and discretion on the one hand, and transparency on the other. Transparency or rather disclosure per se is positive and therefore cannot be renounced. It is the distinguishing feature of democratic, as opposed to authoritarian regimes.[31] It supports and lends legitimacy to flexibility and discretion. For functional reasons, it is not possible to exclude that public policy implementation, especially regarding home affairs, may have its times of opaqueness. However, should this prove persistent and prevalent, in the long run, public policy implementation would lose its very rationale. Clearly, disclosure is not tantamount to adherence to strict, predetermined rules. But it must at the very least mean that policy guidelines and concrete measures are subject to *ex post* checks, on the basis of unambiguous criteria. This is the prerequisite of accountability.

8. Implications for the Union's Foreign Policy

Strengthening cooperation in the fields of justice and home affairs, even through avant-garde initiatives, also has implications for the Union's Common Foreign and Security Policy.

The global dimension of issues arising in the field of enforcement and security requires that parallel strengthening be undertaken in the external dimension of the European Union. This can be achieved through both informal and formal agreements through special agreements with third-party countries, as with the United States in the weeks that followed the 11 September 2001 attacks on New York and Washington. Much has already been achieved, but much remains to be done in this field, including with

---

[30] On this, see Ackerman (2006, p. 51).

[31] See Bobbio (1986, p. 175). See also Curtin (2001, p. 35).

other NATO member states, and in particular with Turkey (this might, incidentally, help develop cooperation with a view to possible accession). At the same time, the Union can, and probably should, exercise jurisdiction by promoting agreements with other third-party countries as well as with intergovernmental bodies,[32] within which the common position of member states would be defined, as specified in TEU Article 37 (former Article K.9).

Thanks to the Amsterdam Treaty, there are no doubts as to the ability of member states to enter into such agreements under the Third Pillar. The issue is rather whether all member states are automatically bound by such agreements. One possibility could usefully be explored and expounded upon by other fora: it involves the opting-out provision of which member states may avail themselves for specific reasons linked to their Constitution (TEU Article 24, former Article J.14), when specific agreements are entered into. This allows for agreements with differential implementation and for developments in line with a mix of united progress and trail-blazing initiative. One may therefore assume that countries agreeing to cooperate more closely in order to exercise public order functions will also enter into agreements with third-party countries. Obviously, customary validity requirements will need to be met: non-interference with the interests and functions of the Community, compliance with the general principles of Community law, opening of accession procedures to all member states with the political will to do so, provided they meet the requisite criteria and preconditions specified by contracting parties.

References

Ackerman, B. (2006), *Before the Next Attack. Preserving Civil Liberties in an Age of Terrorism*, New Haven & London: Yale University Press.

Adam, R. (1999), *La cooperazione in materia di giustizia e affari interni*, in *Il Trattato di Amsterdam*, Milan: Giuffrè.

Amato, G. (2007), "Unione: Le tentazioni sbagliate", in *Il Mulino*, No. 2, p. 229.

---

[32] In this respect, Opinion No.1/07 handed down by the Court of Justice on 7 February 2007 is significant, insofar as it allows for a new convention on judicial cooperation in civil matters with Switzerland, Norway and Iceland.

Bianchi, A. and Y. Naqvi (eds) (2004), *Enforcing International Law Norms Against Terrorism: Achievements and prospects*, Oxford: Hart Publishing.

Bobbio, N. (1986), "Il potere invisibile e la democrazia", in N. Bobbio, *Il futuro della democrazia*, Turin: Einaudi.

Brady, H. (2005), "An Avant-garde for Internal Security", in *CER-Bulletin*, No. 44, October-November.

Cassese, S. (1997), *Lo Stato introvabile*, Rome: Donzelli.

Curtin, D.M. (2001), "The Developing Rights of Citizen Access to Information on Asylum and Immigration Decision-Making", in E. Guild and C. Harlow (eds), *Implementing Amsterdam: Immigration and Asylum Rights in EC Law*, Oxford: Hart Publishing.

della Cananea, G. (2009), "Global Security and Procedural Due Process of Law Between the United Nations and the European Union", *Columbia Journal of European Law*, Vol. 15, No. 3, p. 511.

Delmas-Marty, M. (ed.) (1996), *What Kind of Criminal Policy for Europe?*, The Hague, London andBoston: Kluwer Law International.

Diez-Picazo, L.M. (2005), *Hacia una teoria de la coación en el derecho de la Union Europea*, in L. Ortega Alvarez (ed.), *La seguridad integral europea*, Valladolid: Editorial Lex Nova.

Ehlermann, C.D. (1997), "Différentiation, flexibilité, coopération renforcée: les nouvelles dispositions du traité d'Amsterdam", *Revue du Marché Unique Européen*, 3.

Giannini, M.S. (1990), "Sovranità", in *Enciclopedia del diritto*, Vol. XLIII, Milan: Giuffrè.

Guild, E. and C. Harlow (eds) (2001), *Implementing Amsterdam: Immigration and Asylum Rights in EC Law*, Oxford: Hart Publishing.

Guild, E. and S. Peers (2001), "Deference or Defiance? The Court of Justice's Jurisdiction over Immigration and Asylum", in E. Guild and C. Harlow (eds), *Implementing Amsterdam: Immigration and Asylum Rights in EC Law*, Oxford: Hart Publishing.

Klliker, A. (2005), *Flexibility and European Unification: The Logic of Differentiated Integration*, London: Rowman & Littlefield.

Monar, J. (2003), "Cooperation in the Justice and Home Affairs Domain: Characteristics, Constraints and Progress", in *European Integration*, Vol. 28, No. 5.

Monnet, J. (1976), *Mémoires*, Paris: Fayard.

Ortega Alvarez, L. (2005), "Hacia un concepto integral de seguridad europea", in L. Ortega Alvarez (ed.), *La seguridad integral europea*, Valladolid: Editorial Lex Nova.

Peers, S. (2005), "Governance and the Third Pillar: The Accountability of Europol", in D.M. Curtin and R.A. Wessels (eds), *Good Governance and the European Union. Reflections on Concepts, Institutions and Substance*, Antwerp-Oxford: Intersentia.

Peers, S. (2008), *EU Justice and Home Affairs Law*, Oxford: Oxford University Press, 2nd edition.

Satta, I. (2003), "La cooperazione di polizia e giudiziaria in materia penale", in G. Bonvicini and G.L. Tosato (eds), *Le relazioni internazionali dell'Unione europea dopo i Trattati di Amsterdam e Nizza*, Torino: Giappichelli.

Siegel, S. (2008), *Courts and Compliance in the European Union: The European Arrest Warrant in National Constitutional Courts*, Jean Monnet Working Paper 05/08 (available at www.JeanMonnet@Program.org).

Slaughter, A.M. (2005), *A New World Order*, Princeton, NJ: Princeton University Press.

Stone Sweet, A. (1998), *Integration, Supranational Governance and the Institutionalization of the European Polity*, in W. Sandholtz and A. Stone Sweet (eds), *European Integration and Supranational Governance*, Oxford: Oxford University Press.

Tosato, G.L. (2000), "Atti giuridici vincolanti e competenze della Corte comunitaria nell'ambito del 'Terzo pilastro'", in R. Aliboni, F. Bruni, A. Colombo and E. Greco (eds), *L'Italia e la politica internazionale*, Bologna: Il Mulino.

Volcansek, M.L. and J.F. Stack (eds) (2005), *Courts Crossing Borders: Blurring Lines of Sovereignty*, Durham, NC: Academic Press.

von Bogdandy, A. (2006), "Doctrine of European Principles", in A. von Bogdandy and J. Bast (eds), *Principles of European Constitutional Law*, Oxford: Hart Publishing.

Weiler, J.H.H. (1999), *The Constitution of Europe*, Cambridge: Cambridge University Press.

Ziller, J. (2004), *La nouvelle constitution européenne*, Paris : La Découverte.

Ziller, J. (2007), *Il nuovo Trattato europeo*, Bologna: Il Mulino.

14. THE ROLE OF PARLIAMENTS IN THE DEMOCRATIC LIFE OF THE UNION

ANDREA MANZELLA

1. The democratic principles of the Union and national parliaments within the European parliamentary system

The role of national parliaments in the 'proper functioning' of the Union is considered in the new Treaty of Lisbon as an informing principle of European democracy. Together with the principles of democratic equality (the 'equal attention' shown to all citizens by Union institutions), representative democracy (the 'direct representation' of citizens in the European Parliament) and participative democracy (legislative initiative, consultation, citizens' dialogue with the Union's institutions), we now have this principle of national parliamentary democracy, which is generally anchored to the guiding concepts of subsidiarity and proportionality, and more specifically linked to a variety of co-decision procedures regarding the area of freedom, security and justice, constitutional revision and new member state accession.

Deciding to give national parliaments a direct role (without government intermediation), which is listed among the fundamental principles of European Union action, meets a political requirement. Opposition to the Union's oft-mentioned 'democratic deficit' did in fact reach its acme with the French and Dutch referenda. A visible and popular way of increasing the European constitution's 'democraticity rate' somehow had to be devised. Granting more power to national parliaments was the easiest way forward, for a double, reassuring reason.

First of all, this helped convey the message that the 'distant constitution' (a symbol, however, of countless perils such as the dismantlement of the welfare state, the free circulation of out-of-control migration, industrial relocation...) was being subjected to the supervision of age-old, familiar national parliaments. Secondly, this helped reduce, through 'parliamentarisation', the scope of 'handed-down' institutional innovation and its constitutional features, in an attempt to avoid further recourse to referendum-based adventures (always dangerous when ratification of international treaties is at stake; it is no accident that this is an area non-eligible for referendum in Italy's 1948 Constitution).

The anti-referendum function was the dominant reason underpinning the Union's decision. The "no" of French and Dutch voters had in fact first and foremost been a disavowal of national governments and parliaments - who favoured, by an overwhelming majority, the Constitutional Treaty. A further refusal by referendum therefore risked challenging the very representativeness of national governments and parliaments. In other words, by taking on a direct safeguard role in the EU's decision-making mechanisms, the latter were in the end protecting themselves against a domino effect of de-legitimisation.

These substantial political reasons are however not equally valid in institutional terms, insofar as the powers granted to national parliaments can actually produce a blocking effect in the EU's already laborious decision-making process.

The new role given to national parliaments in the Union has in fact two different dimensions corresponding to two different - actually, opposite - views of democracy in Europe. It therefore all depends on whether the Union's 'democracy' is to be measured by the yardstick of systematic connections between various democratic legitimacies (governments, the European parliament, national parliaments) taking part in Union decisions, or conversely by a parameter linked to old strictly national decision-making powers conferred to national parliaments on community issues, or to pre-federal concepts (direct election of the President of the European Commission, transnational lists for the European parliament, European referendums...). As the old convergence-of-extremes rule would have it, these two opposite concepts have in fact both contributed to the birth and growth of the democratic deficit myth: which clearly appears impossible to correct if one reasons in terms of such parameters, and not in terms of European Union history and institutional status.

Regarding the first aspect, the role of national parliaments takes on three different modalities, concerning:

a) the powers granted to national parliaments in specific procedures. The principal innovation consists of the right to take part in the 'conventions' for Treaty revisions. Of higher strategic significance because of their impact on the 'ordinary' integration motors appear the powers of national parliaments related to the flexibility provisions inserted into the Treaty: the bridging clauses leading to simplified revision and voting procedures (Article 48 of TEU) and the "historical" clause permitting an extension of the Union powers (Article 352 TFEU);

b) the right of national parliaments to receive Community information directly; and

c) their right to exercise advisory and policy orientation functions either through COSAC, the body bringing together the national parliament committees dealing with Union policies, or more importantly through 'effective' and 'regular' inter-parliamentary cooperation involving national parliaments and the European Parliament.

As to point a) above, the German Constitutional Court has evidenced, by means of its recent decision of 30 June 2009, how the involvement of national powers may significantly aggravate the European integration process in its entirety. The Court has confirmed the openness to Europe of the German constitution and what may be described as the 'communicating vases' theory (the powers taken out of national parliaments can be compensated by those vested in the European Parliament). Nevertheless, the stringent request for prior approval of the German parliament will cause an 'indirect' rigidity of European decisions on numerous areas.

As to points b) and c) above, these are powers and rights not only appropriate to the Union's multi-tiered constitutional model but actually essential to the Union's proper functioning. Joint and equal institutional communication is indeed indispensable in order to give actual substance to the interplay between various institutions. Each institution requires channels of interference with all the others, as this is how the Union's decision-making process fully and seamlessly acquires legitimacy. Likewise, the principle of loyal cooperation among various institutions within the system requires visible inter-institution connections and interfaces (through 'inter-parliamentary conferences', short-hand for which could be the 'COSAC formula', where special delegations from the European Parliament and relevant national parliamentary committees meet with a view to expressing a majority opinion on specific topics). On this last point, the most significant from the point of view of the system's institutional equilibrium, the new "Protocol on the role of national parliaments" interestingly includes an indirect broadening of European Parliament jurisdiction to issues of "common security and defence policies". Organising inter-parliamentary conferences on such topics with the specialized committees of national parliaments actually confers to the European Parliament a potential right to scrutinise areas that the treaties still consider to be the exclusive prerogative of national parliaments (as shown by a later and almost maniacal statement according to which treaty provisions regarding CSDP do not prejudice the specific nature of member states' security and defence policies).[1]

Setting aside specific problems, the Protocol's mention of inter-parliamentary conferences is in line with the interaction required for effective cooperation, typical of multi-tier constitutional systems. Clearly this multilateral consultative participation in the decision-making process is the key to the Union's democraticity, insofar as it specifies the connections of the various democratic legitimacies exercising different powers but equally 'responsible', through their different investiture mechanisms, vis-à-vis Europe's voter constituency.

Regarding the second aspect, national parliaments' role under the new Protocol involves procedures regarding the appropriate application of the subsidiarity and proportionality principles. These procedures may include, depending on the number of national parliaments supporting any given initiative, simple checks leading to requests for review (with a quorum of one third of national parliaments) of draft legislative acts (proposals by the European Commission, initiatives from a group of member states, initiatives from the European Parliament, requests from the Court of Justice or recommendations of the European Central Bank). But they may tantamount to the exercise of an actual veto right, however

---

1 One should add that if these 'conferences' were to be held with the degree of regularity generally called for in the Protocol, the survival of the already weakened WEU Parliamentary Assembly would become very difficult to justify within the general framework of European bodies. As to the Union itself, providing for future "structured cooperation in the field of defence" raises issues regarding the participation of members of the European and national parliaments representing member states not party to this cooperation (clearly a sensitive institutional issue for all 'enhanced cooperation' groups, even if cooperation in the area of common defense is only open to states with significant military capacities).

'concealed' by a cumbersome procedure (the quorum required then is a majority of national parliaments) with respect to draft legislative acts subject to the general co-decision rule. The two procedures are obviously radically different. While monitoring through requests for review is a mechanism perfectly consistent with the Union's specific multi-tier constitutionalism, the same cannot be said of the 'veto' powers, which are de facto connected to the emergence of a majority among national parliaments (that is, to quantitative data, two votes per parliament, no weights for national demographics – however relevant they are to the Union's institutional organisation).

The fact that national parliaments could block a draft legislative act being processed according to the regular legislative co-decision rules does indeed disrupt the multi-tier constitutional balance. Under an albeit complex procedure, concealed behind Community legislation's *coactus tamen volui*, one of the system's components has thus been granted an improper right to interfere in decision-making. Clearly this interference cannot be mistaken for the regular, cooperative version typical of modern constitutional systems (national systems included, where under the probable influence of EU procedures such 'federalist' practices are becoming increasingly common). On the contrary, this is a genuine invasion of the Union's decision-making ground, which does indeed upset the system's balance by assigning to national parliaments the (albeit indirect) power to paralyse the highly sensitive area of legislative initiative. An area where the appreciation of Community-wide public interest and the need for Union legislative action can best be grasped by the current initiative incumbents (first and foremost the Commission, but also the European Parliament, as well as groups of member states who in their collegiality do express views that are not strictly nationalistic) – certainly more so than by a majority of national parliaments, and their chance convergence on a negative blocking stance. One could add to this, as some have done, a number of pointed observations on the deficiencies of enhanced parliamentarisation as a yardstick for Union democratisation. Or, to put it differently, as a means of appraising a system where interest representation is organised through checks and balances combining legitimacy and efficiency – a model far removed from the parliamentary one currently prevalent in Europe.

One can however object - and this should be borne in mind for any comprehensive appreciation of the injury involved - that this monitoring or check only applies in areas where the Union does not have exclusive jurisdiction, but shares authority with member states. Well, even taking this objection on board, it is quite clear that (national) parliamentarisation of decision-making in such areas corresponds on the one hand to a hollowing out of the Union's legislative powers - and more specifically of the role played by governments within the (European) Council of Ministers - and on the other, to the slotting in, albeit with negative powers, of a third legislator figure within the EU's complex institutional balance. The resulting imbalance is clear to see, even disregarding the perils of decision-making paralysis entailed by the new procedure in an already 'stressed-to-the-limits' system (knowing that waning of legitimacy always comes in the wake of a loss in efficiency...).

The procedure moreover does nothing to increase the Union's democraticity rate. National parliaments are already entitled to resort, within their national systems, to effective instruments to control and possibly block their governments-acting as co-European legislators (think of Italy - but not only - where the 'parliamentary reservation' argument can be used against the government upstream of all European decisions...). The procedure clearly impacts the fullness of player legitimization however (European Parliament, Council, European Commission) within the regular legislative process. In other words, this is a negative sum game especially as regards the so-called democratic deficit that it somehow set out to correct.

2. The political nature of the subsidiarity and proportionality principles

The above comments yield an even direr conclusion when one reflects on the eminently political nature of the subsidiarity and proportionality principles. This intrinsic political nature is first of all linked to the fundamental role played by the subsidiarity principle in the concrete identification of the most appropriate level of government for a given task (the bias favouring 'close to the citizen' political action is nothing but a very general base criterion, always open to waivers for the higher levels of government, in order to accommodate requirements of provision scope and efficiency). The displacement of decision-making levels is clearly a political act per se, and one of the more significant ones.

This reading is emphasised by the absolutely political criteria that run through the definition of these principles. Consider the concepts of 'sufficiency' of member state action, of better achievement by the Union of its goals, of decision scale and effects assessment and, as regards the proportionality principle (which must however be viewed as an internal limitation of the subsidiarity principle, as we shall see later in more detail), the requirement that Community action not go "beyond what is necessary to achieve the objectives (of this Treaty)". These are all parameters the legal effectiveness of which is deeply dependent on their strictly political appreciation.

One element however provides at least a partial corrective to this primacy of the political sphere, namely the jurisdiction given (under Protocol Article 8) to the Union's Court of Justice. The Court shall indeed have jurisdiction in actions on grounds of the subsidiarity principle infringement brought by member states or transmitted by states on behalf of their parliaments. This provision, which should take on a key role in the system, calls for at least three comments.

The first concerns the fact that the Court of Justice (following the tested road taken by authoritative constitutional case law at the national level) may decide it is the ultimate judge of the appropriateness of levels at which decisions are made. Even if the legal system assumes that appeals come from below, it is quite obvious that the Court of Justice can provide (as in a boomerang effect) legitimisation and consolidation to the Union's decision-making over that of appealing states (and their parliaments).

The second comment concerns the possible juridification via case law of criteria that are per se open to considerable political discretion. The Court is indeed *the* authority that can provide legal meaning to the justification requirement (stated in Protocol Article 5) imposed upon those bodies entitled to put forth draft legislation. Creative constitutional case law is indeed the only way to provide legal certainty and finality to requirements to submit "detailed statements", "qualitative and wherever possible, quantitative indicators", not to mention the taking into account "of the need for any burden, whether financial or administrative, falling upon various levels of government as well as "economic operators and citizens" to be minimized, etc. These requirements, were they to remain entrusted to political decision-makers, would lend themselves to very volatile and ambiguous application.

The third comment concerns the peculiarity of a provision - the text and context of which are both based on the elimination of member state government intermediation - specifying, with respect to the Court of

Justice, that member states are empowered to seek legal remedies (or empowered to do so on behalf of their parliaments, should parliaments take the initiative of an appeal under the subsidiarity principle).

In other words, it is only on the Court's very threshold that the subsidiarity principle eludes the rules of an entirely political game, with decisions taken on the basis of the balance of power struck at a given point in time among Union bodies and national parliaments. At the current juncture in the ups and downs of European integration the pendulum's swing seems to be favouring, at least at symbolic moments, the granting of decision-making powers to national parliaments, including in matters of community significance. A provision such as Protocol Article 8, isolated in its 'orthodoxy', provides a measure of the political and re-nationalisation effects inherent in the rest of the mechanism.

3. The irresistible political expansion of proportionality control

National parliament monitoring is exercised solely over draft legislative act compliance with the subsidiarity principle (Articles 6 and 7). But all Union institutions shall ensure constant respect for the principles of both subsidiarity *and* proportionality (Article 1). And draft legislative act justification concerns both the subsidiarity and the proportionality principles (Article 5). That said, both the title and the 'whereases' of the Protocol speak indifferently, when addressing "application" and its monitoring system, of both principles.

Another very relevant factual clue has to be borne in mind. Namely that during the preliminary try-outs of the new monitoring system promoted by COSAC, the reasoned opinions of participating national parliaments frequently invoked proportionality, as a principle of political conditionality applicable to positive assessments of subsidiarity, with quite stringent provisions - inspired by national concerns - regarding Union action.[2]

[2] Trial subsidiarity and proportionality checks performed under COSAC auspices on 17 July 2006 and 31 October 2006 focused on the draft directives regarding applicable law and jurisdiction in matrimonial matters, COM(2006) 399, and postal services liberalisation COM(2006) 594.Twenty-two national chambers from 17 member states took part in the first check (on law and jurisdiction in matrimonial matters). Almost all, with the exception of the Dutch House of Parliament and the

In the face of these formal and substantive elements, one wonders whether limiting national parliament monitoring solely to subsidiarity[3] is really defensible. And whether conversely the 'release' provided by comments concerning proportionality couldn't actually be seen as a contribution - clearly more political still - to the drafting of legislative acts: but without the delays and other problems connected to the exercise of subsidiarity checks per se.

In all fairness one has to bear in mind that the proportionality principle plays out in a field that can in no way be reduced to a legal dimension, and dealt with solely by the courts. As an internal and subsequent criterion for the review of 'subsidiary' legitimacy it aims in fact to check that the content and form of action do not go "beyond what is necessary to achieve the objectives" of the Union. It therefore recalls, in this matching of means and end, of power and abuse thereof the basic tenets of a rigorous administrative judicial process, per se irreconcilable with the 'constitutional' review of competences, covered by Protocol Article 8 (laden as it is with other difficulties, regarding access and reference parameters...).

That said, practical experimentation in any event suggests the advisability of an 'extensive' reading of the Protocol: on the one hand, there is this rigorous fencing in of legally effective controls (whether *ex ante* and political, or *ex post* and juridicial) to the sole area of subsidiarity, while on the other there is the admissibility, in the absence of any specific legislation, of a parliamentary practice of 'observations' based on the proportionality

---

Lower House of the Czech Republic, expressed favourable opinions with respect to the proportionality principle. The second trial check (on postal services) elicited participation by 27 national chambers representing 21 member states. Luxemburg's Chambre des Députés was the only parliament to raise an issue of subsidiarity principle breach, while 5 chambers pointed out the inadequacy of the Commission's justifications in this respect. Seven chambers pointed out a breach of the proportionality principle and expressed corresponding reservations.

[3] This limitation is the outcome of the reasoned confrontation between 'reductionists' and 'amplifiers' that took place within the Giscard d'Estaing Convention's Working Group I on the Principle of Subsidiarity (see, in this connection, the Group's report to the Members of the Convention, CONV 286/02, 23 September 2002).

principle, with an obligation for the institution submitting the draft legislation to respond to such observations in its final justification.

The rationale for this would appear to be the need to avoid having national parliaments transform their comments on a given project's 'proportionality' into observations regarding its 'subsidiary' legitimacy, for fear the former would not properly be taken into account. The setting up, through practice, of a parallel and *soft* procedure regarding proportionality could therefore be an appropriate counter-measure geared to a trend that has begun to emerge (as an early warning sign...) in national parliamentary practice. This trend is well-known to some aspects of administrative law when it comes to fuzzy lines separating excess of power and legality vices.

4. The improper interaction of quorums

The main threat of divergence from the legal paradigm that, through crises and standstills, has nevertheless allowed unprecedented inter-state integration does not however come from *individual* national parliaments. The new Article in the Treaty on European Union regrouping the previously scattered powers bestowed upon national parliaments provides them with an enhanced configuration. The powers concerned correspond however to areas of community law of intergovernmental relevance and national parliament intervention here 'mirrors' that of corresponding governments.

This applies in particular to participation in the mechanisms geared to assessing Union policy implementation in the area of freedom, security and justice, with a view to encouraging the full application of the mutual recognition principle. In this same 'area' national parliaments are said to be "associated" to the monitoring of Europol activities and to the evaluation of judicial cooperation activities performed by Eurojust. Similar considerations also apply to the normal Treaty revision procedure. In this framework each national parliament has the power to ratify or reject. The same also applies to national requests of accession to the Union.

The specificity introduced by the mechanisms signalling subsidiarity (or proportionality) infringements - to the breaking point of the system's logic - stems from the *collegiality* requirement they set for national parliament action. The legal effects of compliance checks as performed by individual parliaments are in fact dependent on there being a quorum of national parliaments. This necessary collegiality has echoes of a yet un-materialised 'third chamber' (after the European Parliament and the

European Council of Ministers). And the quorum requirement in an area where the political rate is extremely high, as mentioned earlier, is what risks upsetting the Union's unified institutional make-up.

The concern continues to apply even when the 1/3 of national parliament votes quorum[4] simply allows for a check resulting in a request for review. This may apply to all draft legislative acts (proposed by the Commission, the European Parliament, a group of member states, the Court of Justice, the European Central Bank or the European Investment Bank). The concern however takes on far more serious relevance when a quorum equal to a majority of national parliaments can ultimately block draft legislation, because of the 'politically' unstoppable trigger of a simple majority of national parliaments deciding to oppose a draft[5] under the 'regular legislative procedure' that is, the basic co-decision procedure giving the Commission a monopoly over initiative and where the 'European legislator' is made up of the Council of Ministers and the European Parliament.

If the Commission then upholds its draft, despite a contrary vote by a majority of national parliaments, review of the project does get blocked, in the case of a procedural - not substantive -vote of 55% of all members of the Council of Ministers or a majority of expressed votes in the European Parliament.

Requests for a 'third Chamber' made up of national parliamentary delegations and designed to be a 'subsidiarity Chamber" have been recurrent in the ongoing controversy over the Union's democratic deficit. They have however run into strong doctrinal and practical objections, as reflected in the following passage:

> The setting up of a new institution representing national parliaments would not increase the system's democratic legitimacy. On the contrary, it would risk reducing it. This "chamber" would indeed be made up of national representatives elected by the parliaments of individual Member States. It would

---

[4] Currently at 54 votes: one third therefore equals 18 votes, that are brought down to 13, i.e. one quarter if the topic is the area of freedom, security and justice.

[5] In the current 54 vote configuration this majority would be equal to 28 votes, corresponding to 14 member states: Protocol provisions make no mention of any computation of the corresponding population.

therefore not have a direct popular mandate, as does the European Parliament, but some sort of "democratic legitimacy of second degree", as does the Council. This would therefore increase the system's complexity without any real counterpart. Conversely, it would almost certainly engage in competition with the European Parliament.[6]

On the basis of the legitimisation inferred from the new subsidiarity monitoring mechanism, the 'third Chamber' might thus take on a 'diffuse' form, its variable geometry changing from time to time, with one quorum for review requests, and another for procedural blockage. There actually is a forum for the convergence into legal quorums of individual parliamentary positions (a forum actually set up to encourage such operation). This is the COSAC Secretariat, which despite strong resistance on the part of successive Italian delegations in recent years (only initially supported by European Parliament delegations) and the objective limitations that have thus been brought to bear on both its numbers and its functions, nevertheless is a sufficient forum for the bringing together (if not the promotion) of the requisite quorums.[7]

---

[6] See.Verola (2006, pp. 206-207).

[7] See COSAC Rule of Procedure 11bis, in the latest version submitted to the Lisbon Conference, 15-16 October 2007: "The COSAC Secretariat shall be composed of officials from the Parliaments of the Presidential Troika, and a permanent member who supports the Secretariat in its activities. The officials from the Parliaments of the Presidential Troika shall be appointed by each of the relevant Parliaments for a non-renewable period of eighteen months. The permanent member shall be appointed by the COSAC Chairpersons on the proposal of the Presidential Troika. He or she shall be an official of a national Parliament and shall remain in office for two years with the possibility of one renewal. The COSAC Secretariat shall assist the Presidency and the secretariat of the host Parliament in all its tasks. The members of the COSAC Secretariat shall perform their duties under the political responsibility of the COSAC Presidency and the Presidential Troika or according to the decisions taken by COSAC meetings. The permanent member shall coordinate the activities of the COSAC Secretariat under the direction of the Parliament holding the Presidency. The cost for seconding the permanent member of the Secretariat to Brussels and other necessary technical costs of the Secretariat are jointly borne by Parliaments wishing to contribute." (According to the report submitted by the Working group on the co-funding of the permanent member of the COSAC Secretariat, dated 11 September 2006, there is an agreement providing

In this context the issue of whether the mechanism "should be activated by subsidiarity challenges to different points in the proposed act, or whether a quorum is required on the same point" takes on considerable significance[8].

All things considered, subsidiarity checks cannot be equated with point checks of draft legislation. Contrary to the proportionality principle, which lends itself more readily to point assessments, the subsidiarity principle - in this specific case focused on the appropriateness of the proposed level of public decision-making - per se only implies a comprehensive assessment of finalities. In both letter and spirit, provisions relative to subsidiarity checks therefore rule out a blow-by-blow analysis of the various provisions making up any draft legislation, unless the process is geared to clarifying the goal pursued by the draft.

All in all, under subsidiarity checks, the assessment parameter - here too exquisitely political - lies in the draft legislation justification rather than in the rules contained in the draft per se. If anything, the rules serve as counter-proof (to strengthen or weaken justifications, depending on governments' likes or dislikes...) for the actual goals pursued. But this is a teleological element, to be used in the end to support the decision-maker's legitimate choice. Clearly, a goal-oriented assessment along these lines therefore refers to the draft in its entirety, which rules out any point-by-point analysis. And this provides an argument additional to the one put before, regarding the practical usefulness of opening a channel for observations relative to proportionality, so as to avoid their 'emergence' - politically possible, however inappropriate - into the area of subsidiarity.

---

for the co-funding of COSAC administrative expenditure. This includes computers and telecommunications, stationery... The European Parliament puts furnished premises at COSAC's disposal, free of charge. It has been agreed that the total amount of cost contributions linked to the permanent member should not exceed €80,000 a year).

[8] The question appears in the following document: "Il progetto di mandato alla Conferenza intergovernativa per la riforma dei Trattati europei", Italian Senate, Relations with the European Union Division, No. 59, 16 July 2007, p. 12.

5. Conclusions: Early warning for the early warning

In order to conclude this analysis very briefly, one could say that a breach has clearly been opened with the subsidiarity monitoring mechanism, which could allow neo-nationalistic positions to erupt both in the Union's values and in its multi-tier constitutional system. This system requires and multiplies functional interferences with a consultative purpose, but would however rule out any impingement on decision-making powers - whether positive or negative - as laid out in the treaties.

The mechanism introduced is clearly influenced by public opinion sentiment assigning to difficult Community-wide decisions - with obvious factual misrepresentations - a whole set of political and social problems that have almost always been due - in terms of severity - to causes external to the Union. The preferred solution has been to address the lingering democratic deficit issue not through more mature controls to be exercised by national parliaments over governments and by the European Parliament over the action of the Union as a whole, but rather through direct national parliament activism with respect to community legislative procedures

In order to restore balance, governments will therefore have to exercise 'control' over their parliaments, and if necessary, rein them in. This shows how choosing the wrong tack to combat the so-called democratic deficit can lead to a democratic paradox. If the Union's institutional balance is to be safeguarded, with a view to exorcising the peril of a fragmentation of its decision-making processes by national parliaments - of all perils, this is certainly the most severe.

References

Senato della Repubblica (Italian Senate) (2007), *Il progetto di mandato alla Conferenza intergovernativa per la riforma dei Trattati europei*, Ufficio dei rapporti con le istituzioni dell'Unione europea (Relations with the European Union Division), No. 59, 16 July, p. 12.

Verola, N. (2006), *L'Europa legittima,* Florence: Passigli Editore.

15. The Shape of post-Lisbon Europe

Gian Luigi Tosato

1. The new Treaty's structure

The Lisbon Treaty's structure is the result of a compromise between opponents and supporters of the previous Constitutional Treaty. Its opponents gained the upper hand with regard to form and its supporters with regard to content. Formally, what we have is a revision treaty, like those of Amsterdam and Nice. It simply modifies existing treaties (the Treaty on the European Union and the Treaty establishing the European Community), without replacing them; it is, as its official description reads, a 'Reform Treaty'. In substance, the new treaty includes many of the innovations of the Constitutional Treaty rejected by the French and Dutch referenda. The nature and number of changes are such as to have a profound effect on the existing treaties.

Form and substance do not mesh well in the new treaty in view of the clear contrast between container and content. The container, a mere amending instrument, seems unsuited to accommodate the content that has been poured into it, in view of the scale and significance of the reforms. The immediate consequence is that the new treaty is difficult to decipher. The document produced is long and complex and requires a labourious comparison between the new revision text and the old amended texts, and between the latter and a text (the constitutional text) that has formally been abandoned. The document's meaning is all the more difficult to grasp as it is supplemented by several additional protocols and declarations intended to supplement, clarify and sometimes even depart from the text's provisions. Two significant examples are the goal of free and fair competition, initially eliminated from the text, then salvaged in an additional protocol; and the primacy of Union law over domestic law, also removed initially and later slipped back in through a declaration, which refers to consolidated Community case law in this area.

These aspects of the treaty have elicited an avalanche of criticism. Initial commentators spoke of its labyrinthine nature, rife with cross-references and legalisms: just the opposite of the calls contained in the Nice and Laeken Declarations on the Future of Europe (in January and December 2001). Simplification and transparency, two key words in these documents, were to have been the guiding principles for the future development of European integration. Instead, after a labourious gestation of over six years, what has been delivered is a text that is neither simple nor transparent and which is certainly difficult to understand for the European citizens it was intended for.

It is hard to deny that this criticism has a point; the new treaty is really obscure and tortuous. One should however not dwell only on these more visible aspects of the new treaty. The criticism summarised above only reflects a first level of analysis. Going beyond the revisional method used and looking at the new Treaty not in itself, but rather from the point of view of its impact on the existing treaties and the overall architecture of the Union, a different picture emerges, which marks substantial progress in the areas of simplification and re-organisation of the current system.

2. A simplified and re-organised system

After Lisbon, two founding treaties still remain. But previously, each related to a different entity (Union and Community), and a distinct legal system (Union law and Community law), not to mention the three pillars (two inside the Union and the third represented by the Community). Now, despite there still being two treaties, we have a single entity (the Union), with a single system and a single set of institutions, where the distinction between pillars has been (almost) abolished. This marks the end of the absurd dualism between Union and Community produced by the Maastricht compromises, the elimination of which was long overdue.

This represents a significant simplification of the European architecture. Of course the approach had already been included in the Constitutional Treaty and thus to some extent can be considered as already having been accepted. But it is a good thing for it to have been given further and, one hopes, final endorsement. The Treaty of Lisbon introduces another new ingredient in the re-organisation of the system, which goes beyond the Constitutional Treaty and holds potential for promising future developments.

As just mentioned, despite the fact that there are still two founding treaties, they now refer to a single entity. The primary rules of the Union are thus distributed between two distinct texts: the Treaty on the Union and the Treaty on the Functioning of the Union. And even though it is pointed out that both have equal legal value, in fact they differ in terms of content and formal legal regime.

The first treaty contains the principles and fundamental rules of the Union; it establishes its goals, values, competences, institutional structure, relations with member states and with European citizens and procedures for amendment, accession and withdrawal. The second treaty lays down the rules under which its various bodies will operate, the way in which the domestic market is regulated as well as provisions governing the implementation of common policies. The provisions of the second treaty concerning policies and deliberative procedures are subject to a simplified amendment procedure. The intergovernmental conference stage is by-passed and, in the case of deliberative procedures, internal ratifications are considered as granted unless individual national parliaments formally dissent. One could borrow a term used for the European Coal and Steel Community (ECSC) to define this simplified procedure as 'small revision', to distinguish it from regular and solemn amendments.[1]

Admittedly, the way provisions are distributed between the two texts is not always consistent. Some of the provisions of the Treaty on the Union should really have been placed in the other treaty, like the 'specific' rules relating to common foreign and security policy. Greater simplification of the 'small revision' procedure would have also been preferable. The simplified procedure only applies to some of the provisions of the second treaty, and yet it still requires approval on the part of all member states at government and parliamentary level. Nevertheless, we find ourselves with a major innovation. The Union's primary rules are not only grouped into separate documents, they are also distinguished by significant differences of a substantive and formal nature.

Ever since its inception, the process of European construction featured the intermingling within the same treaty of basic institutional

---

[1] The 'small revision' expression has been used within the ECSC with reference to the revision procedure set out in Article 95 of the Treaty. By means of a 'small revision' an adjustment to the powers of the High Authority could be enacted.

elements together with rules applicable to specific sectors. This may have been justifiable at the time of the ECSC, which dealt with a clearly defined sector, but became increasingly pointless with the European Economic Community (EEC) and the European Union and the progressive extension of their competences.[2] The Constitutional Treaty provided no remedy to this problem, which now seems in the process of being solved.

We now have on the one hand a basic treaty, the Treaty on the Union, the provisions of which establish its fundamental law; and on the other hand an implementing treaty, a kind of 'organic law', the Treaty on the Functioning of the Union. This gives rise to a two-tier system, with the implementing treaty in a subordinate position to the basic treaty. In view of their nature, the provisions of the basic treaty (fundamental law) require a more stable consensus over time; they therefore should not be open to opt-outs on the part of individual members and it is reasonable that they require a more stringent amendment procedure. On the other hand, the provisions of the implementing treaty (organic law) are such as to require more frequent adaptations, in line with changes in circumstances and prevailing political positions; in this case, therefore, there appears to be a rationale for a more flexible amendment and opt-out system.

It is hard to say whether the system described is intentional. The concern addressed was likely of a different nature, connected to the ratification process and the referendum risk. Emphasis was deliberately laid on the discontinuity between the new treaty and the constitutional one, the former an amending treaty, the latter a treaty replacing its predecessors. As a result, two treaties remain, despite the fact that they refer to a single entity. But what might appear to be an incongruity, ascribable to happenstance rather than intention, ends up producing a positive innovation. It brings about the re-organisation and simplification of the system, basing it on two separate groups of primary rules.

It will now be easier for the two groups of rules, and their respective treaties to evolve independently of each other. In particular, it will be possible to amend the sectoral regulations of the Union without affecting its institutional structure. This all leads to a double-positive effect –

---

[2] Not surprisingly, the Laeken Declaration of 15 December 2001 indicated the desirability of making a distinction between a basic treaty and other treaty provisions.

endowing the system with greater flexibility and opening new areas to political debate. As has been rightly pointed out by Micossi (in this volume), the policies of the Union have become normal policies, and political divisions may now take shape around them, in line with traditional left/right divisions. This will certainly contribute to strengthening the Union's democratic life (and thereby its legitimacy).

3. The 'constitutional' issue

The new treaty eliminates any trace of constitutional names or signs. The terms 'constitution', foreign 'minister', 'law', 'framework law' are all banished; the symbols of the Union (flag, anthem, motto) are equally discarded, as is any explicit reference to the primacy of Union law. This is tantamount to a full-scale requiem for the European Constitution, almost a kind of *damnatio memoriae.*

The countries that had rejected the Constitutional Treaty through referendum or that in any case were opposed to the text have thus been given the tangible sign they wanted of a break with the past. They can now tell their publics that the new treaty is radically different from its predecessor. On the other hand, countries that were in favour of the Constitution had to accept this 'sacrifice', because otherwise no agreement would have been achieved. But what is the real effect of deleting the constitutional names and symbols? A clarification appears desirable.

The 'constitution' concept can be understood in a number of different ways.[3] Some believe it has a very specific and highly circumscribed historical meaning; that its purpose is to identify the basic law of a political community with features specific to modern State systems. Outside of this context, it would be mistaken to use the term, as it would lose its distinctive nature and give rise to misunderstandings. If that is so, there is obviously no justification for using the term in a European context. As the Union is not a State, its founding act cannot be a constitution. And the fact that the term is used, as in the previous treaty, does nothing to change its nature: it remains a treaty and not a constitution.

One can argue, however, that issues of modern constitutionalism also apply to supranational political entities endowed with authority over

---

[3] On this point see Cassese (2002) and Amato (2003).

member states and individuals. It would then be quite proper to recognise the constitutional nature of those Union norms that govern fundamental aspects of the Union (institutions, competences, procedures, guarantees, etc.). Therefore the European Court of Justice made no mistake in its past rulings (*Les Verts* judgement, 1986; SEE opinion, 1991) when it referred to the Community Treaty as a constitutional charter; and it is equally not mistaken to use the same term today with regard to the Treaty establishing the Union, despite the deletion of all and any constitutional terminology.

So it all depends on which concept of constitution one takes as a starting point. Clearly, its applicability to the Union is to be ruled out assuming that there is an inseparable link between constitution and State. This only means, however, that the Union is not a State-type entity; and not that the Union can be equated with common international organisations, regulated by international covenants. Conversely, under the other line of reasoning, the founding act of the Union can be deemed to have a constitutional character, but this does not mean assigning State identity to the Union. The two issues – the nature of the Union and the definition of its founding act – remain separate.

So far, we have examined the issues from a legal standpoint. However, signs and symbols also carry political weight. And as the adoption of constitutional terminology provided momentum for a closer integration of the peoples of Europe, discarding it now moves in the opposite direction. It signals a retreat back to national values and interests, or at least a moment of uncertainty with regard to the outcome of the process of European construction. That said, some symbols, such as the Union's flag, remain solidly in place, despite the attempt to dispatch them with the stroke of a pen – a warning that reality is much stronger than any attempt to force matters through regulations.

4. Institutions and decision-making efficiency

In the area of institutions, we had become accustomed to the Community trio or triangle: Parliament, Commission and Council. In the unified structure of the Union we now also have the European Council, which did actually already exist but without a clearly defined position. The trio has been converted into a quartet and the triangle into a rectangle. At the lower corners we find the European Parliament and the Council; at the upper corners, the Commission and the European Council. On one of the two vertical sides we find institutions with a supranational vocation – the

European Parliament and the Commission; on the other, intergovernmental institutions – the two councils. Each institution interacts with all the others; relations therefore develop not only along the sides of the figure but also along its diagonals.

The new treaty also ushers in a new player, national parliaments. For better or for worse (see Manzella, in this volume), the quartet thus evolves into a quintet. Hard to say exactly where the newcomer should be placed. Formally, this player is not one of the Union's institutions, but it has become a stable part of its legislative procedures and may exercise a blocking influence on new legislation. It is also difficult to decide whether to position national parliaments on the supranational or the intergovernmental axis. They contain a bit of both: as democratic bodies representing the people, national parliaments appear to be comparable to the European Parliament; at the same time they express national rather than supranational interests. What is clear is that the institutional dynamics of the Union now include a new player interacting with all the others.

The picture just outlined is a mere sketch; it would require a detailed account of the tasks and duties of the various players. However, it delineates a particularly complex institutional system. Certainly this could be described in positive terms, as an increase in fora, scrutiny and guarantees within the Union. But if the yardstick is decision-making efficiency, the assessment may be somewhat different. What seems to be emerging is a consensus-based system, more effective at stalling decisions rather than facilitating them, and at encouraging deferral and (unavoidably small-scale) compromise solutions, rather than ensuring promptness of action and the prevalence of European interests. This is aggravated by the voting procedures in the two councils. All European Council decisions have to be unanimous and the same applies to major Council decisions. Furthermore, defining a new system for calculating majorities within Council is practically postponed until 2017, or even later because of the reference to the 'Ioannina' approach.

Summing up, the Union's decision-making procedures feature a plurality of players and an unavoidable requirement for general consensus among national governments, with all the implications this has in today's 27-country Europe. Decisions are therefore likely to remain labourious and uncertain in outcome and the problem of decision-making efficiency (so central and vital for Europe) may remain unresolved even after the reform.

5. Three candidates for the role of Mr (or Ms) Europe

The discussion over institutions calls for an appendix, of not negligible importance. Who will be *Mr (or Ms) Europe* in the new Union structure? There are a number of candidates for the part. The three frontrunners are the President of the European Council, the High Representative for Foreign Affairs and Security Policy and the President of the Commission. As a matter of fact, one could also add the rotating President of the Council and the President of the European Parliament. But the position of the President of the Council is weakened because of the continuing half-yearly rotation. As to the President of the European Parliament, although the Parliament is certainly of increasing significance as a legislative and political body, it can't as yet compete with the traditional governing institutions of the Union (Councils and Commission). Therefore the race can be narrowed down to the three main contenders.

Each has both strong and weak points. The President of the European Council is backed by the weight of the most authoritative government institution, and will have the task of establishing the body's agenda and implementing it. However, s/he does not have autonomous decision-making powers. The President of the Commission can rely on the resources and structures of a well-established institution, on its prerogatives over foreign trade and a special relationship with the European Parliament. To some extent, it is the recognised voice of economic and supranational Europe. Major issues of foreign (and domestic) policy however remain the province of national governments and consequently of the councils representing them. As far as the High Representative is concerned, despite the change in name, s/he basically inherits the role and functions assigned to the minister for foreign affairs under the Constitutional Treaty. S/he will therefore be responsible for conducting the Union's foreign, security and defence policy, taking advantage of his two hats as Vice-President of the Commission and President of the Council on External Relations, combining the functions of the two positions in his person. S/he will furthermore be able to make use of a dedicated structure, the embryo of a European diplomatic body. The position of the High Representative however appears to some extent subordinate to those of the President of the Commission and the President of the European Council.

In light of the above considerations, two scenarios are possible: either that following a competition between the three figures, one prevails and becomes the true *Mr (or Ms) Europe*; or else that positive cooperation is established between the three, so that Europe is represented by a troika rather than a single individual. Also possible are dual solutions, in which case the High Representative would hold the balance of power. It is difficult to predict how this will play out. It will in part depend on the personalities of the people chosen for the three positions and in part on the balance between governmental and supranational institutions; more importantly, the weight of facts and realities may well exercise a decisive influence. One can only hope that the three figures will not hinder each other in the pursuit of personal visibility and success and that a spirit of cooperation will prevail. Until we have one person jointly holding the presidency of the European Council and the Commission (something that is not ruled out in the new Treaty),[4] the aforementioned troika could, if united and cohesive, provide a powerful engine for initiative and action. The Union stands in great need of such a boost in authority in order to overcome national resistance and take on a leading role on the world stage.

6. The market: Between competition and general interest

Turning from institutions to the Union's common policies, the list of open issues grows. One example, in the economic area, relates to competition policy.

Market and competition rules have characterised 50 years of European integration, being its main driving force. But today competition has been removed from the list of Union goals. These now include sustainable development and balanced economic growth, more generally the economic and social well-being of its citizens. Competition has been downgraded to a mere instrument (together with others) in the pursuit of such goals. The importance of this instrument is however reiterated in a special protocol. One may thus wonder what the future role of competition will be.

We need to understand whether the previous open and competitive market approach will continue to prevail, as would seem to be required by the protocol; or whether this is the beginning of a new season in the relations between politics and the economy, between the market and the

---

[4] Under the Lisbon Treaty the office of President of the European Council is incompatible solely with a national office (see the new Article 15 of the Treaty on the European Union).

public interest, as would seem to be suggested by the elimination of competition from the goals of the Union. The Treaty of Lisbon gives contradictory signals in this area and future developments are not easy to predict. For the time being, we can but note the conflicting views of those advocating greater flexibility in competition law implementation in order to give greater scope to industrial policy goals and public concerns (environment, consumers, employment) and those who fear the onset of a new course featuring regulatory constraints that may hinder free market dynamics.

The same question arises with respect to general interest services. The current Community Treaty has two provisions concerning these services: one has existed since the establishment of the Community (Article 86), whereas the other derives from the Amsterdam amendment (Article 16). The first establishes that enterprises providing public services must be fully subject to market and competition rules, provided this does not hinder their mission. Should this be the case, an exemption applies, which the Commission and the Court long interpreted very restrictively. The second provision, from the Amsterdam text, emphasises the importance of public services and urges the Community and its member states to ensure they operate adequately. Following the adoption of this provision, the exemption has been interpreted less restrictively. With the new treaty, the two provisions remain in force and a special protocol has been added thereto, which recognises national authorities' broad discretionary powers in organising services of general interest.

How should the protocol be read? It states that its provisions are purely interpretative, but in that case why insert them? This may be deemed nothing more than a redundancy in the new treaty without any concrete implications. Or it may be a signal akin to the elimination of competition from the goals of the Union. In which case the special regime for public services would be strengthened and such services would make up a sort of 'free zone' set aside for state jurisdiction and to a large extent unaffected by the constraints of EC competition rules.

7. A foreign policy for the Union?

In foreign policy (and so we come to the heart of political Europe), uncertainties and ambiguities prevail regarding the respective powers of the Union and its member states. The treaty text appears to go in one direction, and a declaration appended to the final act, in quite another.

The treaty contains a number of significant innovations: the Union's international legal personality, the occasional resort to majority decision and the creation of a figure entrusted with handling common foreign policy as a whole. We have already referred to the latter. Whereas the Constitutional Treaty spoke of a Minister for Foreign Affairs, the title is now more modest: High Representative. Its terms of reference however remain the same; they include submitting proposals to the Council on Foreign Relations, presiding over it, implementing its decisions and speaking on behalf of the Union before the United Nations. The High Representative will be supported by an embryonic European diplomatic service. All these measures are aimed at strengthening the ability of the Union to develop its own foreign policy and speak abroad with a single voice.

The appended declaration, however, contains a number of *caveats* in defence of state prerogatives. According to the declaration, treaty provisions do not affect the responsibilities and powers of individual member states in shaping and handling their own foreign policy, do not compromise their relations with other countries or international agencies, do not hinder the tasks and roles of its diplomatic representations, do not restrict the freedom of action of the holders of permanent seats on the Security Council and do not confer any new Common Foreign and Security Policy responsibilities on the Commission or the European Parliament.

The emerging picture is contradictory. Which should we give more credence to: the treaty, which directs the Union to develop its own foreign policy or the declaration, which makes this goal very difficult to achieve? From a legal standpoint, declarations, unlike protocols, are not binding, but they do carry political weight. In this case, there is a risk that the CFSP will continue to be a separate pillar within the Union. A pillar that is rigorously intergovernmental in nature requires the unanimous support of all member states before any common initiative can be taken and leaves them freedom of action to protect their national interests.

Hopefully the Union will succeed in asserting itself as a single entity on the international stage. But uncertainties still exist and concerns are justified. There is a danger that the Union will only be allowed to handle minor issues, with high-profile foreign policy matters remaining the absolute prerogative of member states (see Merlini in this volume).

8. Two conflicting concepts

The examples of ambiguity and uncertainty described previously can (almost) all be traced back to the two conflicting concepts that have marked the process of European construction since the beginning: on the one hand a political (and not just economic) entity, with federal connotations; on the other, a confederal, intergovernmental institution mainly (though not exclusively) entrusted with economic matters.

At times the first concept nearly prevailed: consider the Defence Community in the 1950s, Spinelli's parliamentary project in the 1980s and, more recently, the Constitutional Treaty. But none of these initiatives succeeded. On the other hand, the repeated attempts at giving Europe a purely intergovernmental nature (the Luxembourg compromise, the creation of the European Council, the second and third Maastricht pillars) have also failed. Europe over time has maintained its ambiguity, setting it apart from all existing models; it combines federal and confederal, integration and cooperation, supranational and intergovernmental elements.

Thanks to the many positive innovations introduced to the Nice texts, the Lisbon Treaty certainly marks a new step on the way to "an ever closer Union". In this sense, Lisbon is in line with Maastricht, Amsterdam and Nice. But as its predecessors also did, it leaves the Union's finality unclear. And pending the settlement of this basic issue, from which all others stem, ambiguity and compromise will remain unavoidable, as clearly explained by Giorgio Napolitano on 27 November 2007, in his Berlin *lectio magistralis* (see Napolitano, 2007).

The reform process can therefore not be considered complete. It is no coincidence that the European Parliament, while endorsing the new treaty, immediately mentioned new amendment initiatives.[5] More significant still is the establishment of a group of wise men to reflect on the future of Europe. A decision taken by the European Council, the very day the Treaty of Lisbon was solemnly signed.[6] According to the Heads of State and Government, the wise men should not concern themselves with institutional issues. But they can hardly address the major issues of the new

[5] Resolution of the European Parliament of 11 July 2007, at point 21.

[6] European Council of 14 December 2007, Presidency Conclusions, at points 8 to 13.

century - sustainable development, the environment, energy, immigration, combating terrorism and international crime - without reasoning in terms of resources, structures and powers, in other words without considering which instruments will be best suited to the implementation of the policies required. Institutional issues appear unavoidable; and with them also the need to "overcome the deadlock between conflicting concepts of the European project" and "eliciting a new common political will", as stressed by President Napolitano in the lecture cited above.

9. A look into the future

The contruction of Europe is thus not complete; but what tools will one need to move ahead?

Over the last two decades we have seen a continuing process of revision: the Single Act, followed by Maastricht, Amsterdam, Nice and now, by Lisbon. A series of revision treaties that have marked the successive stages of the integration process. The last stage proved particularly lengthy and laborious, characterised by a resounding failure (the rejection of the Constitutional Treaty) and the serious crisis that ensued. One can thus easily predict that member countries will think twice before embarking on a similar adventure again. Getting 27 members (or even more, if there is further enlargement) to agree appears extremely difficult; and, after all, the compromises and resources of diplomacy have their limits. Europe has not reached its final destination, but its method for solemnly revising the founding treaties may well have.

In the future, changes will more likely be made solely to the second-tier treaty, on the functioning of the Union. As mentioned earlier, such revisions can be addressed through simplified procedures that bypass the intergovernmental conference stage. But even the so-called 'small revision' will not have an easy time, as it requires the consent of all national governments and parliaments (which was not the case with the ECSC).

Beyond formal revision procedures, instruments may over time be perfected within the Union, through inter-institutional agreements or case law. Inter-institutional agreements have in the past been used to introduce quite significant innovations in legislative and budgetary procedures, relations between institutions and the protection of basic rights. They may be used again in the future. Although one should not underestimate the fact that Council approval will be required, with the unanimous agreement of governments this entails; and a further obstacle might stem from national parliaments, following the recent *Lisbon* judgement of the German Constitutional Court.

As for case law, it is superfluous to recall its driving force in the integration process; and it is unthinkable that the evolving and creative interpretation of European judges could be somehow blocked. The new Treaty however establishes explicit barriers to the expansion of EU competences via judicial decision: from the meticulous re-assertion of the principle of conferral to the recurrent clarification that the legal personality of the Union, the Charter of Fundamental Rights, support competences and the residual competence under Article 308 in no way allow for new powers to be conferred upon the Union. In fact, European judges themselves have shown caution and restraint in recent times.

And then there is differentiated integration – already a fact within the Union: consider Schengen, the euro or the defence policy. This phenomenon has expanded in the new Treaty, as illustrated by the opt-outs granted on issues of basic rights and in the area of justice and home affairs. In any case, the key issue is clear to all and cannot be eluded. On the one hand, some countries are not prepared to go for any further integration, whereas on the other, matters requiring a European response are increasingly pressing. It is therefore inevitable that if all do not feel ready, initiatives will be taken by smaller groups, either through enhanced cooperation within the Union (as in the euro approach), or through agreements outside the Union legal system (the initial approach to Schengen).[7]

Increasingly, differentiated integration appears to be an appropriate way forward. The dissent of a few countries cannot be allowed to hold up all the others. Europe therefore faces a future of unity and diversity, as stated in the Constitutional Treaty. Admittedly, the two terms are difficult to reconcile. The tasks and challenges ahead are therefore clear: Europe must be allowed to move forward on a differentiated basis without compromising its unitary construction and without losing sight of its hopefully still common final goal.

---

[7] On the euro model see Ciampi (2004).

References

Amato, G. (2003), "Verso la Costituzione europea", in *Rivista italiana di diritto pubblico comunitario*, No. 2.

Cassese, S. (2002), *La crisi dello Stato*, Roma-Bari, Laterza.

Ciampi, C.A. (2004), *Dall'Europa all'Euro dall'euro all'Europa*, edited by F. Galimberti, Roma, Treves Editore.

Napolitano, G. (2007), *Sciogliere l'antico nodo di contrastanti visioni del progetto europeo. Far emergere una nuova volontà politica comune, Lectio Magistralis*, Università Humboldt-Berlin, 27 November.

ABOUT THE AUTHORS

Stefano Micossi (co-editor), General Director of Assonime in Rome, Professor of Economics at the College of Europe in Bruges and Member of the Board of Directors of the Centre for European Policy Studies, Brussels.

Gian Luigi Tosato (co-editor), Professor at the University of Rome "La Sapienza" and member of the Executive Committee of the Istituto Affari Internazionali, Rome.

Carlo Bastasin, Columnist at Il Sole 24 ore.

Ginevra Bruzzone, Deputy Director General of Assonime in Rome.

Rocco A. Cangelosi, Director of the Office of Diplomatic Affairs of the Italian Republic.

Sabino Cassese, Professor of Administrative Law at University of Rome "La Sapienza" and Judge of Constitutional Court.

Mario P. Chiti, Professor of Administrative Law at University of Florence and Chairman of the Italian Institute of Administrative Science.

Giacinto della Cananea, Professor of Administrative Law at the Faculty of Political Science of University "Federico II" in Naples.

Maurizio Ferrera, Professor of Social Policy and Chairman of the Graduate School in Social, Economic and Political Sciences at the State University of Milan and Director of the Research Unit on European Governance (URGE), Collegio Carlo Alberto di Moncalieri, Turin.

Fiorella Kostoris, Professor of Economics at the Department of Economics of University of Rome "La Sapienza".

Andrea Manzella, Director of Centro Studi Parlamentari at Luiss University in Rome.

Cesare Merlini, Deputy Executive Chairman of the Council for the United States and Italy and President of the Board of Trustees of the Istituto Affari Internazionali, Rome, of which he was previously Director (from 1970 to 1978) and President (from 1979 to 2001).

Pier Carlo Padoan, Deputy Secretary-General of the OECD.

Alessandro Pansa, Joint Director-General of Finmeccanica and Professor at Luiss University in Rome.

Luigi Prosperetti, Professor of Economic Policy at Faculty of Law, Università degli Studi in Milan.

Stefano Sacchi, Assistant Professor of Political Science, University of Milan and Acting Director, Unit on European Governance (URGE), Collegio Carlo Alberto di Moncalieri, Turin.

Ferdinando Salleo, Secretary-General of Italian Ministry of Foreign Affairs 1994-1995 and Italian Ambassador in Moscow 1989-1993 and Washington, 1995-2003.

Valeria Termini, Director of Scuola superiore della Pubblica Amministrazione; Professor of Economic Policy; Chairman of the Intergovernmental Committee for Energy and Environment of the Presidency of Italian Council and Representative for Italy to the G8 and UNFCC on these issues.